Baron James

Baron James

The Rise of the French Rothschilds

Anka Muhlstein

The Vendome Press

New York Paris

Designed by Marlene Rothkin Vine

First published in the United States of America by
The Vendome Press, 515 Madison Avenue, N.Y., N.Y. 10022
Distributed by The Viking Press, 40 West 23rd Street, N.Y., N.Y. 10010
Distributed in Canada by Methuen Publications

Library of Congress Cataloging in Publication Data
Muhlstein, Anka.
    Baron James: the rise of the French Rothschilds.
    Translation of: James de Rothschild.
    Bibliography: p.
    Includes index.
    1. Rothschild, James, baron de, 1792–1868.   2. Bankers
—France—Paris—Biography.   3. Jews—France—Paris—
Biography.   4. Paris (France)—Biography.   I. Title.
HG1552.R816M83   332.1'092'4 [B]   82–6989
                                                AACR2
ISBN 0–86565–028–4
Printed in the United States by
The Lakeside Press, R.R. Donnelley & Sons Company

Acknowledgments

This book could never have been written without the aid of Baroness Élie de Rothschild in Paris and Lord Rothschild in London. The one, Liliane, allowed me to poke about in old mementoes, account books, and personal objects once owned by James, all the while responding to my endless questions with a characteristic mixture of enthusiasm and exactitude. The other, Victor, opened the family archives in England for my perusal—on the sole condition that the references be precise! With warmest affection, I dedicate to him the notes at the end of the text. I also acknowledge a debt of gratitude to all of James' descendants: Guy, Alain, and Élie, who gave me access to their files; Philippe, who sent documents on the Restoration; Eric for a useful and most enjoyable sojourn at Château Lafite; and Baroness de Becker for illustrations now interleaved with the text.

I thank my publisher, Alexis Gregory, for his encouragement and my editor, Daniel Wheeler, for his patience and devotion. In addition, I reserve a *grand merci* for François Nourissier, who read the original manuscript with fraternal vigilence.

I want also to express my gratitude to Professor Richard Kuisel for his suggestions on how to handle the monetary equivalents; to Hans Bertram-Nothnagel for his translations of Ludwig Börne; to Robert Dujarric and his statistics; to Stéphane Dujarric and his calculator; and to Yvonne Moss, of the Rothschild Archives in London, without whom I would never have been able to decipher the letters of Leonora.

Finally, I want to thank my husband, Louis Begley, who read, reread, and read yet again.

For my sons,
Robert and Stéphane,
and in memory of my father,
Anatole Muhlstein

Contents

Mayer Amschel Rothschild (1743–1812)
m 1770
Gudule Schnapper (1753–1849)

Jeannette (1771–1859)
m 1795
Moses Worms (1772–1824)

Amschel Mayer (1773–1855)
m 1796
Eva Hanau (1779–1848)

Salomon Mayer (1774–1855)
m 1800
Caroline Stern (1782–1854)

Anselm Salomon (1803–74)
m 1826
Charlotte (1807–59)

Mayer Anselm Léon (1827–28)

Julie (1830–1907)
m 1850
Adolph Karl (1823–1900)

Hannah Mathilde (1832–1924)
m 1849
Wilhelm Karl (1828–1901)

Sara Louise (1834–1924)
m 1858
Raimondo Franchetti (1829–1905)

Nathaniel Mayer (1836–1905)

Ferdinand James (1839–98)

Evelina (1839–66)

Salomon Albert (1844–1911)
m 1876
Bettina (1858–92)

George Anselm (1877–1934)

Alphonse Mayer (1878–1942)
m 1912
Clarice Sebag-Montefiore (1894–1967)

Albert (1922–38)

Bettina (1924–)
m 1943
Matthew Looram (1921–)

Gwendoline (1927–72)
m 1948
Roland Hoguet (1920–)

Louis (1882–1955)
m 1946
Hildegard von Auersperg (1895–)

Miriam (1908–)

George Lane (1915–)

Eugène Daniel (1884–1976)
m 1925
Cathleen Wolf (1885–1946)

Elizabeth Charlotte (1909–)

Jeanne Stuart (1908–)

Victor (1910–)
m 1933
Barbara Hutchinson (1911–)
m 1946
Teresa Mayor (1915–)

Charlotte Esther (1885)

Kathleen (1913–)
m 1935
Jules de Koenigswarter (1903–)

Valentine Noëmi (1886–1969)
m 1911
Sigismund von Springer (1875–1928)

Oscar Ruben (1888–1909)

Betty (1805–86)
m 1824
James Mayer (1792–1868)

Alice (1847–1922)

Charlotte (1807–59)
m 1826
Anselm Salomon (1803–74)

Leonora (1837–1911)
m 1857
Alphonse (1827–1905)

Evelina (1839–66)
m 1865
Ferdinand James (1839–98)

Lionel Walter (1868–1937)

Charlotte (1873–1947)
m 1899
Clive Behrens (1871–1935)

Rosemary (1913–)
m 1934
Denis Berry (1911–)

John Seys (1914–)

Charles (1877–1923)
m 1907
Rozsika von Wertheimstein (1870–1940)

Edmund (1916–)
m 1948
Elizabeth Lentner (1923–80)

Naomi (1920–)
m 1941
Jean-Pierre Reinach (1915–42)
m 1947
Bertrand Goldschmidt (1912–)

Lionel Nathan (1808–79)
m 1836
Charlotte (1819–84)

Nathaniel Mayer (1840–1915)
m 1867
Emma Louisa (1844–1935)

Lionel (1882–1942)
m 1912
Marie-Louise Beer (1892–1975)

Leopold David (1927–)

Alfred Charles (1842–1918)

Leopold (1845–1917)
m 1881
Marie Perugia (1862–1937)

Evelyn Achille (1886–1917)

Anthony (1887–1961)
m 1926
Yvonne Cahen d'Anvers (1899–1977)

Renée (1927–)
m 1955
Peter Robeson (1929–)

Anne Sonia (1930–71)

Anthony Nathan (1810–76)
m 1840
Louise Montefiore (1821–1910)

Constance (1843–1931)
m 1877
Cyril Battersea (1843–1907)

Annie (1844–1926)
m 1873
Eliot Yorke (1843–78)

Nathaniel (1812–70)
m 1842
Charlotte (1825–99)

Nathalie (1843)

James (1844–81)
m 1871
Thérèse (1847–1931)

Hannah (1815–64)
m 1839
Henry FitzRoy (1807–59)

Hannah (1851–90)
m 1878
Archibald Rosebery (1847–1929)

Mayer Amschel (1818–74)
m 1850
Juliana Cohen (1831–77)

Mayer Albert (1846–50)

Arthur (1851–1903)

Isabella (1781–1861)
m 1802
Bernhard Sichel (1780–1862)

Louise (1820–94)
m 1842
Mayer Karl (1820–86)

Henri (1872–1946)
m 1895
Mathilde Weisweiller (1874–1926)

Evelyn Robert (1931–)
m 1966
Jeannette Bishop (1940–)
m 1973
Victoria Schott (1949–)

Jeanne Charlotte (1874–1929)
m 1896
David Leonino (1867–1911)

James (1896–)
m 1923
Claude Dupont (1904–64)

Yvette Choquet (1939–)

Nadine (1898–1958)
m 1919
Adrien Thierry (1885–1961)

Babette (1784–1869)
m 1808
Siegmund Beyfus (1786–1845)

Adèle (1843–1922)
m 1862
Salomon (1835–64)

Philippe (1902–)
m 1935
Elisabeth de Chambure (1902–45)

Emma Louisa (1844–1935)
m 1867
Nathaniel Mayer (1840–1915)

Clementine Henriette (1845–65)

Georges Halphen (1913–)
m 1950

Philippine (1935–)
m 1961
Jacques Sereys (1928–)

Hannah (1962–)
Beth (1964–)
Emily (1967–)
Nathaniel (1971–)

Sarah (1934–)
Jacob (1936–)
m 1961
Serena Dunn (1935–)

Miranda (1940–)
m 1962
Boudjemaa Boumaza (1930–64)
m 1967
Iain Watson (1942–)

Emma Georgina (1948–)

Benjamin (1952–)

Victoria Katherine (1953–)

Amschel (1955–)
m 1981
Anita Guinness (1957–)

Katherine (1949–)
m 1971
Marcus Agius (1946–)

Nicholas David (1951–)

David Lionel (1955–)

Charlotte (1955–)

Jessica (1974–)

Anthony (1977–)

David Mayer (1978–)

Nicole (1924–)

Monique (1925–)
m 1945
Jean-François Drach (1924–)

Nathan Mayer (1777–1836)
m 1806
Hannah Cohen (1783–1850)

Lionel Nathan (1808–79)

Nathaniel (1812–70)

Charlotte (1807–59)
m 1826
Anselm Salomon (1803–74)

Mayer Karl (1820–86)

Nathaniel (1812–70)
m 1842

Charlotte (1825–99)

(1808–79)

Karl Mayer (1788–1855) m 1818 Adelheid Herz (1800–53)
- Mayer Karl (1820–86) m 1842 Louise (1820–94)
  - Thérèse (1847–1931) m 1871 James (1844–81)
  - Hannah Louisa (1850–92) m 1878 Agenor de Gramont (1851–1925)
  - Margaretha Alexandrine (1855–1905) m 1882 Alexandre de Wagram (1836–1911)
  - Bertha Clara (1862–1903)
- Adolph Karl (1823–1900) m 1850 Caroline Julie (1830–1907)
- Wilhelm Karl (1828–1901) m 1849 Hannah Mathilde (1832–1924)
  - Georgine Sara (1851–69)
  - Adelheid (1853–1935) m 1877 Edmond (1845–1934)
  - Minna Caroline (1857–1903) m 1878 Maximilian Goldschmidt (1843–1940)
- Anselm Alexander (1835–54)

Julie (1790–1815) m 1811 Meyer Beyfus (1790–1860)

Henriette (1791–1866) m 1815 Abraham Montefiore (1788–1824)
- Charlotte (1825–99) m 1842 Nathaniel (1812–70)
  - Bettina (1858–92) m 1876 Salomon Albert (1844–1911)
  - Lionel James (1861)
- Alphonse (1827–1905) m 1857 Leonora (1837–1911)
  - Charlotte Béatrix (1864–1934) m 1883 Maurice Ephrussi (1849–1916)
  - Édouard (1868–1949) m 1905 Germaine Halphen (1884–1975)
    - Alphonse (1906–11)
    - Guy (1909–) m 1937 Alix Schey von Koromla (1911–1982) m 1957 Marie-Hélène van Zuylen de Nyevelt (1927–)
      - David (1942–) m 1974 Olimpia Aldobrandini (1955–)
        - Lavinia (1976–)
        - Stéphanie (1977–)
        - Alexandre (1980–)
      - Édouard (1957–) m 1981 Mathilde Coche de la Ferté (1952–)
    - Jacqueline (1911–) m 1930 Robert Calmann-Lévy (1899–) m 1937 Gregor Piatigorsky (1903–76)
    - Bethsabée (1914–) m 1948 Donald Bloomingdale (1913–54)

James Mayer (1792–1868) m 1824 Betty (1805–86)
- Gustave (1829–1911) m 1859 Cécile Anspach (1840–1912)
  - Octave (1860)
  - Zoé Lucie Betty (1863–1916) m 1882 Léon Lambert (1851–1919)
  - Aline (1867–1909) m 1887 Edward Sassoon (1855–1912)
  - Juliette (1870–96) m 1892 David Emmanuel Leonino (1864–1936)
- Salomon (1835–64) m 1862 Adèle (1843–1922)
  - André (1874–77)
  - Robert (1880–1946) m 1907 Nelly Beer (1886–1945)
    - Diane (1907–) m 1932 Anatole Muhlstein (1889–1957) m 1952 Giuseppe Benvenuti (1898–1967)
      - Béatrice (1939–) m 1962 Armand de la Beaumelle (1929–64) m 1981 Pierre Rosenberg (1936–)
      - Eric (1940–)
    - Alain (1910–82) m 1938 Mary Chauvin du Treuil (1916–)
      - Robert (1947–)
    - Cécile (1913–)
    - Élie (1917–) m 1942 Liliane Fould-Springer (1916–)
      - Nathaniel (1946–) m 1975 Nili Limon (1951–)
        - Raphael (1976–)
        - Esther (1979–)
      - Nelly (1947–) m 1970 Adam Munthe (1946–)
  - Hélène (1863–1947) m 1887 Étienne van Zuylen de Nyevelt (1860–1934)
- Edmond (1845–1934) m 1877 Adelheid (1853–1935)
  - James (1878–1957) m 1913 Dorothy Pinto (1895–)
  - Maurice (1881–1957) m 1909 Noémie Halphen (1888–1968)
    - Edmond (1926–) m 1958 Veselinka Gueorguieva (1927–) m 1963 Nadine Lhopitalier (1932–)
      - Gustava (1952–) m 1970 Marc Leland (1938–)
      - Benjamin (1963–)
  - Miriam (1884–1965) m 1910 Albert Max von Goldschmidt (1879–1941)

**Line of descent
through the male progeny
of Mayer Amschel Rothschild**

Rich as a Rothschild? An Introduction

It would be pointless to begin this book by stating that James de Rothschild was wealthy, a millionaire many times over. The fact has long been a matter of public knowledge. But just how rich was he? And compared to whom was he rich? Herein lies an interesting question, one however that yields to no easy answer. Still, given the nature of this story, I must attempt to provide some practical way of estimating James' relative wealth, so as to save the reader the nuisance of wondering what the modern equivalent may be every time a monetary figure appears in the text.

First, it is important to know that from 1815 until 1868, the year James died, the value of the French franc remained constant. This permits us to understand, once the Baron's worth has been estimated at 120,000 francs in 1815, at 20 million in the years before 1830, at 40 million under Louis-Philippe (1830–48), and at 150 million in 1868, that the phenomenal growth of the Rothschild fortune in France was real and not a product of inflation. But what does it mean in terms of today's money? To imagine the wealth of Fouquet, whose vast fortune so antagonized Louis XIV that the young monarch confiscated it, is not the same thing as reading about the financial empire of Dassault, the twentieth-century magnate who led France's booming aeronautics industry. The fact that James bought an eighteenth-century mansion on the Place de la Concorde for slightly more than a million of his francs and that an Arab Sheik recently spent 50 million of our francs to acquire a similar eighteenth-century mansion on the same square provides us with information of two quite different orders. While the second figure is tangible enough, the first remains an abstraction for the contemporary mind. Comparison therefore fails as a technique for resolving the worrisome problem of how to translate old money into current values. Moreover, it is not enough merely to multiply Louis-Philippe's franc by 6.30, the rate established in a 1979 study of France's price index,[1] in order to obtain a true sense of an equivalence in contemporary francs.

To begin with, nineteenth-century fortunes were considerably smaller, in both size and number, than modern ones. Wealth began to grow at an accelerating rate only about 1830, when it truly soared, as can be seen in the curve of the French nation's real per capita income.[2] Stated in another way, the fortune of an early nineteenth-century millionaire, when measured in constant money, would appear quite insufficient to the great tycoons of today. Bernard Delessert, one of the richest men in France, left an estate worth 11 million at his death in 1847. Now, even 69 million (the value of the Delessert fortune when multiplied by 6.30) would not place the owner among the wealthiest people of his time. Conversely, it was possible in 1840 to live, albeit badly, on a subsistence income of 40 francs a month. In 1983, no one would dare claim that 250 francs (30 dollars or 20 pounds) constitute even a minimum monthly wage.

Then, too, a fortune is more than just a statistic; it is essentially the power to purchase so many acres of land, to employ so many workers, to maintain so many residences, or, on a different level, to dine in a certain style and take a certain kind of vacation. But little that money can buy has failed to change in relative value during the past century. Indeed, the price of a haircut may be the only thing that continues unmodified to any significant degree.[3] Most goods and services cost a great deal less than they did a century ago. The real price of a hectar of French farm land, for instance, has gone from

6,550 to 703, a Paris-Toulouse train ticket from 1,360 to 27, and a good seat at the Opéra from 57.8 to 8.6. The cost of a postage stamp or a newspaper reflects even more spectacular reductions. Only servants' wages have evolved in inverse proportion. An experienced valet, for example, once earned about 600 francs a year, with a maid receiving some 350 francs, and this in the best houses. The great Carême, the most celebrated chef of the nineteenth century, earned an annual salary of only 2,000 francs during his reign over James' kitchen. Meanwhile, the minimum wage in 1830 was considered to be 450 francs a year. By the very nature of things, of course, servants enjoyed rather considerable advantages, and one need not shed too many tears for Carême, since it was a notorious fact of the time that "the rake-off at M. de Rothschild's was equal to the income from a large farm."[4] Still, even lower middleclass households could boast one or two domestics.

This reveals yet another difficulty for those determined to compare living standards, a difficulty that stems from fundamental changes in consumption. The luxury of 1830 is the necessity of 1980; what was once rare has become commonplace. Heating costs, all but nonexistent in the budgets of our forebears, are substantial today, and this is true for everybody, whatever his place in the socioeconomic scale. Sugar, coffee, and even salad (think of the rapture experienced by Zola's Gervaise at the prospect of eating lettuce) were practically unknown in the meals of nineteenth-century workers and peasants. Out of an annual salary of 450 francs, the Parisian laborer devoted 347 francs to food, with 110 of them going for bread. Today, the cost of bread is almost imperceptible in the budget of a working man's household. And few would now classify a cup of sweetened coffee among the great luxuries of life.

The evolution of prices simply contains too many disparities for it to serve as a basis for calculating living standards or purchasing power. Depending on the commodity being considered—sugar or flour, for instance—one can arrive at quite different conclusions. With a million francs, James in 1848 could have bought 780 hectars of good land; today, when the average price of a hectar of arable land is 19,350 francs, 783 hectars would cost him 15,350,000 francs.[5] Meanwhile, if we take the price of James' mansion as reference point, it becomes apparent that what cost a million around 1830 would now command a price of 50 million. Clearly, the results of the two comparisons are so different as to be meaningless, even though real estate is an important element in any consideration of purchasing power.

If we must abandon the idea of finding a precise modern expression for a nineteenth-century fortune, there are however a few benchmarks[6] that can help guide us through the financial data that inevitably well up in the life story of a man so utterly preoccupied with money as James de Rothschild. Eighty percent of the population of France around 1840 had a per capita income of 500 francs a year, and fifteen percent between 2,000 to 20,000 francs. The middleclass, with disposable income ranging from 20,000 to 500,000 francs, accounted for only five percent of the population, while the financial aristocracy comprised a mere dozen families, each of which, however, possessed wealth sufficient to generate annual revenues in excess of 500,000 francs. Jacques Laffitte, who for a brief period under the Restoration controlled a fabulous fortune, estimated at close to 30 million, gave his daughter a dowry of 4 million, then regarded as a prodigious sum. To broaden the frame of reference, we should also note that in early nineteenth-century America, anyone with an accumulated wealth of 50,000 dollars was thought to be rich,[7] for in order to live comfortably, an average American family needed only 800 dollars a year. But fortunes grew and multiplied at an incredible rate in the New World, and halfway through the century the affluent had assets averaging from 100,000 dollars to 200,000. There were twenty-five millionaires living in New York, among them the Goelets with 2 million, Cornelius Vanderbilt with 1.5 million,[8] and John Jacob Astor, by far the wealthiest man in North America. At his death in 1847 Astor left an estate worth 20 million,[9] which was about the size of the fortune possessed by James on the eve of the Revolution of 1848. But Rothschild and Astor were peers in another respect, since they had both outstripped their nearest competitors in the financial sweepstakes by a factor of ten.

These then are the figures that the reader should keep in mind as he attempts to comprehend the ambitions and achievements of James de Rothschild.

1
Jew Street

In March 1811, a young man of nineteen, slight-framed, sandy-haired, ill-favored, and sure of himself, arrived in Paris. This was the year the French celebrated the birth of the Roi de Rome,[1] an event that would mark the zenith of the Napoleonic Empire. The capital was awash in *gloire*. But while triumphal arches, classical temples, and colonnades evoked Greco-Roman antiquity and its conquering heroes, another temple—the Bourse (Paris' Stock Exchange), brand new, modern, and sumptuous—made it clear that the nineteenth century would unfold under a different symbol, that of massively accumulated monetary wealth.

The traveler appreciated—indeed relished—the freedom that greeted him upon his arrival. At liberty for the first time in his life to seek lodgings elsewhere than in the ghetto, he cheerfully went to the very heart of the city's finest quarter, to 5 Rue Napoléon, the present Rue de la Paix, at the corner of the recently opened Rue de Rivoli. For the first time in his life he found himself immersed in the crowd. Nothing set him apart as a Jew, not even his clothing, which was indistinguishable from what could be seen on all sides. His accent must have been strong, but the French were too busy to worry about variations of Germanic inflection. To a Parisian, all foreigners were alike, and in the frenzy of the cosmopolitan capital no one bothered to give the young man a second look. No one, that is, except the police, who not only took note of his presence but did so at a high level. "A Frankfurt man who is now in Paris," wrote Mollien,[2] the Finance Minister, to Napoleon, "and who calls himself Rotschild [*sic*], is occupied mainly in smuggling guineas from the English coast to Dunkirk."[3] In reality, his enterprise amounted to considerably more than that, consisting as it did of making money—immense sums of money. Such was his supreme priority, and in this the ambitious James—as Jacob Rothschild chose to be known—was a true son of his father and the pupil of his elder brothers. Money would forever remain the overriding preoccupation—*la grande affaire*—in the life of James de Rothschild.

The first Rothschild to achieve distinction had been the father of James, Mayer Amschel, born in 1744 to a family long established in Frankfurt. The ancestral line has been traced to the beginning of the sixteenth century,[4] despite the difficulties posed for researchers by the fact that Jews did not bear official family names. They were, in principle, known only by their father's name. Obviously, in a ghetto as populous as the one in Frankfurt, which contained some five hundred families all inextricably related to one another, such an imprecise system of denomination could only foster confusion. In the seventeenth century, therefore, patronyms began to appear signifying a place of birth, a city of origin, a profession, or membership in a family of rabbis. Sometimes the husband joined his wife's name to his own. It was even possible for several different names to coexist within the same family, and the same person might well be known by different names, depending on the time or the place. Occasionally a name would have only a fleeting life, which may be seen on tombstones engraved with one name for the father and another for the son. The place of residence—or rather the signboard attached to a house, since numbering did not exist in the ghetto—provided the most stable patronyms. Thus the name Rothschild originated in a red signboard—*Rot Schild*—identifying a house the family occupied in 1563. It survived a move in 1685, possibly because the new dwelling was called "The Casserole." Finally, the name stuck when Mayer Amschel failed to change its color even after he had taken up residence in a house displaying a green signboard.

The Rothschilds constituted a sizable group in eighteenth-century Frankfurt. A good twenty of them have been identified in the generation of Mayer Amschel's parents, all engaged in buying, selling, speculating, or otherwise dealing in money, since, as Jews, they had no right to practice any other trade. Thus the parents of Mayer Amschel, like so many others, ran a tiny foreign-exchange business, a type of commerce essential to eighteenth-century Germany. In this political mosaic, with its 350 different principalities each of which coined its own currency, the small size of the individual states meant that almost any movement from place to place entailed the crossing of frontiers and thus an exchange of money. Mayer Amschel, the eldest of three sons, learned to help his parents at a very early age, and by the time he was ten the boy could easily convert ducats, gulden, and thalers, obtaining the precise weight of the metal pieces from the sensitive scales enthroned upon the counter.

A year later, in 1755, Mayer Amschel lost both his parents, carried off by an epidemic of smallpox. Now the boy was sep-arated from his brothers and sent by maternal relatives to a rabbinical school at Furth. Ill-suited to the monotony of study and the long hours devoted to textual commentary, Mayer Amschel soon found that not even the respect attached to the role of rabbi could hold him, and at thirteen he launched forth into the world. The Oppenheimers gave him a clerical job in their bank at Hanover, but as he learned the business he came to realize that money-changing would never make him a for-tune. To succeed, it would be necessary, above all, to obtain the protection and patronage of a Prince and then to deal not only in currency exchange but also in loans and trade. After a six-year apprenticeship with the Oppenheimers, Mayer Amschel felt secure enough to try going into business for him-self. He now left Hanover, returned to Frankfurt, one of the major centers of European commerce, and set to work.

In 1762 Frankfurt, the site of the election and coronation of the Holy Roman Emperors, was a free city governed by a coun-cil of notables. With a population of forty thousand, it counted among Europe's largest cities, equal to Antwerp, Brussels, Strasbourg, and Prague at a time when Vienna could claim almost two hundred thousand souls and Paris something like six hundred thousand.[5] This republic of tradesmen, which in the Middle Ages had been the regular host to a famous fair, profited by its crossroad situation to become the receiver and redistributor of English exports, consisting mainly of colonial produce, manufactured goods, and textiles. The city, which thus functioned as a giant warehouse, contained one of the oldest and most important of Germany's ghettos. Created in the twelfth century, the Jewish quarter had at first come under the protection of the Emperor and only later that of the city council. Every three months its inhabitants found themselves obliged to pay for the right to occupy the *Judenstrasse*—"Jew Street." This tax benefited the Jews by granting them freedom of the city, provisional of course and always subject to revocation, but nevertheless sufficiently established to permit continuity in their lives and work.

Mayer Amschel therefore had good reason to seek a career in Frankfurt. As a means of sustaining everyday life there, he opened a foreign-exchange shop and placed his brothers in charge of it. To raise the operation above the ordinary, he began to stock cloth, tobacco, and wine, whenever such products could be procured at a good price. Finally to vault right into the merchant hierarchy, the budding tycoon expanded the collection of antique coins and engravings he had begun in Hanover, arranged for a catalogue to be printed, and initiated a search for clients "of quality," his effort aided by General von Estorff, a powerful contact young Rothschild had made while working for the Oppenheimers.

General von Estorff, a great collector of medals and coins, had learned to appreciate Mayer Amschel's advice and did not forget its worth when he left Hanover for Hanau and entered the service of Prince Wilhelm.[6] A small city quite close to Frankfurt, Hanau was a fief of the heir to the Landgrave of Hesse, the region's most important Prince, the possessor of a significant fortune, and, moreover, the nephew of both the King of Sweden and the Tsar. Prince Wilhelm also took an interest in numismatics, which was what prompted him to send for the young Jew, whom von Estorff had so warmly recommended.

Sizing up his opportunity, Mayer Amschel responded to the Prince's summons and proved himself a man of intelligence, prudence, and finesse by selling His Highness the best pieces in his collection—at a loss. The distinction that would come to him by virtue of a regular association with a powerful personage far outweighed the value of an immediate profit. Conscious that he should not betray any impatience or greed, Mayer Amschel waited four years before making a petition to Wilhelm, and when he did the Prince could easily be accommodating inasmuch as it cost him nothing. Rothschild wanted simply to be named supplier to the Hessian court. All this earned him in the short term was the esteem, if not the jealousy, of his neighbors and the goodwill of a merchant in Frankfurt's Judenstrasse, Salomon Schnapper, who finally consented, in 1770, to give the young man his daughter, Gudule,[7] in marriage.

Gudule was worth her own weight in gold. Energetic and shrewd, endowed with a sense of economy that endured even in wealth, proud but intolerant of ostentation, she was to work hard at her husband's side, raise ten children to be respectful of familial traditions, and survive until 1849. At the age of ninety-six, she still had the strength to joke with her doctor when he declared himself powerless to make her young again. Her only wish, she swore, was to grow still older. On her deathbed Gudule, in a manner worthy of a banker's wife, responded to the forced optimism of her children: "I know very well that I'm going to die. Why should God take me at ninety-nine when he can have me at ninety-six?" But in 1770 Gudule and Mayer Amschel were beginning their life together and had no thought of death. The younger brothers left the house, a dwelling much too cramped to shelter them all. And as Mayer gave his wife full power to run the shop, keep an eye on the exchange business, and supervise the clerks carrying in and out the large cases that choked every corner and passage of the house, he himself turned unreservedly toward the world outside.

Mayer Amschel's business affairs developed rapidly. One success led to another, and such was the reign of thrift within the Rothschild household that financial gains were never spent but immediately reinvested. Mayer Amschel would take on anything that could be traded: muslin, linen, wool, clothing, engravings, and pictures, coffee, tea, wines, and tobacco, nails, tools, sugar, and rabbit skins. Anything was worth buying and anything worth selling once it offered the possibility of a profit. Gradually, Mayer Amschel began to broaden his horizon, to the point where he took the first steps toward becoming a real banker. In this he made some timid use of his relationship with the Hessian court.

The client, Prince Wilhelm, had succeeded as Landgrave of Hesse in 1785, a change that did nothing to soften this temperamental aristocrat, a *débauché* of legendary avarice. Mayer Amschel, owing to his origins and the inherent fragility of his situation as a Jew, did not feel secure or brave enough to deal directly with Wilhelm. He made his approach through the Landgrave's financial advisor, Karl Buderus. Mayer Amschel succeeded because he knew a rare coin when he saw one and understood when it was desirable to share the benefits of a good deal. He had mastered the art of giving and seeking advice. Buderus and Rothschild, similar in their ambitions, formidably tenacious, patient, and secret, had a meeting of minds and decided to enter into an arrangement of mutual assistance.

A torrent of gold flowed toward Kassel, the capital of the landgraviate of Hesse; a flow perhaps somewhat tainted with blood, but neither the Prince nor his bankers let that bother them. The ruler made an immense profit by hiring out his subjects. Mercenaries recruited in Hesse had long been offered to the highest bidder, and after years of experience, the Hessians had refined their contract to the point of perfection. It stipulated that the Prince receive a lump sum at the onset of military activity, then a supplementary payment for each soldier wounded, and a still larger amount every time one was killed. The lease did not expire when a truce was declared, nor even with the restoration of peace, but only a full year after the conscripts had returned home. The number of men rented in this way, mainly by England,[8] has been estimated at between 12,000 and 17,000 a year. Part of the payment remained in England, where it was invested, with only the interest going to the Landgrave of Hesse, in drafts negotiated by the local bankers. That portion of the fees actually transferred to Kassel provided capital for high-interest loans to the various German

Princes. The scheme resulted in a tremendous movement of funds into and around Kassel, a labor-intensive activity since to lend money in the eighteenth century meant literally transporting metal from one place to another. It took long years and much patient work by Mayer Amschel before he could insinuate himself into this profitable merry-go-round.

Prince Wilhelm cost Mayer Amschel a lot of time. The court would summon him, make him wait, and then send him away, only to insist that he come straight back. At last, he would be favored with the opportunity to dun a recalcitrant debtor. Mayer Amschel managed to endure it all with a smile. Is it possible that he dreamt of being asked to perform the functions of Court Jew, the title sometimes conferred by a King or sovereign Prince when appointing a Jew to an official position, usually that of Secretary General of Finance? These Jews, and these alone, had the right to leave the ghetto and live wherever they wished. They could even wear a sword, and no prohibition restricted the way they dressed. To work on behalf of the court provided the sole means by which Jews might escape their condition without also compromising their faith. Mayer Amschel yearned for this supreme reward, so coveted by all the ghetto's petty bankers. But knowing he was not indispensable to the reigning Prince, he had no illusions and was intelligent enough to place himself simultaneously at the disposal of another powerful family, the Princes of Thurn und Taxis, who in the sixteenth century had initiated a postal service that covered the whole of Europe. Being Prince and supreme postmaster did not automatically eliminate the need for money, and Mayer Amschel offered to lend it at an attractive rate of interest. In this he was following the policy that had already proved successful. The arrangement was advantageous to the borrower in the short term, but it promised to be invaluable to Rothschild in the long.

In 1800, as the price of services rendered, Mayer Amschel requested that he be named Imperial Agent of the Crown. The title, which was granted, gave him greater freedom to travel about the Empire, a precious asset for anyone engaged in placing loans and collecting interest, and one that few Jews, his direct competitors, enjoyed. This super-passport had the added advantage of liberating its bearer from certain of the taxes imposed upon Jews. Finally, by becoming familiar with the postal system, the Rothschilds learned the fundamental importance of secret and swift communications. Certainly they discovered the latitude that the Thurn und Taxis allowed themselves in unsealing letters, possibly divulging their contents, and, according to their own interests, delaying or accelerating delivery.

Thus Mayer Amschel developed his affairs in as many directions as possible, and did so with obvious success, although the extent of this is difficult to measure in the absence of actual figures. We know, however, that until 1794 he was estimated to have assets worth about 2,000 gulden (800 dollars), on which the community imposed a tax of 13 gulden (or 5 dollars).[9] By 1795 the valuation had been increased tenfold. This made the income flowing to Mayer Amschel more or less comparable to that enjoyed by the Goethes, a well-off bourgeois family also resident in Frankfurt. In 1796 Rothschild found himself one of the most prosperous Jews in the ghetto. Further evidence of a fortune that would henceforth remain significant came in 1795, when his eldest daughter married Benedict Moses Worms and bore him a dowry of 5,000 gulden. But already, several years before, Mayer Amschel had succeeded in moving his household, no easy matter in the overpopulated ghetto, and in renting, since the Jews did not have the right to own property, a dwelling that boasted a water pump in the kitchen and a whole range of excellent hiding places, in addition to secret, underground passages that linked it to neighboring houses.

The "beautiful house" that Mayer Amschel and his family moved into would have horrified their economic peers, the upper-middleclass parents of Johann Wolfgang von Goethe. These solid citizens could scarcely have appreciated the "advantages" of the narrow structure that the Rothschilds were forced to share with another family.[10] The congestion within the three dark rooms would have struck the Goethes as inhuman. Since Jewish children had no right to play in public parks, they spent the day penned up at home, away from the quarter's single street. In this malodorous, unhealthy lane, devoid of pavements and thronged with a population of four thousand, a shaft of sunlight scarcely ever penetrated beyond the steep, serried roofs. At nightfall, guards locked the gates and sealed the street, making it impossible for anyone to enter or depart. Such was the law that governed the ghetto. The confinement it imposed, however, constituted a protection as well as a persecution, in that the walls which imprisoned the Jews also kept any possible enemy outside. Frequently the portals of the ghetto were fitted with locks on the inside, so as to give the inmates additional security in the event of hostile manifestations from without. In 1711 fear and suspicion on the part of the Jews had reached such proportions that when a great fire broke out in the Frankfurt ghetto, the inhabitants refused to open the gates and thus allowed the quarter to burn down.

This quarantine of the Jews had the effect of rigorously preserving their cohesiveness and culture. The apparent disorder of the ghetto concealed a fierce discipline that, paradoxically, fostered the community's spiritual and psychological flowering. To resist the repression imposed upon them by the outside world, the Jews learned to control every aspect of their existence. It was this astonishing effort of organization—these cultural, religious, and social constraints—that kept them from succumbing. They had a world unto themselves, a structured universe, complete and demanding, where the individual melted into the whole. For anyone who had no occasion to go out of the enclosure, life within it, overregulated and unrealistically secure, could assume a suffocating monotony. "These obscure, humble people had one great advantage over us," wrote Albert Einstein. "Each of them belonged in every fiber of his being to a community, in which he was wholly absorbed, in which he felt himself a privileged member, which asked nothing of him that was contrary to his natural habits of thought. Our forefathers of those days were pretty poor specimens intellectually and physically, but socially they enjoyed an enviable spiritual equilibrium."[11]

The municipal government, moreover, considered the ghetto to be a totality and responsible to the city as such. Thus taxes were to be paid by the community, not by each Jew individually. This meant that the group's own leaders determined the amounts owed and then covered them as they thought best. As a result, the wealthiest members ended up paying for everyone else. By making all families subject to a central authority, either as beneficiaries or contributors, the financial arrangement simply strengthened the ties that bound the community together. At the same time, it gave those in charge an intimate knowledge of everyone's affairs, thereby increasing the influence of the well-off—the bankers and the merchants. This occurred all the more decisively in the eighteenth century by virtue of the diminishing quality of intellectual life in the ghetto.

The strict isolation suffered by the Jews condemned them to live as if sealed in an airtight chamber, their closeness and overpopulation growing to intolerable proportions. Cut off from the intellectual movements of their time—the Age of Enlightenment!—they devoted themselves exclusively to study of the Torah and the Talmud. It was impossible for Germany's Jews to take their own measure against contemporary minds of equal stature. Intellectual exchange, so indispensable to the development of thought, was prohibited. Ironically, the only Jews who came into contact with the exterior world were the dealers in money. It was they who would extricate themselves from the soft cocoon of habit, show initiative, and summon up the courage to face Christians on their own ground, those Christians whom the Jews had been taught from early childhood to fear and detest and to hold responsible for all their woes. One may well believe that it was the psychological security engendered by the warmth of the ghetto that gave the Jewish financiers the strength to fight for their place in the world.

Another benefit accruing to the ghetto's merchants was the relay system made possible by the compact clusters of Jews scattered throughout Europe. As soon as they arrived in a strange city, Jewish businessmen knew immediately where to go, which was straight to the ghetto. There contacts occurred quite naturally. The unique quality of this Jewish society derived from the fact that it was fixed and turned in upon itself, yet at the same time linked to outposts all over the world. Small Israelite entities could be found in Europe and Asia; soon they would develop in North America and Africa as well, all offering safe haven to the Jewish traveler. Allied by the similarity, if not the uniformity, of their education, by their analogous ways of living and thinking, by their use of the same ritual language, most of all by a kind of writing so inaccessible to outsiders that it served as a secret code, the Jews compensated for the difficulties of life in an alien and often hostile environment by developing a formidable *esprit de corps*, which explains the strength and durability of their network of reciprocal aid.

Mayer Amschel did not venture particularly far afield, limiting himself to specific sorties required by his different clients. On his home ground, however, he entered into the most varied activities. He did this all the better by reason of the backing he soon received from his children. Gudule had lost no time either in producing infants or in setting them to work, girls as well as boys. "Go forth, my dear children, along different paths, and with a common fervor seek your fortunes at full speed." This precept, so often inscribed upon the signboards hung out by midwives, had most certainly been adopted by the Rothschilds. Beginning in 1771, Gudule gave birth annually for about eighteen years. Ten of the children survived, and all took part in the family business. Mayer Amschel employed outsiders only when in need of talents unavailable among his own and always for limited periods. There was, for example, a decree requiring that Jews keep their accounts in German. Mayer Amschel and Gudule spoke only Frankfurt Yiddish, a hybrid dialect of German marked by peculiarities of pronunciation and expressions drawn from Hebrew. Moreover, they wrote exclusively in Hebrew characters. This made it necessary for them to hire accountants better educated than they were. Soon it became essential to know English since trade with Great Britain was developing rapidly. Then too, Mayer Amschel placed great store by the style of his letters, fully aware that the skillful nuancing of a polite formula could bring off a deal, that a knowing use of flattery might prove determining. But even the Rothschild children, girls and boys alike, had not gone beyond the elementary school organized in the local synagogue, which taught nothing more than the rudiments of Hebrew. Thus they had no mastery of Roman script. Profit outweighing prejudice, Mayer Amschel engaged a young Christian woman to draft his letters for him.

Having early discerned his children's aptitude for helping him in all essential matters, Mayer Amschel refused to involve his numerous other relatives in the family business, even though this generated more than enough work to go round. He excluded cousins, nephews, and, most particularly, sons-in-law. The Rothschild daughters married, one after the other, as soon as they reached the age of about twenty-five. No one married young in the ghetto owing to the rigorous control exercised by cities over Jewish marriages. At times only the eldest son received authorization to take a wife, and occasionally even this was determined by the number of deaths that had occurred. The Rothschilds probably felt less pressure to marry off their daughters because the young women played an important part in their father's business. They kept the books with exemplary precision, which gave them the upper hand in disputes with their brothers. Once they had married, however, the Rothschild ladies departed the paternal house forever. And they all took their leave accordingly, marrying the sons of Frankfurt bankers—Worms, Sichel, Beyfus—though the youngest daughter married only after Mayer Amschel's death and did so in England.[12] The German in-laws conducted regular business with the Rothschilds but never enjoyed a privileged relationship. Daughters-in-law, on the other hand, found themselves immediately adopted and just as quickly put to work, having been chosen with the greatest care by old Mayer Amschel. He was guided more by the young women's connections than by sentiment—at least according to Amschel, the eldest Rothschild son, who complained to the end of his life that his father had refused him permission to marry the woman he loved.

Mayer Amschel honored all the traditions, and however great his commercial success, it in no way altered his style of life. Modesty and economy remained the dominant characteristics of the Rothschild house, which functioned not only as a home but also as office and warehouse, where clerks and clients jostled one another for space. Gudule wrote to Karl, then in London staying with Nathan: "Bring me whatever is lying around in Nathan's dwellings . . . whatever he has no use for, because I make use of everything here."[13] Gelche, the wife of Salomon, who was to become Baroness Caroline once the Rothschilds had attained their glory, dissuaded her husband from bringing back a new hat since she already owned a hat. The shirts worn by the men, for which Gudule took personal responsibility, were recut, mended, and used until threadbare.[14] And piety continued to reign in this household. Far from allowing his wealth to serve as a dispensation from religious practice, Mayer Amschel observed all the Hebraic laws more regularly than ever. This virtue, together with his professional triumph, earned Rothschild the respect of the whole Jewish community.

Throughout most of his childhood, James witnessed the irresistible expansion of the Rothschild business, an advance whose frenzied rhythm was set as much by political events as by Mayer Amschel's own qualities. The Napoleonic wars, by isolating the Continent, generated an urgent demand for precisely the manufactured goods and textiles that Rothschild was importing from Great Britain. Even the hazards of war served the interests of the Frankfurters. Thus, when the French invasion of the Low Countries resulted in the closing of the Amsterdam Stock Exchange, then the most important such institution in Europe, it brought a powerful new stimulus to the activity of every financier in the German city. Even the bombardment of Frankfurt itself and the destruction of the ghetto had happy consequences for the Jews, who now gained the right to rent sheds in the Christian city. Since it was only by maintaining warehouses that merchants could stock goods for sale at the most opportune moment, the possibility of enlarging their storage capacity held the promise of tremendous benefits. Needless to say, Mayer Amschel lost no time in taking advantage of the occasion.

In 1805, upon reaching the age of thirteen, James ceased to be regarded as a minor and took his place in the community of men. Like his brothers, he had spent hardly any time at school, responding instead to the need at home. "Our Jacob is already working in our *comptoir*," wrote a proud Mayer Amschel to Nathan.[15] The boy must have been quick, engaging, and reliable, for his father took him along on all his travels across Germany. Mayer Amschel had had himself built a carriage honeycombed with secret drawers to contain and conceal payments collected on behalf of the Landgrave of Hesse. None of this, however, could protect the Rothschilds from countless humiliations, and James learned to toughen himself as he encountered them. Every time the Jews crossed one of the frontiers separating all those little principalities, they found themselves required to pay a special duty called *Leibzoll* (a sort of head tax). They might even be forced to offer a set of dice, or to forfeit the equivalent in money, in atonement for what had been won on Christ's garments at Golgotha. Some cities would admit the Jews only by day. When it came to taking an oath before a tribunal, they had to do it *more judaico*, which entailed a complicated and degrading ceremony.[16] Constantly harassed in this way, no Jew could ever forget the inferiority of his status.

However considerable his fortune and excellent his reputation, Mayer Amschel always remained in the uncertain position of a Jew. He had to beg for the right to make a business trip to Kassel, and this despite his privileged relationship with the Landgrave. Although he tenaciously challenged the justice of the taxes that were heaped upon him, it availed the elder Rothschild little or nothing. He had to appeal endlessly, and always in the most obsequious terms, in order to consolidate his gains. Every privilege granted him was personal, and therefore could be withdrawn. He enjoyed no legal protection whatever. And James, acutely sensitive to the contrast between the importance of the negotiations underway and the cavalier manner in which the clients treated his father, was under no illusion about the precariousness inherent in his origins.

For the same reason, James always appreciated returning to the ghetto and the consideration accorded his father there. The rich man had by now acquired an undeniable dignity. Making money in such a hostile world endowed him with an aura of the heroic and absolved all displays of arrogance. The community gloried in every one of Mayer Amschel's successes. This explains why persecutions suffered outside the ghetto in no way undermined the self-confidence of young James. He enjoyed, moreover, a rock-solid strength and stability, built up by his family, that family simultaneously closed tight like a fist, united by mutual confidence and an invincible wall of secrecy, yet wide open to the outside world. Such was the cohesion of the Rothschilds that the removal of one or more of them left no gap in their common defenses.

Several years earlier, in 1798, Nathan, the third brother and without doubt the most astute and enterprising Rothschild of his generation, had decided to depart for England in order to take charge of the exports to the Continent. He settled first in Manchester and then in London. His father, who believed that "the best way to make money in big business is to have some already,"[17] gave him 20,000 pounds to get started. Although chronically disorganized (an attribute that drove Mayer Amschel mad) and incapable of writing legible script or correctly numbering the cases he expedited, Nathan began to increase his stake with an apparent facility that could only disconcert his competitors. Conscious of the support available from his family, he repeatedly asked that Salomon or Karl should come and reinforce him with their own presence. For James, Nathan represented a broad, European spirit, a breakthrough, the possibility of fleeing Frankfurt without severing the tie that bound him to his own kind. In that promising mixture of daring and prudence, moreover, James resembled his elder brother to a remarkable degree. Contact with his father's clients had made James a young man of rare aplomb. So "scrupulously did he carry out his assignments" that soon he found himself entrusted with matters of the greatest importance.[18] As early as 1808, Mayer Amschel, eager to avoid a police inquiry into certain shipments from Hamburg, had sent James to look over the situation and then attached great importance to his advice.[19] The Rothschild family quickly began to treat their cadet as an equal.

Events in Germany itself were evolving at a quickening pace. In 1805 came the Battle of Austerlitz and the collapse of Austria. The following year saw the defeat of Prussia. "My intention," decreed Napoleon, "is that Hesse be wiped off the map." Wilhelm IX, who only three years earlier had been elevated to the dignity of Elector, was forced to beat a hasty retreat and seek refuge at Prague. Needless to say, his sudden flight sowed consternation among Frankfurt's bankers, who made their living from the negotiation of the Prince's receipts and loans. Mayer Amschel, however, was unaffected by the debacle. Buderus, Wilhelm's confidential agent and long an accomplice of the Rothschilds, remained at his post. It was later stated that the departing Landgrave had entrusted his wealth—most particularly certain cases filled with precious objects—to Mayer Amschel. Nothing of the sort happened. Rothschild received for safekeeping only four cases, which he hid in his own cellar. What he gained from the Prince's departure, thanks to Buderus, was his appointment as the only person authorized to collect interest on loans made by the Landgrave of Hesse to Austria, to discount the installments from England or Copenhagen, and to pay, on commission, the agents and soldiers of Wilhelm IX. For the Rothschilds, therefore, the French occupation signaled expanding professional activity; it also meant a social revolution, born of reforms imposed by the conquerors.

Napoleon had organized the states of Western Germany into the Confederation of the Rhine. Frankfurt, which had always gloried in its independence, found itself incorporated, though saved from total humiliation by being designated the residence of the Primate of the Confederation, Archbishop von Dalberg.[20] This was the first change of regime that James lived through, the first in a long series that continued into the Second Empire (1852–70).

The Jewish question immediately came to the fore. In principle, the Jews of Germany were offered unconditional freedom just as the Jews of France had been in 1791. The imperial armies hastened to impose French-style liberty on all the conquered lands. Napoleon, it seems, imagined that emancipated and grateful Jews would rally to his cause. He was mistaken. German Jews, especially those of Prussia, preferred to identify with Germans rather than to join the forces of liberty and revolution. Moreover, Germany was too diverse to permit uniform treatment of Jews throughout all the various states.

At Kassel, capital of the Kingdom of Westphalia that Napoleon had just created for the benefit of his brother Jérôme, unrestricted rights were granted to the Jews. Relieved of all discriminatory taxes and interdictions, Westphalian Jews could now live wherever they wished and their sons might aspire to careers in medicine, law, even teaching. At Frankfurt, however, a reform of this magnitude was not possible. Archbishop von Dalberg, an open-minded man who himself was so aware of the usefulness of the Jews that he appointed one to be Chief of Police, knew only too well the virulent anti-Semitism of the city's long-dominant patricians and could not risk complete emancipation after the manner of Westphalia. He therefore undertook merely to protect the Jews "against insult and injustice, and declared that full equality could not be granted until they had proved themselves worthy of it by abandoning their special practices and adopting the customs of the country."[21] In other words, Frankfurt's Jews would be regarded as foreigners—treated like human beings but not as citizens. They continued to pay special taxes, and despite the partial destruction of the ghetto by French artillery, were not allowed to live elsewhere in the city. Thus the Jews had reason to view the improvement in their lot as no more than relative. The situation was open to negotiation, however, and the Jewish leadership wasted no time in driving every bargain possible.

Simultaneously, the younger Jews began to question the merits of total submission to the dictates of their religion. The children of Mayer Amschel were especially eager to pass through the door now opened to them. With the exception of Amschel, the eldest son, they abandoned the Orthodox style of dressing and the traditional beard. They took liberties with the sacrosanct laws which required rest on the Sabbath. "I write while hiding from Amschel. Today it's Saturday," confessed Karl in a letter to James,[22] who himself needed no encouragement along the path to revolt. His travels had revealed to James the delights of a forbidden cuisine, a taste which now made a journey with the pious Amschel almost intolerable. "Amschel is so religious that he always insists upon eating kosher,"[23] James wrote to Salomon in 1814, "and even though he knows that I care nothing for [dietary rules], he forces me to take my meals with him. . . . I can no longer abide that awful food."[24]

The younger Rothschilds also attacked the problem of language. Struggling to perfect their German and to learn both English and French, they rose before dawn and set about studying. They refused to be put off by any laughter their accent might provoke. They also refused to limit their dealings with Christians to matters of business. Once usury ceased to be the main activity of the Jews, and their funds served to reinforce the capital of merchants and entrepreneurs, the business of credit lost its ugly character. The obligation to reimburse a loan and to pay interest became less onerous to men whose affairs had flourished as a result of the borrowed money. The Jewish lender ceased to be a bloodsucker; often, indeed, he became an associate of the borrower. The winds of freedom set moving by the French armies had swept away the prejudices of old Germany.

The Jews of Berlin, among them the poet Heinrich Heine,

organized a society designed to help overcome the cultural isolation of their coreligionists, to encourage them to venture into careers outside commerce, and to be flexible in the exercise of their faith so as to allow them to integrate with society at large, without betraying their most fundamental beliefs. At Frankfurt, Salomon belonged for several years to a Masonic lodge where Jews and Christians could meet on neutral and friendly ground. This by no means meant that local anti-Semitism had evaporated, however. Of the five hundred members of Salomon's lodge, no more than twenty-five were Christians, and only one of these lived permanently in Frankfurt. All the others were officers or soldiers in the occupying army, and when the French departed the lodge had to be dissolved. But even the brief contact it provided with the non-Jewish world sufficed to persuade the Rothschild boys that they were not irrevocably destined to lead the same existence as their father.

Mayer Amschel did indeed live in a world apart. The fact that he dealt with Princes in no way diminished his exclusion. His personal life remained rooted in the ghetto. Language, education, taste, diet, all prevented the elder Rothschild from sharing a meal with a Christian, while his long black caftan, round fur hat, and full beard served to build a wall between him and others. For Mayer Amschel, to break with custom and abjure all that made up his universe would have been unthinkable. (It was no mere quirk that Gudule, who survived her husband by thirty-five years and could have lived in Europe's most beautiful palaces, never wanted to leave her house in the ghetto. For her too, Jew Street represented warmth, humanity, and shelter from a hostile world.)

Once successful, Mayer Amschel took pleasure in feeling his authority and duties grow within the heart of the ghetto. These meant so much to him that he sometimes neglected his own affairs for those of his people. "If I have not written to you in greater detail," the elder Rothschild explained to James in 1808, "it's because I spent all last week on the problems of our community. . . ."[25] Thus Mayer Amschel, along with a group of other prosperous Jews, began intensive discussions with the authorities designed to bring about genuine reforms. First, they requested that the various taxes imposed upon the

Jews should be combined into one annual excise. Then, taking advantage of the government's financial needs, they offered to pay in advance a lump sum equal to twenty years' taxes, in exchange for their civic rights. The proposal was accepted and a decree issued declaring that all Jews resident in Frankfurt, their children, and their descendants would henceforth enjoy the same liberties and privileges as the city's other inhabitants. After this success, Mayer Amschel was regarded as the official leader of the Jewish population; all the more so since he personally had paid a full quarter of the ransom. But however great this responsibility, it did not make Rothschild forget the demands of commerce. On the contrary, his activity grew more intense and diverse as a consequence of the Napoleonic reorganization of Europe, which had changed every rule in the book.

When the Continental Blockade was mounted, so as to cut off all communication with Great Britain, it seemed to promise slow but certain death to trading cities like Frankfurt. For the more resourceful, however, it also offered great opportunities. If one could outwit the authorities, including the French customs, and smuggle merchandise that, because of its scarcity, had gone up tenfold in price, one might realize profits on a prodigious scale. The situation proved to be one in which the Rothschilds could exercise their genius for extracting advantage from apparently unpropitious circumstances. This was made possible by Nathan's presence in England and the mobility of Amschel, Salomon, Karl, and James on the Continent. Mayer Amschel's sons found themselves caught up in the rude life of traveling salesmen, making regular runs from Gravelines, where a collection point for English contraband had been established, to Hamburg, Amsterdam, and Berlin. Along the way they slept in bad inns, endured the discomfort of poor roads and worse carriages, and wrote endless doleful letters to Frankfurt, ungratefully complaining about the weight of the cakes with which Gudule had lined their bags. But despite tormented stomachs, headaches, the sadness of nights alone, they ploughed on across Europe, taking charge of incoming shipments, chasing clients or lenders, forever cultivating their business relations. The order books kept by Nathan reveal some fifty contacts, not only in Germany but also in Basel, Brussels, Copenhagen, Lyons, Metz, and Nancy. He exploited everyone related to him, his brothers-in-law Beyfus, Sichel, and Worms, the Hanaus, the parents of Eva, Amschel's wife, and the Sterns, the parents-in-law of Salomon, not to mention his own wife's family, the Cohens, who were solidly established in London and Amsterdam. A service rendered to a Jew was never wasted, Mayer Amschel loved to repeat, since it invariably came back a hundredfold through the new business it generated. The Rothschilds made the most of their connections, based on mutual confidence and unimpeded by any frontier.

If the Rothschilds reaped profits more substantial than those of their rivals, it was because they had adopted the simplest kind of commercial policy. Holding to the principle that it was better to borrow in order to purchase rather than to remain on the sidelines, they obtained money at the best rate going, bought heavily, and sold everything as quickly as possible. The corollary to this practice was their determination to undersell all competitors. "I can procure anything manufactured in England and guarantee that I will make you a price 10 percent lower than that of any other house in Frankfurt," Nathan insisted to a client in Antwerp. Since he was known to be as good as his word, Rothschild quickly concluded the deal.[26]

Trading of this kind had for some years constituted an important part of the Rothschilds' business, but always it had been carried on as an adjunct to their financial operations. These, of course, arose mainly from the business of their old client, the Elector of Hesse, now a refugee in Prague, and they illustrate the importance of astute calculation of risk. Because of the war, Prince Wilhelm could not collect the considerable sums that had accrued to him in Great Britain. Nathan pondered how he might make good use of those funds. Supported by his father and the faithful Buderus, who profited from the Prince's distrust and timidity, Nathan became manager of the Elector's English fortune. Wilhelm insisted, against all advice, upon having the whole amount invested in government bonds. Nathan, for whom Buderus had arranged power of attorney, proceeded to pay the Prince the official rate of interest, while "borrowing" the capital in order to invest it for a much higher return. The Elector was never the wiser, but even if he had been, he could hardly have complained of disobedience. In fact, Wilhelm turned increasingly to the Rothschilds and used their services more and more.

Amschel soon began spending more time at Prague than in Frankfurt. By remaining close to his client, he succeeded in making himself the sole intermediary used by the Elector in his communications with Buderus in Kassel, a position that Amschel retained throughout the French occupation. Apart from the purely financial advantage of this relationship, the Rothschilds acquired a reputation that led to their first contacts with the Hapsburg court. Every Prince in Germany, including the Austrian Emperor, sought to borrow from the Elector of Hesse. It did not take them long to discover that the best guarantee of success was to gain the confidence of Wilhelm's Jewish bankers. The power of the Rothschilds had been perceived, and soon Finance Ministers were approaching them direct.

All this activity, whether it concerned contraband or the finances of the Elector, Napoleon's declared enemy, had to be carried out in a clandestine manner. Mayer Amschel soon found it expedient to maintain two sets of accounts, for the expansion of his commercial interests had been too spectacular not to be noticed by the authorities. An inspection of his books resulted in the seizure of vast quantities of indigo, but, after paying a heavy fine, the Rothschilds went on with their smuggling. Then came another alarm.

Napoleon's police, with good reason, began watching the activities of the Elector of Hesse, suspecting him of financing resistance to the French occupation of Germany. It seemed only prudent to place the Rothschilds under similar surveillance, and a search of their premises was fixed for May 1809. Dalberg, who regularly borrowed from Mayer Amschel, warned the latter and gave his Jewish creditors time to prepare themselves. As always in such cases, the inhabitants of the ghetto closed ranks and displayed their full solidarity. Mayer Amschel disposed of his most compromising papers by passing them to his neighbors. But what was he to do with the four large chests consigned to him by Buderus in 1808? Too massive to be transported through the secret passages leading from one cellar to another, they had to be emptied and their incriminating contents burned. The elder Rothschild, with the help of his wife, children, and daughters-in-law, completed the task in the nick of time and then took to his bed, there to await the arrival of the inspector. He had undergone surgery the year before, Mayer Amschel explained to Savagner, the Chief of Police, and had not felt well since. His memory was failing, and he hoped to be forgiven if his responses seemed a bit vague.

Savagner turned to Gudule, but the poor woman knew nothing, mere housewife that she was. Salomon and James, confined in the kitchen, kept to the agreed line. True, their older brother was in Prague, but solely on the personal business of the Elector. They could not imagine what else he might be doing. All these dullards found their wits, however, once Savagner confessed that he was in financial difficulties. Miraculously, the requisite sum was found straight off and offered— at, no doubt, a reasonable rate of interest. This was not the first time the Rothschilds had lent to the French. What better way, after all, to assure their goodwill? The method proved infallible. Whenever Mayer Amschel and his sons were on the verge of being caught out, some highly placed person stepped in and stopped the investigation.

The Rothschilds changed course constantly during this period, always maneuvering to avoid any kind of political commitment. Although the French still appeared all-powerful, they failed to win the support of Frankfurt's leading financiers. Yet Mayer Amschel and his sons did not hope for a straightforward restoration of the old order. This is apparent in their attitude toward the Elector. Wilhelm, ever hopeful of recovering his throne and his power, asked that one of the Rothschild brothers should remain permanently at his side. Mayer Amschel, moved by a sure instinct, refused. He declined to oblige one of the richest grandees in Europe, the Prince whose favor he had so ardently courted in the early years, whose patronage he had most humbly solicited, waiting all those hours in the antechamber. He refused this secure and remunerative post even though to have filled it would still have left him four sons. And this he did because he had come to perceive that the future lay not with the little courts of Central Europe but with the triangle defined by London, Paris, and Vienna, and that it would have been absurd to limit himself in exclusive service to a single sovereign, thereby making this client the sole beneficiary of the

Rothschilds' international contacts. On the contrary, the Rothschilds must establish themselves as a family, a homogeneous
firm, on an international footing able to serve governments
everywhere, in Germany, in Great Britain and France, in Austria and Italy. The loose, unsystematic organization that bound
its individual members into a random web of clients and busi-
nesses would transform itself into a well-integrated structure
capable of gathering information and carrying out complex,
unified operations. The precision with which Mayer Amschel
drafted the clauses of his will attests to the elder Rothschild's
foresight. The dispersion of his sons would in no way affect
the essential reality, which was that the House of Rothschild
constituted a single firm. It just happened to exist physically
in different locations.

In his will, the broad outlines of which had been drawn up
in 1810, Mayer Amschel provided that a fraction of his total
fortune should be reserved for the benefit of his wife, that some
25,000 gulden (10,000 dollars) should go directly to each of his
five daughters, and that all the rest should remain with his five
sons, who were to continue in close association. An understanding had been reached that none of the boys would have
the right to withdraw his portion of the capital from the whole
and that each of them should take from the annual profits no
more than was strictly necessary for his household expenses.
Each of the partners was entitled to sign on behalf of the firm.
As a precaution against discord, Rothschild specified that the
brothers might refer their differences to a court of law only
after depositing a substantial sum of money. Finally, the will
stipulated that neither daughters nor sons-in-law would have
the right to examine the accounts.

Nathan most certainly had some influence upon the structure of this document, for in 1811 he was already beginning to
reorient the family business. Contraband had become increasingly risky since the annexation of Hamburg, Bremen, and
Lubeck by France. At the same time, however, the ubiquity of
the Rothschilds on the Continent helped their brother in England to implement a plan for transferring funds, something
that the British government desperately needed in order to
provide regular sustenance for Wellington's troops in Spain
and Portugal. The system, which Nathan quickly perfected,

had James and Salomon shuttling between Paris and Dunkirk, taking delivery of the gold pieces sent by Nathan, and converting them through Parisian bankers into drafts on Spanish banks, which then disbursed the proceeds to Wellington. Karl, meanwhile, posted himself temporarily in southwestern France, whence he supervised the final transfer of the funds across the Pyrenees.

The arrangement made it imperative for a Rothschild to be officially installed in Paris. James had long since proved his abilities. Indeed, Nathan had already wanted to involve him more thoroughly in his schemes, but Mayer Amschel had refused to let his youngest son go. Now, in 1811, Nathan renewed his appeal. So tricky and dangerous was the mission in Paris that it justified the assignment of James, not only in recognition of his boldness and good sense in matters of business, but also because of his curiosity and openness of mind. Nathan found him, of all his brothers, the one with the greatest aptitude for mixing easily in society, a quality indispensable for anyone intent upon becoming established in France. Finally, James himself wanted to take up the challenge and leave Frankfurt.

The only problem that remained was the considerable one of obtaining the necessary permission from the authorities. For this Mayer Amschel counted on the vanity of Dalberg. It so happened that the Primate wanted to be in Paris for the baptism of the Roi de Rome, a noble assembly at which he felt it imperative that he should cut a fine figure. This was sure to be costly. First, Dalberg approached the Frankfurt merchants' guild for a loan of 160,000 francs—around 32,000 dollars. The good tradesmen refused, thereby giving Mayer Amschel his opportunity. Undaunted by the amount, which represented one-tenth of his liquid assets, Rothschild offered to lend the money at a rate of five percent—plus a small supplement, the passport needed by James. Dalberg, who according to an inspector's report was in no position to refuse the elder Rothschild anything,[27] was delighted to clinch the deal. And so, even though the French police had their suspicions about the Rothschilds, and Napoleon's spies knew well that the traffic being carried on by Mayer Amschel and his sons would be facilitated by the permanent presence of a Rothschild in France, despite the fact that the authorities inveighed against the "extreme cunning" of these Jews, who succeeded in having friends at every court, James was able to depart unhindered. Once again, shirts and cakes went into the luggage. This time, however, Mayer Amschel dispensed with advice, so confident did he feel about his boy. Instead, he simply gave the traditional blessing. Thus, with his young niece, the daughter of Salomon, extracting a promise that he write regularly, James set forth towards new horizons.

2
A New World

James, more than his brothers, had wanted to leave Frankfurt and follow in the footsteps of Nathan. The departure he made in 1811 was final. The suffocating congestion of the ghetto, the intrusions of neighbors with their suspicious and constant control over his movements, and the primitive conditions in which the Jews lived had weighed too heavily on James for him ever to return. The great gift the Frankfurt ghetto bestowed upon him was adaptability, a quality matched by the driving force of his ambition, his prodigious energy, tremendous powers of concentration, and determination to get even. James set out to make his place in the world.

For all his promise, however, James Rothschild made a start in Paris that fell somewhat short of total triumph. True, he enjoyed his liberty and rejoiced in his professional success, but at the same time he suffered very real emotional isolation, unlike his brother on the other side of the Channel. Nathan—thanks to his marriage to Hannah Cohen, an English Jewess "of great distinction and capacity for holding her own at the most elegant gatherings,"[1] a young woman whose father was a well-established City banker with access to London's Jewish patriciate—had been immediately adopted and supported by a rich and powerful clan. The services that he rendered the British government during the Continental Blockade ensured that his naturalization came easily. Nothing of the sort happened to James who, until the Restoration in 1815, remained hostile to the government and could not enter Parisian Jewish society for the simple reason that none existed.

Whereas London had been host to a thriving, prosperous Jewish community of some six thousand people since the sixteenth century, pre-Revolutionary Paris contained no more than a handful of Jews. Despite their undeniable talent in commerce and industry and the utility of their countless contacts in Europe's urban centers, Jews had not succeeded in establishing themselves in the French capital. In 1789, the year the Bastille fell, only five hundred Jews could be found in Paris, a tiny minority without legal status or unity. Divided as they were among Germans from Alsace, "Portuguese" from Bordeaux, and Avignonnais from Provence, half of Paris' Jews spoke Yiddish while the other half spoke Spanish or Ladino, a medieval Spanish tinged with Hebrew. The three groups had so little affinity with one another that they did not even share the same temple or use the same rites, all of which reflected the disparateness of France's Jewish population.

To understand this, we must retrace a bit of history. Jews appeared in Gaul at a very early time. Evidence of their presence on the Mediterranean coast dates back to the fourth century, and it seems that until the twelfth century they lived on peaceful terms with their neighbors. The Carolingians even created the office of *magister judaeorum* to protect their interests. Nevertheless, society evolved in ways that did not favor the Jews. Caught in a web of loyalties based exclusively on religious faith, medieval man was troubled by the presence and activity of people he regarded as heretics. "In this strictly hierarchical society, a role was assigned to each class of person: The feudal lord should bear arms and govern; the priest should pray and glorify God; the serf should labor. And the Jew? He had no place in the system."[2] Excluded from the guilds and corporations, the medieval Jew had no choice but to become a money lender. This occupation, however useful, led all too easily to the role of scapegoat, once the Crusades generated an atmosphere of religious intolerance. From the twelfth to the fourteenth century, as persecution increased, the Jews of France often sought safety in exile.

In 1394, Charles VI ordered a general expulsion of Jews. This, however, did not mean the total elimination of all Jews from France. The order affected only the royal domains, which left the expelled Jews free to resettle in less hostile provinces, such as Dauphiné, Champagne, Provence, and Guyenne, none of which came directly under the jurisdiction of the King. Thus progressively, as the crown annexed more and more territories, the royal authority found itself confronted with deeply rooted Jewish communities, each very different from the other. The Jews of Alsace and those of Bordeaux formed the extremes.

The two concentrations of French Jewry were dissimilar in every way. The so-called "Germans" lived in an area, on the west bank of the Rhine, that had only come under French rule in 1648, after the Thirty Years War, and had always been subject to anti-Semitic prejudices comparable to those that raged throughout Central Europe. Prohibited from living in town, they huddled in rural settlements, wretched and despised, and took no part in the cultural life of France. More fortunate were the "Portuguese," those refugees from the Inquisition in fifteenth-century Spain and Portugal who observed their own— Sephardic—rite and suffered no discrimination whatever. Established in Bordeaux itself and sufficiently respected by their neighbors not to isolate themselves, these Jews constituted an intellectual élite acknowledged by all. From them came the most famous doctors of the eighteenth century; Louis XV would have no other. The Bordelais Jews, moreover, were frequently offered such positions as librarian or interpreter to the court. Rich, powerful, and securely based in a province which had formed an integral part of France since the reign of Louis XI, they achieved a position of such prominence that the Estates General invited them to submit a list of their grievances when that body convened in 1789. Needless to say, the situation of the Bordelais had nothing in common with Jews elsewhere in France, whom the lucky few heartily scorned.

Then came the Revolution. The Parisian Jews—those few who had been intrepid enough to risk life in the capital where, barely tolerated, they were subject to continuous and brutal police surveillance—suddenly found themselves filled with political zeal. Even before the emancipation decrees, a good quarter of them enlisted in the National Guard. Some actually offered to serve on the district committees. They strenuously campaigned for and finally succeeded in having the Jewish question placed on the agenda for the Constituent Assembly. The toleration cause was then taken up by a priest, Abbé Grégoire, as well as by three members of the high nobility: Mirabeau, Clermont-Tonnerre, and Castellane. The initial victory came when the Jews of the Midi gained their civil rights. A year later, on September 27, 1791, the Assembly granted full citizenship to all Jews born and domiciled in France. For the first time in Europe, Jews were accepted without restriction of any kind into a national community. As they saw a whole new future opening before them, the Jews of France also heard from Robespierre words that soothed old wounds like a healing balm: "Things have been said about the Jews that are infinitely exaggerated and often contrary to history. How can one blame them for the persecution they encounter among all peoples? Everyone imputes to them vices, prejudices, a sectarian and usurious spirit, and in the most exaggerated way. But to what can we impute these things if not to our own injustice?"[3]

Now the Jews' enthusiasm for public life knew no bounds. "Here we are, thanks to the Supreme Being and to the sovereignty of the nation, not only men and citizens but Frenchmen. What a happy change! . . . From lowly slaves, simple serfs, a type of humanity scarcely tolerated in this realm, subject to enormous and arbitrary taxes, we have suddenly become children of the fatherland and can now share in its rights and responsibilities,"[4] exclaimed Isaac Cerfbeer, one of the most notable of the Alsatian Jews. France's Jews became captains in the National Guard, police lieutenants, justices of the peace. Countless numbers of them volunteered for the Revolutionary army, and when forced to choose between the Orthodox life and service to their new *patrie,* many did not hesitate. Jews began thronging to Paris, and by the end of the Revolution the capital's Hebraic population had swelled to around three thousand.

These new Parisian Jews rapidly distinguished themselves in the widest variety of fields. Furtado and Worms de Romilly were elected to the Chamber of Deputies, Worms also serving as mayor of Paris' third *arrondissement*. Venture, a specialist in Oriental languages, would become secretary and interpreter to Bonaparte during the Egyptian campaign. When the latter learned of Vivant Denon, formerly curator of Louis XV's medal and coin collection, he appointed him Director General of France's museums. The Jews blossomed no less vigorously under the Empire, for Napoleon quickly reaffirmed all their civil liberties. The Emperor even convoked a general assembly of Jews, which became the Great Sanhedrin, a body whose function was to facilitate the assimilation of the Jews while at the same time leaving them free to practice their religion.

Nevertheless, the bright new world that greeted the Jews in post-Revolutionary France was not without its shadow, cast by the "infamous decrees" designed to impose severe restrictions on the freedom of commerce and movement allowed the Jews of Alsace. There were specific causes behind this retrograde step. At the outset of the Revolution, Alsatian peasants had acquired a great deal of nationalized land, but without the liquid assets to make their property flourish, the new owners could only turn to the despised yet envied Jewish money lenders. Times proved hard and uncertain, taxes heavy, and profits less than expected, with the result that the peasants found themselves unable to pay their debts. Hence their anger towards the Jews, their repeated petitions to the Emperor, and the ultimate decision to slow the rise of the Jews. The Parisian Jews, feeling threatened, protested their honor and patriotism and actually managed to gain exemption from the reimposed constraints. Créquet, the Interior Minister, advised the Emperor that among the several thousand Jews in the capital "there were not four who engaged in usury" and that more than one hundred and fifty were fighting under the French flag.

Despite their shock, French Jews submitted to the new regulations. These were based on a hierarchical and centralized system that shattered the old organization of small, individual communities, each gathered about a synagogue and led by a rabbi elected and invested with considerable administrative as well as spiritual and moral power. Now, thirteen consistories, or elected assemblies of rabbis and laymen, came into being for the purpose of directing the affairs of their constituent communities. Over these bodies stood the Central Consistory, endowed with sufficient authority to assure a certain coherence among all the Jews of France. But unification did not proceed without problems. In Paris, for instance, Jews settled largely in the third and fourth *arrondissements*, owing to the necessity for special butchers' shops and markets, but cultural issues tended to fragment the Jewish population. Thus the Germans and the Portuguese built separate synagogues, and while some rabbis officiated in Ladino, others used Yiddish. A few even gave their sermons in French. Not until 1831—forty years after emancipation—did French become standard usage in all the capital's synagogues. Then there was the division that entry into the lay world created between the Orthodox, the Liberal, and the Freethinker. Élie Halévy, a great Hebrew poet recently arrived from Germany, scandalized Parisian Jews when he sent his sons to the Lycée Charlemagne. There was no question but that Halévy considered himself a Jew; he simply hoped for the possibility of being both a Jew and a Frenchman, a position as strongly opposed by conservative Jews, who insisted on maintaining Jewish schools, as it was encouraged by the civil authorities.

Thus the Jewish community that James encountered in Paris was too loosely organized, too fraught with problems more personal than political, and too different from the Frankfurt ghetto, with its solidarity born of the constant need to defend its rights, for young Rothschild to feel any obligation to become part of it. Moreover, no one encouraged him. He was not even asked for a contribution. In his account books, all carefully kept, we find five francs—one dollar—given to a Frankfurt Jew, balanced by five francs given to the parish verger, and this would seem to be the full extent of his charity.[5]

In all likelihood, James simply gave the matter no thought, concerned as he was with his business affairs and the organization of his new life. He soon rented office space in the Rue Le Peletier and then moved into a small apartment above it. He received no visitor, except occasionally his brothers; nor did he return to Frankfurt during that first year, not even for the burial of his father, who died in the autumn of 1812.

Mayer Amschel had collapsed while at the synagogue attending Yom Kippur services. Returning home, he took to his bed, made the final revisions to his will, and died without designating which of his sons he deemed worthy of becoming head of the family. Instead, he exhorted them all to remain unified. Despite their different temperaments—quiet Amschel, scrupulous guardian of tradition, had little in common with dynamic Nathan—the Rothschild sons would never dissolve their relationship. "We are like the mechanism of a watch: each part is essential,"[6] declared Salomon, even while acknowledging that Nathan was probably more essential than the others. "We consider you to be the General and we are your Lieutenants,"[7] Salomon wrote to Nathan. And if they all lamented that their English brother was a commanding officer who treated his troops with impatience and insensitivity, a General more determined than his Lieutenants to live solely for business, the subordinates never dreamed of dissociating themselves from him. James, at the outset, would literally make no move except on orders from Nathan.

From London came the impetus that enabled the Rothschilds to raise themselves above the ruck of merchant bankers to the level of state bankers. When they began to penetrate government circles, it was Nathan who made it possible, as his brothers knew full well. "I realize," Salomon wrote to Nathan, "that if we're regarded as bigwigs, we owe it to your prestige and to all the business that we have obtained through you."[8]

The operations carried out by the Rothschilds at this time are exceedingly difficult to sort out. Their correspondence, always carried on in faulty German transcribed into Hebrew characters with all but unreadable handwriting (Nathan's was so illegible that ten years earlier his father had instructed him to engage a secretary), became deliberately more obscure once the authors began dealing in confidential or illicit matters. The brothers filled their letters with deletions and additions designed to mislead the unsuspecting reader. Moreover, they made generous use of code names; thus Metternich became "uncle," the Tsar the mysterious owner of "Gervais," and Nathan someone named Langbein. In the secret world of the Rothschilds, Rabbi Mayer functioned as the Duc de Richelieu! They also used the names of rabbis to signify English guineas. To break all their codes would be like deciphering the Rosetta Stone. Consequently, no one is certain precisely when the

Rothschilds began to be regarded as true agents of the British government. It is evident, however, that by 1813 they had become an important factor in the war machine mounted by the anti-French coalition, and that they were playing a primary role in the transfer of subsidies from Great Britain to its Continental allies. Certainly this was the period when the Rothschild brothers made the most money, increasing their net worth tenfold, a rate of growth they would never again equal.[9] Since the exact means by which this was accomplished can no longer be worked out, we must resort to conjecture. According to John Herries, a high official at the British Treasury, more than half the funds sent by his government to the Continent was handled by the Rothschilds, the process obviously controlled by Nathan. Together the brothers succeeded in outclassing all competitors by their speed and reliability, their information, and their skill in profiting from rates of exchange. Soon there would be no minister in Europe who did not know about the Rothschilds.

It was now that Nathan set up a private courier system that would surpass all others. At first the service ran between Dover and Calais, but then it expanded to link London with Paris, Vienna, and Frankfurt. For the English Channel, with its frequent bad weather, he recruited fearless captains, prohibited their accepting passengers, and, by promising large bonuses, induced them to take great risks. As a result, a Rothschild charter often crossed when no other boat would. But the family acquired a formidable reputation on land as well. During the winter the Rothschild courier took six days to go from Paris to Vienna, whereas the mail coach, the express service of that period, which had absolute priority over all other relays, required ten days. Thus the Rothschilds had the news before anyone else, including ministers; they also understood how to make use of it. Talleyrand swore, with some irritation, that thanks to the Rothschilds the British envoy to Paris knew everything ten to twelve hours before the dispatches from the French Ambassador in London could be delivered.

Financial operations, particularly those involving the transfer of funds from one country to another, did not always proceed without some friction developing among the associates. The slightest delay—the least hesitation—could result in heavy losses. Nathan's scathing letters to his brothers date from this period. Salomon, who always became the spokesman for the Rothschilds at critical moments, complained that the harangues delivered from London were making him ill. When the bickering subsided it was usually through appeals to sentiment rather than pure reason. This was because, however violent their invective, the brothers remained in full agreement concerning goals and the means used to achieve them. The problems almost invariably arose over some momentary failure to maintain their books in exemplary order, a failure that now seems inevitable given the near-uncontrollable growth of the Rothschild fortune.

Nathan, always forward-looking in his ideas but never able to express them with clarity, lost patience whenever he was not immediately understood. Then, incapable of measuring the impact his letters would have on the sensitive, united family in Frankfurt, he became angry and wrote whatever came into his head.

The few friends intimate enough to know about these dramas strove to calm the troubled spirits by invoking the specter of discord and ruin: "As long as a house is like yours, and as long as you work together with your brothers, not a house in the world will be able to compete with you, to cause you harm or to take advantage of you, for together you can undertake and perform more than any house in the world. But if such a family disintegrates, it makes a big difference and through your correspondence it could, God forbid, come to it, that your brothers will feel too insulted."[10] Still, the disputes continued, always fueled by the confusion in their accounts, but without ever reaching the point of rupture. "Thank God, we are, it seems to me, rich enough not to quarrel over three or four thousand pounds,"[11] pleaded Salomon, supported by Hannah, Nathan's sensible wife. The brothers continually played at frightening one another, all the while too mindful of their common interest to break up. Moreover, they honored their father's tradition and declined to involve friends or relatives in their speculations. Nathan, who received many appeals, found himself warned by James: "Suppose Nathan buys for Davidson shares worth twenty thousand francs. If they rise, Davidson would say, 'I speculated and I had luck.' If they fall, he would say, 'My boss has ruined me.' What would poor good Nathan do then? Either he would pay the loss from his own pocket, or he would buy enough of the security in question to drive the price up."[12]

In Paris, James had no trouble keeping his friends separate from his business since he had no friends. He realized, however, that such isolation could prove counterproductive and that he would need to embellish his somewhat uncouth appearance. It was now that he gave up the name Jacob as too Biblical and instead adopted James, the English sound of which seemed to strike a more suitable note. During the Restoration everything fashionable was *à l'anglaise*. This meant that James Rothschild ought to order his clothes from London, but when Nathan had him sent a frockcoat, he returned it with thanks: "I can't wear a garment so ill-cut and made of such coarse cloth. . . . I want exactly the same as that made for M. de Roure."[13] Meanwhile, James lamented his clumsy dancing and feared he might look ridiculous at a ball. He also thought he should learn to ride. This, unfortunately, led to a fall and a broken ankle, which prompted not sympathy but sarcasm from Nathan, angrily complaining that he wanted to hear about the stock market, not about a foot. Nevertheless, James persevered, convinced—and correctly so—of the importance of cutting a fine figure in society. He took pains to explain himself to his exasperated brother: "Dear, good Nathan, don't be bad-tempered. . . . I think of nothing except business; if I attend a society party, I go there to become acquainted with people who might be useful for the business. I swear this is true. . . ."[14] Despite his prodigious financial success, James remained unassuming. He merely rented his quarters in the Rue Le Peletier and recoiled from the cost of a real establishment. "A porter, a clerk, a pair of domestics, a coachman—all that is expensive, and it frightens me," he confessed to Salomon.[15] He constantly worried about his reputation, fearful that he and his brothers might be thought of as gamblers, and he did not underestimate the talents of his French competitors. "You have no idea," he wrote to Nathan, "how astute all these merchants are."[16] Desperately eager to be accepted by his colleagues, he was occasionally polite to the point of obsequiousness. But such was the diversity of this milieu that James, save for his self-consciousness, would have had no cause to imagine that he might fail to penetrate it.

The financial aristocracy of France, established by Napoleon and powerful enough to remain there after his fall, constituted a far from homogeneous ensemble.[17] Le Couteulx, from an old and eminent legal family related to the Noailles, and owner of one of the oldest banks in Paris (founded in 1670), sat on the Board of Regents of the Banque de France next to Jean-Pierre Germain, the son of an Avignon baker. Also on the board was Guillaume Mallet, a member of the foremost family in Geneva, as well as Louis Pierlot, the offspring of poor peasants. The great majority of the forty-three Regents had speculated in nationalized land and, on these grounds, could consider themselves children of the Revolution. The most characteristic member of the group was Jacques Laffitte. Apprenticed to his carpenter father in 1779, he had over a period of forty years amassed a fortune then thought to be one of the largest in France.

Among such professionals a new arrival like James had no reason to feel out of place, all the more so since there was nothing narrowly nationalistic about the financial establishment in Paris. Indeed, many of the financiers represented foreign interests. Jean-Frédéric Perrégaux, a Protestant from Neuchâtel, had done his apprenticeship at Mulhouse, then at Amsterdam, and finally in London. Moreover, he remained sympathetic to the British point of view. Jean-Conrad Hottinguer, another Protestant, this time from Zurich, had begun his career before the Revolution as a petty clerk under Le Couteulx. After returning to Switzerland during the Terror, he went on to London where he married a rich American from New England. This led to several years in the United States and an association there with Talleyrand. He returned to France under the Consulate. However endowed with energy and daring spirit, these *nouveaux riches* could not be said to have included social graces among the gifts they brought into the world.

This was the period of what Charles de Rémusat called the "mercantile salons," the stupefying dullness of which almost outweighed the value of the information available there. The denizens of this parvenu circle had come to power freighted with all the habits of their profession and native origins, and the manners they displayed fell far short of the lofty heights to which they had climbed. No group could have been more remote from the *fermiers généraux*—those eighteenth-century financiers who bankrolled the crown by collecting taxes for a good percentage of the "harvest"—with their wit, their brilliance, and their touch of decadence. The salons frequented by the new money men were "useful," places where one heard and spoke not about literature but about politics. And they attracted James, vulgar, ignorant but quick to learn, saying little and never anything foolish, a young man whose sound judgment appeared remarkable. After some groping, he would find his place.

In 1814, just before the first Restoration, James decided to establish himself on a more solid footing in Paris, and registered his banking house with the Commercial Court. Until then he had merely represented the Frankfurt firm. Of course, the new formalization in no way altered the internal family relationship that joined the three branches of the Rothschild business—Frankfurt, London, and Paris—in one unified organization. It did, however, permit James to expand his activity in the French capital by facilitating his contacts with the agents of the French Treasury and the tax collectors. And when the great political reversals came—with Napoleon's Hundred Days following the original Restoration, only to give way to the more permanent Bourbon Restoration in 1815—James seems to have carried on without interruption. Waterloo, contrary to legend, did not yield fantastic profits for the Rothschilds, since Nathan, who of course learned of the Emperor's defeat before anyone else in London, chose to inform the Prime Minister immediately without exploiting the occasion to play the market. However, the great battle did mark the beginning of a very fruitful period for James. He now enjoyed the gratitude of the new government, the return of whose King, Louis XVIII, the Rothschilds had financed.

3
Old France and Young Barons

The Bourbon Restoration brought radical changes to the affairs of James Rothschild. Having finished his game of wits with a government he was trying to undermine, he would now range himself openly on the side of the rehabilitated monarchy. Here was a regime altogether to his liking. An unshakable prejudice, based less on his own experience than on that of the ghetto, caused him to prefer monarchy to a republican government, since the latter depended upon the people, and the people had never expressed anything but malice toward the Jews. Throughout the ages, only the protection of Princes had saved his forebears from the violence of the Gentile masses. Beyond this, James had no political views. Intellectual speculation on the best type of government was totally alien to him, which explains the facility with which he passed from one regime to another. By instinct, however, he identified most comfortably with counter-revolution. At this time, counter-revolution meant the Restoration, which in addition offered him a double advantage. Not only was it a conservative regime, installed by the Great Powers that he and his brothers had loyally served, but it also represented a society so transformed by the Revolution and Empire that it accepted with alacrity even the parvenu Jew, the uncouth immigrant that James still was.

In France, new traditions were being born and would create a social situation unique in Europe. The aristocracies of Russia, Great Britain, and Central Europe had retained their lands, their wealth, and their arrogance. The Prussian élite, dominated by the proud, austere Junkers, could hardly have presented a more striking contrast to the ruling classes of France. Here, due to an electoral system based on wealth, it was income that had become the foundation of all political power, and it was also income that determined the individual's social position. "You will be much more noble once you have money,"[1] the clear-sighted Balzac taunted the "old owl-like Marquis . . . dumbfounded by everything, a tiny society, new yet old, clownish yet sad, juvenile yet senile,"[2] a world that was just then waking up and rubbing its eyes. The truth of this observation would be readily apparent to the more perceptive of the émigrés who returned from exile in 1815.

The nobles, for whom nothing but the allure of military exploit could rival the charms of leisure and disinterested culture, were poorly prepared to resist the inexorable rise of the industrial and mercantile bourgeoisie. Thus it was to the latter class that every preferment went. The spirit of economic initiative replaced that of knightly valor in the race for success. The spectacular breakthroughs achieved by Napoleon's Generals—Ney, the son of a Sarrelouis cooper; Murat, a former innkeeper; or Bernadotte, an Adjutant in 1790 yet a King in 1815—were legends from the rapidly receding past. In the aftermath of Revolution and Empire, the army no longer provided the great social springboard it once did. The result was a confrontation between the aristocrats, rightly convinced that without money they would not survive for long, hence all the more determined to reclaim their properties and political power, and those men of commerce whose fortunes the titled gentry envied and from whom they had much to learn.

The more the ascendant bourgeoisie gained strength and self-respect, the less they felt inclined to seek alliances at any price with the old nobility. Marrying one's daughter for the prestige of a name ceased to be the capstone of a career in finance. The situation suited James perfectly since, for the moment, he dreamed only of developing his business to the fullest extent possible.

With peace restored, the great obsession of the bankers was to participate in the loans that the French government would be compelled to float in order to settle all the war indemnities. The Allies had in effect condemned France to pay them 700 million francs and to support the armies of occupation until the debt had been satisfied. This put French financiers in a state of high tension and excitement. From London, Nathan exerted the whole of his influence to help James gain access to government circles. First, he obtained for Louis XVIII the 5 million francs necessary to ensure the old monarch a dignified return. He then persuaded the British Prime Minister to bring pressure upon the Marquis d'Osmond, France's Ambassador in London, to recommend James to the Duc de Richelieu, the new Premier in Paris. Richelieu resisted. Certainly, bankers would be needed, but it seemed absurd to favor one instead of allowing them all to compete. Irritated by Osmond's insistence and by the intervention of the Austrian Ambassador, Count Esterhazy, Richelieu finally declared: "I don't understand why the Rothschilds are not happy with me. I have seen and received them in a perfectly correct manner. They visit me incessantly, and we babble away in German."[3]

But James was unhappy because he was impatient. "One must be forever on the run here," he wrote to his English sister-in-law. "In this respect, Paris is bigger than London. People live far away from one another, and if one goes to see a minister, one must spend hours in the hall. Very often it is most difficult to control one's temper."[4] He believed he had less access to the seats of power than did Nathan in London. "You can't imagine," he confided to his elder brother, "how difficult it is here to call on a minister if one has nothing new to propose. Could you go and see Lord Liverpool[5] every day if you had nothing to say?"[6] James did not even dare call on Wellington[7] after this man of the hour arrived in Paris, since, he explained, the Duke "is very busy and I don't like to approach him unless he has sent for me . . . because well-meaning friends spread it around that I am paid by foreign masters."[8]

Social snubs bothered him even more than the problems of

his profession: "Laffitte gave a great ball. I was not invited. From envy, they don't want us to become bigger than we are. . . . I have no home in which to receive. A house without a wife is like a ship without a captain."[9] He seemed downcast and disappointed not to be making faster progress. From Frankfurt Amschel played the big brother and tried to reason with him and assuage his attacks of depression: "My good James, you do not want to understand that in peacetime one has to be more than glad of a profit of half a percent."[10] He must learn to submit to the will of God and never forget the responsibilities that fell to them all. This was why Amschel personally opposed every kind of risky undertaking, since "we cannot jeopardize our fortune and the honor of the Jewish community."[10a] However, nothing short of success would bring calm to the life of James Rothschild.

Where James proved most effective, during the early part of the Restoration, was in paving the way for the future. He made a real coup when he gained the patronage of the Duc d'Orléans, the future Louis-Philippe, thanks once more to the good offices of Nathan. "The Duc d'Orléans," James wrote to his brother in London, "intends to pay his father's debts once he has recovered his fortune. We could buy these debts at a very advantageous price. You should have me recommended to [Orléans] by Prince Leopold of Coburg."[11] By another brilliant stroke, James managed to become intimate with Decazes,[12] Louis XVIII's favorite. Ill at ease with the Duc de Richelieu and distrustful of Corvetto, the Finance Minister, James preferred to save his most valuable information for Decazes, the Chief of Police, who in return promised to keep Rothschild informed. As it happened, Decazes was to replace Richelieu in 1818. Bit by bit, James elbowed his way through the crowd and moved towards the center of things. If he played no part in the 1815 loan, he did succeed in becoming an agent in the transfer of the French indemnity earmarked for Austria. The Rothschilds were especially involved in making payments to the Austrian troops stationed at Colmar (in Alsace). Such movement of funds could be extremely profitable for anyone capable of executing it with skill. The lack of security on the routes constituted so real a risk that the Messageries, the regular postal service, refused to be held responsible in the event of armed robbery, a situation that justified the large commissions demanded by bankers as a means of insuring themselves against loss. With the Rothschilds, it was not a question of knowing how far they could go—how much they could obtain—but, rather, of proposing a rate slightly under that of their competitors, while at the same time offering the maximum degree of security. What permitted them to do this so easily was that they did not transport actual coin. Instead, they arranged to raise the necessary money in Alsace, which automatically eliminated risk on the highway and enabled them to pocket their commission in peace. The wave of new money that now flowed into their coffers began to swell rapidly, for soon they would be made transfer agents for the funds going to London, Vienna, and Berlin.

No sooner had this money come in than the Rothschilds recycled it for lending, an activity in which they became specialists. Every petty German Prince with problems went to the House of Rothschild. Moreover, it was as representatives of these Princes—the Princes with "small claims" on France—that Karl and Salomon attended the Congress at Aix-la-Chapelle in 1818. The sheer effectiveness and availability of these financiers would open to them a much more important market, a wider field of operation in which they would underwrite huge loans for Prussia, Russia, Austria, and Naples. Here their technique was to provide additional security by introducing the practice of making the bonds repayable in London, at a fixed date and at a fixed rate based on the value of the pound. In this way foreign bonds became much more attractive and secure for British capitalists. Such grandiose operations did not, however, make the Rothschilds lose sight of the benefits to be gained from dealings of a more discreet order. Salomon, in particular, understood how to lend an attentive ear to important persons whose needs often exceeded their means. In this way he earned the gratitude of Gentz, the most influential advisor in the entourage of Metternich.

Friedrich von Gentz, Prussian, brilliant intellectual, and former student of Kant, had become a political commentator, publishing such astute analyses that they circulated all the way to London. But Gentz had a weakness that prevented his becoming the impartial oracle that he could have been: he liked money, or, to be more precise, he liked women, the good life, fine furniture, and precious bibelots. This meant that Gentz would take money wherever he could find it, and he never had enough. He was always for sale. Salomon understood the great man at first glance and proceeded to gratify him with exquisite delights procured by what he called "pleasant financial operations." This became the channel through which Rothschild gained direct access to Metternich and gradually established a position of monopoly in the financial affairs of Austria. The proud Chancellor, despite his visceral anti-Semitism and a sensibility so acute that the very sight of a Jew sufficed to turn him against the most beautiful landscape,[13] would soon swear by no one more than "his dear Salomon." Indeed, so great was his goodwill towards Salomon that Metternich gave him—and his family—an asset that would be difficult to evaluate in financial terms: a title of nobility.

Elevating a tribe of Jews to the nobility took courage, and the Emperor did not confer the title out of gratitude, but only as a result of skilled negotiation. Austria, all but ruined by the end of the Napoleonic wars, wanted to put its finances in order by drawing a sizable advance against the indemnity owed by France, which was to be settled in stages over a five-year period. The Rothschilds disposed of sufficient funds to extend the loan,[14] but they were demanding quite a high rate of interest. This was when the Austrian Finance Minister, Stadion, conceived the idea of recompensing the Jewish creditors by offering them a particle (adding *von* to their name, which of course became *de* in French), to be followed two years later by the title of Baron, granted to all the descendants of Mayer Amschel Rothschild. So keenly did they feel themselves awkard and socially vulnerable, that the Rothschild brothers accepted the deal with joy.

Despite their wealth, the Rothschilds resented their lack of place, let alone rank, in society. Their irritation grew as their wealth increased. At moments they believed themselves to be on the verge of escaping the constraints imposed by the ghetto, but even then they suffered from not knowing what position they should try to occupy or how they would be accepted whatever approach they might take. It was not simply a question of entering high society, but rather of acquiring a dignity that would permit them to forget the exclusion and humiliation of the past and to identify with a different social milieu. The very length of the deliberations carried on prior to their ennoblement proved that the Rothschilds were not wrong in preferring permanent social advancement to immediate financial gain.

Stadion's proposition created great embarrassment within the Austrian government. The ministers feared not only the jealousy of Gentile bankers but also repercussions affecting negotiations then underway concerning the rights of Jews. To favor certain Jews just when every city in Germany was determined to reduce the advantages already gained by the outcasts during the French occupation seemed illogical to certain officials. An inquiry was made as to whether an imperial gift, richly ornamented snuffboxes for example, might not suffice as evidence of the Emperor's gratitude. Finally, to cut it short, the monarch turned the problem over to Metternich. Informed by Gentz of the prodigious skill of these "vulgar, unmannered Jews [whose] . . . professional instinct . . . [and] admirable common sense permitted them always to come out on top,"[15] and fully conscious of the brothers' influence in government financing, a process vital to Austria, the Chancellor decided in favor of the proposal.

The title was an important symbol. This is evident in a remark made by a German official concerning Amschel, who still did not have the right to buy a house outside the ghetto: "He is one of the richest bankers in Europe; he has no worries, except being a Jew."[16] Becoming a Baron would somewhat mitigate the bitterness of that situation.

The pleasure the elevation brought to the Rothschilds comes through in their letters. The brothers addressed one another as "Dear Baron" and made fun of Salomon, whom they accused of ceasing to work with his customary energy now that he had been ennobled. They also discussed their arms, choosing five arrows symbolizing the unity among the five brothers, and settled on their motto: *concordia, integritas, industria*. On a darker note, Amschel reported the unpleasant reactions of the Gentile community: "They parade in front of the house bawling 'Baron Amschel' and making all sorts of inane remarks. They are furious. Soon, they will calm down, and it will be like France."[17]

The Jews themselves were delighted. Salomon Hamburg, a banker friend, went into ecstasies upon hearing civil servants, those notorious persecutors of Jews, address Amschel by his title. The latter reminded his brothers of an old proverb and then enlarged upon it: "If a Jew owns a garden, every Jew owns a garden. If a Jew is a Baron, every Jew is a Baron."[17a] The pious Amschel rejoiced particularly because he felt certain that the Rothschilds' elevation would check those opportunists among the Jews who sought conversion to Christianity. Only Nathan, in England, would not condescend to use his title. Englishman that he was, he did not consider that a foreign title would bring him any particular advantage. He felt no threat either to his dignity or to his position. Having no desire to escape his own milieu, nor any need of the ceremonial consecrations that marked the social ascent of his brothers, he emphasized, not without a certain style, that he preferred to remain Mr. Rothschild.

In Paris, James got carried away and decided to attempt a major coup. He would invite Wellington to dinner, he announced to Nathan, and "create a sensation."[18] The Duke accepted and the new Baron was thus happily launched on the road to social success. As evidence of his intentions, James moved twice in two years. First he left the Rue Le Peletier for the Rue de Provence, within the Chaussée-d'Antin, the fief of Paris' most prominent financiers, and then on December 10, 1818, he purchased an *hôtel*, or town house, on the Rue d'Artois, now the Rue Laffitte, built for the banker Laborde, a victim of the guillotine in 1794. The dwelling had been occupied successively by Hortense, the daughter of Empress Josephine whom Napoleon had married to his brother Louis and made Queen of Holland, and Fouché, the Police Minister throughout much of the Revolution and Empire. The latter had sold the property to a Viennese banker, Fries, and thence it went to an important merchant from Prague, Lamel, who sold the house to James.[19] This move proved final, for the House of Rothschild would never have any other address in Paris. Like his colleagues, James lived in the main wing, between the forecourt and the garden, and set up his offices in the subsidiary wings framing the forecourt. Thus he was installed in the richest, most animated, and modern quarter of the capital—Paris of the boulevards, of lights, of youth, a district that stood in marked contrast to the Faubourg Saint-Germain, that bastion of the aristocracy with its exclusive, stiff-necked salons.

From this point dates the real social ascent of James de Rothschild. Henceforth all government circles would be open to him. How could anyone not treat with consideration a man whose family, as the Burgomaster of Frankfurt stated bitterly, had become "through their formidable financial operations, through their network of business and credit . . . a veritable power and had gained such control of the international capital market that they were in a position to check or forward as they pleased the activities of the greatest European powers?"[20] Still, the undeniable progress of his integration with society did not prompt James to seek French citizenship.

The political reversals in France caused James to exercise prudence and to assess the advantages of being subject to the victorious Allies. The union of the Rothschild brothers, each established in a different country, obliged them to juggle their political loyalties with great skill. They came down decisively on the side of the Holy Alliance, the coalition formed by Great Britain, Russia, Austria, and Prussia to fight against Revolutionary and Imperial France. But once peace had been restored, the coalition began to break apart, distancing modern, liberal Britain from the monarchies of Central and Eastern Europe, all mired in the old order. Now the Rothschilds found themselves in two different, if not opposite, camps. James felt strongly that the more difficult he made it for others to label him, the more room he would have in which to maneuver.

In France, this gave no offense. James was so manifestly different that it would have been absurd to insist that he become French. He could be accepted as he was. As for his title of Baron, no one took it seriously. The Faubourg Saint-Germain looked upon James with a certain benevolent humor. "Those good Jews are all Barons,"[21] announced the Comte de Castellane, unable to hide his amusement.[22] Napoleonic titles were inciting the same kind of mirth.

Considerable pressure had to be exerted before the ushers at the Austrian Embassy would announce Napoleonic aristocrats by their titles. Under the Third Republic (1871–1940) the habitués of the Legitimist salons, precincts so dear to Marcel

Proust, still chuckled at those Iénas who bore the name of a bridge. But the smiles prompted by James' early awkwardness were indulgent ones. The memoirs of contemporaries betray no trace of anti-Semitism. Castellane found James "frightfully ugly even though he is the Adonis of the Rothschilds."[23] The Count had a right to his opinion which, however unflattering, was fair. James could not be called handsome, to judge by the photographs eventually made of him. Still, these pictures bear little resemblance to the description written forty years later by the Goncourts in their journal: "A monstrous visage, the flattest, squattest, most frightful kind of batrachian face, with bloodshot eyes, swollen lids, a slobbery mouth slit like a piggy bank, a sort of satrap of gold: that's Rothschild."[24]

If the France of this period remained untouched by anti-Semitism, it was mainly because so few Jews had achieved prominent positions, and these had benefited from the intellectual tolerance characteristic of the first years of the Restoration. Despite military defeat and the occupation, which would end in 1818, everyone breathed freely, rejoicing that the dead weight of the Napoleonic dictatorship had been lifted. The political atmosphere was such that the press found itself operating under fewer restraints, which meant that opposition parties of every hue could now abandon some of the extreme caution that had in the past proved essential to their survival. The French reveled in the rediscovered uses of word and pen. "The kind of anarchic disorder that followed immediately upon the Restoration had something new about it that resembled liberty," remarked George Sand.[25] It was more than mere resemblance. Never, except in the early days of the Revolution, had thoughts been expressed with such daring. Statistics reveal that under the Empire, the French press comprised 238 periodicals; under the Restoration, the total rose to 2,278, a tenfold increase.

In the religious sphere, Catholicism had lost ground. France was no longer the first daughter of the Church. The symbiotic relationship of Church and State would not be revived, to the horror of all God-fearing Europeans. "More than a third of the population," Metternich sadly reported to the Austrian Emperor, "has not been baptized. Today the great business of religion is to introduce religion. . . . The only thing to be done here is to send missionaries, like those working to convert savages."[26] In France some very respectable savages found it possible to display their freedom of thought quite openly. For example, the civil burial of the wife of François Guizot, then a professor of modern history at the University of Paris and later a leading statesman, caused not a stir. The great secular lycées kept their students and their prestige. But when the Jesuits opened six schools, hoping to regain their influence, they provoked a storm of anticlericalism. The Duc d'Orléans flatly refused to obey when the King ordered him to withdraw his children from the Collège Henri IV, one of the most important of the secular schools. The French would no longer abide the intolerance of priests. When the curé of Saint-Roch prohibited the celebration of Mass for the burial of La Raucourt, a famous tragedienne, a riot broke out. The church was invaded, the actress' coffin placed before the altar, and Mass said under the surveillance of a surly congregation. If anyone wished to be buried with due religious ceremony, it was not for priests to prevent it. By the same token, no one should feel obliged to follow religious practices of any kind. The grandmother of George Sand, the respected châtelaine of Nohant, never set foot in church and hesitated long before allowing her granddaughter's first communion. The clerical party would revive under Charles X, but at the outset of the Restoration Voltaire reigned as the great man of the enlightened bourgeoisie.

Finally, the Jews saw the consolidation of all their conquests. The decrees against the Alsatian Jews could have been renewed in 1818, but this did not occur. On the contrary, they were annulled, and the vote, albeit cast by a conservative Chamber of Deputies, was unanimous, except for one voice. Moreover, the clerical right uttered not a word throughout the debate.

In this atmosphere James no longer found his origins a liability. He could write to his elder brother, Nathan, that in Paris, unlike Frankfurt, anti-Semitic incidents were as rare as they were surprising. No one refused the invitations sent out by James de Rothschild. When Metternich visited Paris, James gave a large dinner that was attended by all the chief diplomats. Prince von Württemberg and Prince Esterhazy, who in Germany would not have shaken a Rothschild hand, attended along with everyone else, whereupon *Le Constitutionnel* could not refrain from philosophizing about "the power of gold that brings all classes and cults together. Not the least of the curious spectacles to be seen today, a time so rich in contrasts, is that of all the representatives of the Holy Alliance, established in the name of Jesus Christ, attending a banquet given by a Jew." But the perfection with which these feasts were prepared did not lend itself to sarcasm, and the excellent fare demonstrated James' willing rejection of an Orthodoxy that would have embarrassed his titled guests.

As far as his Jewishness was concerned, James had long since learned to appreciate the value of flexibility. Liberated from the ghetto, he no longer lived surrounded by Jews. Most of his employees were Gentile. James became the first of the five Rothschild brothers not to emphasize Judaism in his everyday existence, something made easier for him by the fact that he remained a bachelor. His household sheltered no children in whom he would have felt obliged to inculcate respect for tradition, although he would certainly play the proper role once he had become the father of a family. Nor did James have a wife to afflict him with her imperious piety, or the kind of mother-in-law endured by poor Nathan, who often had to bow before the strict Orthodoxy of the Cohens, his wife's parents. In his religious observance, James departed significantly from the rigidly devout Amschel, also from Karl, who could not get used to the manners of the assimilated Jews of Berlin, all "too fine and much too delicate" for his taste, as well as from Salomon, who, according to Princess Metternich, had engaged "a famous French chef, but who naturally always had himself served separately with his own little dishes."[27] James frowned upon his brothers' practice of frequently allowing religious duties to take precedence over business and their increasing reluctance to change their ways. While he was learning to minimize his cultural differences in order to enjoy Parisian life the more, his fortune began to make such entertainment possible.

Until 1818 James had led a hectic but austere life. His personal account books disclose no expenditure on his own pleasure. All we find are professional expenses, along with immense sums paid out for postage, the totals averaging a good third of his monthly outlay. Here and there a gift is noted, always very modest. He would seem to have been caught up completely in the task of making money. Then, suddenly, he changes. The records show him going to concerts. He takes a box at the Chantereine Theatre. He even pensions an artist, a certain Allard, giving him five francs a month. The Maecenas in James was beginning to emerge. The man whose dominating passion was money had opened his eyes and discovered the refinements of art. We find him acquiring his first painting, Greuze's *Milkmaid*. He subscribes to the *Courrier des spectacles* and then to the *Journal des théâtres*. He has a table at Ledoyen, the fashionable restaurant. Obviously James de Rothschild was discovering the pleasures of living in grand style. And he began to enjoy himself. The servile manner of his early days in Paris, an approach that remained *de rigueur* in his brothers' correspondence with German ministers, had now disappeared forever. When Salomon offered some costly bibelot to Metternich, he felt compelled to wrap the offer in polite formulas that were as humble as they were clumsy: "I have taken the liberty of having a few bagatelles made for your gracious lady and her dear little Princess, objects that bear faint witness to my devoted feelings. May I be permitted to ask Your Highness to become my gracious intermediary so that I may hope to be pardoned for the boldness of my gesture?"[28] But just when James, now granted equal footing everywhere, had acquired self-assurance, he went too far. Recently married, he surprised everyone by taking it upon himself to present his wife to the Duc d'Orléans, thereby committing a major *faux pas*. A foreigner cannot always do the right thing when entering a society whose rules have little in common with anything he has known before. James had to learn the nuances that separate obsequiousness from presumption. His situation in France was nevertheless in great contrast to that of his family in Germany, who were once again being subjected to persecution, anti-Semitism having revived on the other side of the Rhine in a more virulent form than ever.

Hardly had the French armies withdrawn when the German authorities addressed themselves to the urgent problem of putting the Jews back in their place. In Frankfurt the rights legally acquired and dearly paid for by the ghetto population were now abolished. Once again the Jews found themselves treated like unwelcome aliens. They were ejected from the seats they had gained in the assemblies and excluded from the respectable professions they had begun to learn. No Jew would be allowed to enter law, and only four Jews retained their right to practice medicine. As in the past, Jews were denied the chance to marry freely and had to beg for authorization, which was often refused. Realizing that their honor, their liberty, occasionally even their lives were threatened, the Jews of Germany turned to the Great Powers, then meeting regularly at the Congress of Vienna for the purpose of settling all disputes arising out of the Napoleonic wars. One delegation after another appeared in the Austrian capital, struggling against the decrees passed by some cities expelling the Jews. But however valid the arguments, they were in vain. This left Germany's Jews no choice but to resort, as in the past, to clandestine means and thus find, or buy, protection.

Salomon took charge of the Jewish campaign, and suddenly the wallet of Gentz, Metternich's advisor grew fat. This resulted in a suspension of the Austrian edicts of expulsion, along with calming statements from Metternich and Hardenberg, the Austrian Chancellor's counterpart in Prussia. But principles carried little weight among Germans filled with hatred and a desire for revenge. The liberation of the Jews had coincided with the humiliation of Germany's defeat at the hands of the French. It constituted an insult that the courageous conduct of many Jews in the national armies could not efface. Their patriotism inspired no gratitude. Thus the persecutions recommenced, more vigorous than ever, and were not confined to social issues. As in the worst days of the Middle Ages, the Jews had to flee before the violence directed against them. In 1818 anti-Semitic riots broke out everywhere in Germany.

The first disturbance occurred at Würzburg in Bavaria, where an old professor who had made declarations in favor of the Jews was called to account by students at the university. He fled, pursued by the sinister chant of "Hep! Hep!" That cry, an acronym dating from the Crusades and deriving from *Hierosalyma est perdita* (Latin for "Jerusalem is lost"), struck Hebrew ears like a death threat. The city was seized by a mad lust for blood. When their shops were pillaged, the Jews attempted to resist, and a pitched battle ensued, leaving several of the defenders dead. Only military intervention saved the ghetto population from massacre. Next morning the authorities arrived to announce the expulsion of the community. Four hundred despairing families were forced to abandon their worldly possessions and seek refuge in neighboring villages.

Similar scenes erupted all over Germany. Frankfurt staged its protest in August 1818. To shouts of "Hep! Hep!" the Jews were chased from the streets of the Christian city, driven back into the ghetto, and there attacked with stones and clubs. Their houses provided poor shelter as the mob hurled missiles through windows and ripped doors from their hinges. The Rothschild house was not spared. After all, had not the very success of the brothers made them particularly odious to their Gentile competitors? Now the latter could make their feelings known. What a contrast with France! At that very moment, in August 1818, James was giving a large ball graced by the presence of the entire diplomatic corps. The Austrian Ambassador and the Prussian representative would not have dreamt of missing it.

James, of course, identified completely with his family. Events in Frankfurt filled him with revulsion, all the more so as a result of his several years in France, which had proved that constant humiliation of the Jews was not a necessity of nature. In Paris James had become accustomed to living free of the old shackles. The competition in which he was engaged with his colleagues was as an equal among equals. He went about his daily business unburdened by anxiety. Thus he reacted sharply to the new menace in Germany. His family, he insisted, must leave Frankfurt and move to France or England. Why be at the mercy of rioters when one is playing an essential role in the life of the country? Why put up with such prejudice? Why endure personal insecurity when the reestablishment of confidence in the finances of the government was due to them? "If we leave," James wrote, "I am convinced that every well-off person will follow our example. Can you imagine how German sovereigns will rejoice over an exodus that will force them to go to France or England whenever they need money? Who purchases the state obligations in Germany? The Jews. Hasn't our action fostered confidence in the government's borrowing and thus given the Christian firms the courage to invest a portion of their assets? We are reproached for dealing in money even though all other professions are closed to us. Why accept this? . . . If the wealthy cannot live in peace in Germany, they will be forced to emigrate for their own safety. Obviously they would lose all interest in the finances of a state where their lives had manifestly been put in danger."[29] But despite his logic and energy, James failed to convince his brothers.

Amschel, the eldest brother and titular head of the Rothschild family, was a gentle man of forty-five, prematurely aged, and worn down by the sadness of having no son. Still dressed in the old way, with his big hat pitched backward, almost on his neck, he remained faithful to the Hebraic manners instilled in him during his childhood. At the least altercation, this sensitive man assumed a doleful tone and threatened to retire from business: "If you consider me no longer good enough to be a partner, I swear to you on the tomb of our father that I will resign and withdraw. I have no son and will have none. I shall live on my few pennies and I wish you millions and millions."[30] Morbidly anxious, he forever feared a lack of money. Less enterprising than his brothers, he knew that he could not adapt to life in the brilliant capitals of Europe. Moreover, he worried profoundly about the moral effect that the whirlwind style of these cities was having on his brothers and nephews. For his part, he insisted that he never felt truly comfortable except in Jew Street. Bismarck would develop a great liking for Amschel, "because he remained an old Jewish peddler and never pretended to be anything else."[31] Thus the eldest brother rejected the idea of any great dislocation, arguing, with reason moreover, that Frankfurt continued to be a financial center of such importance that it would be absurd not to retain a foothold there. Finally, the Rothschilds, by remaining in Germany despite the alarm set off by the riot, believed that they stood apart. They were Jewish, certainly, but different.

This judgment was not altogether without foundation. At the height of the anti-Semitic crisis, Metternich had made several advances towards the Rothschilds, letting them know that he would be happy to see the family established in Vienna. But the conditions confronting Jews in Austria were hardly attractive. They had no right to own property. They were excluded from government, of course, as well as from the "liberal" professions, such as law, medicine, and teaching. If they had the right, even the obligation, to do military service, they could not be promoted to the higher ranks. In order to visit Vienna, foreign Jews had to obtain a special authorization and pay a tax. No matter. Compromises could always be arranged. When one is as rich as a Rothschild, one is not quite so Jewish as the rest. Soon Salomon would settle in Vienna. Since he could not buy a house, he was reduced to renting the capital's most luxurious hotel, which allowed him the compensating pleasure of refusing the King of Württemberg the apartment he had normally occupied there.

James did not renew his appeal. Metternich's evident power and protection relieved his anxiety. Thanks to the Chancellor, in fact, the Rothschilds would acquire diplomatic immunity. Having already granted them a useful and flattering title, he would now do considerably more. Nathan and James, as the price of numerous skillfully negotiated loans, conceived the idea of having themselves appointed Consuls to represent Austria in London and Paris. A Jew entering the diplomatic corps! It was unthinkable. However, despite the enormity of the proposal, Metternich agreed. Only the evil-minded would suspect some connection between an advantageous personal loan, made by the Rothschilds to the Chancellor, and the latter's signature on the letters of accreditation. Esterhazy too was put in a conciliatory mood. "You should lend the Count several thousand pounds," Salomon advised Nathan, "and obtain the appointment first for yourself, then for James, and finally for Frankfurt."[32] And so it was done, to the advantage, as it turned out, of all concerned. Metternich assured himself the loyal support of the Rothschilds. He also counted on benefiting from the regular courier service maintained by the brothers, also on having at his disposal in Paris and London a "sub-embassy" more pragmatic and effective than the real one. What could better serve Austrian interests? As for the brothers, they had drawn a precious trump card.

"All court functions lead to new business, especially when it has to do with Austria," wrote Salomon, thereby expressing a notion that he had absorbed from his father at an early age. "If James should be appointed [Consul] in Paris, he could, God willing, take charge of everything related to the liquidation of the debt [owed by France to Austria], since the title of Consul would permit him to treat with the King in person."[32a] Being called Baron flattered one's vanity, but to become a Consul assured one an unquestionable rank, a special place at all official occasions. Even the most massive portals opened before a member of the diplomatic corps. It was in this capacity that James, "strutting in his red uniform,"[33] would attend the coronation of Charles X at Rheims. The happiness he felt at donning his uniform expressed more than the simple pleasure of consummating a good business deal.

James had liberated himself from his past with exceptional speed. In barely ten years he had traveled a distance that would take others a lifetime to cover. But his situation differed significantly from that of his brothers: firstly, because France had been more liberal in opening to him the marvelous and disquieting world of free men; secondly, because he was alone, without the shelter of a happy and traditional Jewish community, like the one he would have found in London, a world that had served Nathan like a way station between the ghetto and complete emancipation. Now on the threshold of a new life which promised success, happiness, and dignity, he felt an urgent need to assume a new image. A savage received into a different tribe would have had himself properly tattooed; he would have sacrificed a victim according to a ritual; the new rules of his existence would have been spelled out with precision. For James, the initiation into society was rendered more complicated by the fact that he wanted to have his cake and eat it too. While remaining Jewish, he longed to acquire the style, gestures, and manners of the world to which he aspired. To slip into the uniform of a Consul, a beautiful crimson garment with great golden epaulets, was to acquire a new skin. Seeing him leave a ministry, passersby took James de Rothschild for an English General.[34]

This accounts for the immoderate love of distinctions that possessed the Rothschild brothers. They enjoyed being decorated and even more making it known. "Salomon von Rothschild and his brothers in Paris have received the order of Saint Vladimir in recognition of the loans negotiated for Russia," wrote Gentz to various German newspapers. "It would be well that you publish the news. Make it Vladimir rather than Saint

Vladimir."[35] In 1830 Metternich would write to Count von Neipperg, the lover of the former Empress Marie-Louise, who had placed her financial affairs in the hands of the Rothschilds: "The Rothschilds would like a small Saint George. What vanity! Despite their millions and their generous loyalty, the Rothschilds have an astonishing appetite for honors and distinctions."[36] He went on to explain that the religious character of the decorations prevented their being given to Jews, and that he himself had committed the crime of denying Austrian decorations to the Rothschilds. But, he pleaded "do not betray me. If Rothschild suspects me of being implicated in this affair, he will take me for a cannibal."[36a]

Metternich could not have understood that this desire stemmed precisely from the Rothschilds' millions. Being accepted for their wealth was not enough to satisfy the Jewish financiers. They felt compelled to weave firm ties to these foreigners whom they wanted to resemble, and all the outward symbols of belonging helped advance them towards this goal. Needless to say, Metternich soon raised objections and was duly rebuked by Gentz. But the rain of decorations continued to fall unabated on the ever-thirsty Rothschilds. In 1863, Karl Mayer, the son of Karl, solicited a decoration from Bismarck, doing so in terms of shocking humility: "Your Excellency knows the enduring, proven, and boundless love that I have for him . . . and I turn to Your Excellency, full of confidence in his nobility, his magnanimity, and his omnipotence."[37] In 1867 James' eldest son Alphonse proudly announced to his cousins in London that "the most notable outcome of Bismarck's visit has been the distribution of decorations. My father has received the Great Ribbon of the Red Eagle, the highest and most distinguished decoration. No Jew in Prussia has received it."[38] By this time the Rothschilds were a universally recognized dynasty, a power equal to any in Europe, and yet they still had their hands out begging for symbols of respectability.

Decorations the Rothschilds would never wear were those modified specifically for the Jews. The King of Prussia gave Karl the Red Eagle but made the mistake of having it Judaized by substituting an oval form for the cross that normally served as a base. Karl never pinned it to his lapel; instead, he paraded about wearing either the Greek Order of the Redeemer or the

Spanish Order of Isabella the Catholic. A specially adapted decoration held no symbolic value and was thus of no interest to the Barons.

Should there be any doubt about the keenness of the Rothschilds' social ambition or their eagerness to be treated as persons of dignity and honor, one has only to consider the lengths to which the brothers went in order to prevent criticism and to invent for themselves a less unseemly background. Thus, when a Frankfurt newspaper made a point of regularly attacking the Rothschilds, the latter appealed to Metternich, who ordered Gentz to have the editor brought into line: "The incessant attacks against the House of Rothschild manifestly, and moreover in the vulgarest way possible, affect the Austrian government, which, as everyone knows, maintains important financial relations with that House, which not only has integrity but is very honorable from the point of view of both morality and public interest."[39]

Gentz, moved by the anxieties of that excellent family, a family which understood his needs so well, went even further to help. In 1824 he lent himself to the achievement of a great publicity coup. The *Enzyklopädie für die gebildeten Stände* ("Encyclopedia of Cultured Society"), then a popular publication in Germany, had never made any mention of the Rothschilds. To correct this omission, Gentz, stimulated by a stipend from Salomon (the amount of which, unfortunately, is not known), drafted an illuminating entry. Glossing over the delays and difficulties encountered by Mayer Amschel, Gentz let it be known that the Elector of Hesse, astounded by the genius of the young Jew, had entrusted him with the whole of his financial affairs, and that the Rothschild family subsequently risked their own security in order to salvage the Elector's interests during the French occupation.[40] He stressed the integrity and the absolute disinterestedness of these bankers, who definitely were not to be compared with others of their sort. He virtually insinuated that they were above dealing in anything as sordid as hard cash. The enumeration of all the titles and decorations conferred upon the brothers proved that beyond every doubt the Rothschild firm was the most powerful, glorious, and honorable of all. In his conclusion Gentz truly surpassed himself: "The Rothschilds, now constituting the largest of business firms, are among those who have achieved grandeur and prosperity simply by taking intelligent advantage of opportunities which were equally open to thousands of other persons, and have done so thanks to their spirit of enterprise balanced by the coolness of their judgment." For the greater glory of James, the article appeared in translation when the French version of the social encyclopedia came out in Paris. Proudly sporting his Legion of Honor ribbon, he now turned to the world a face radiant with triumph.

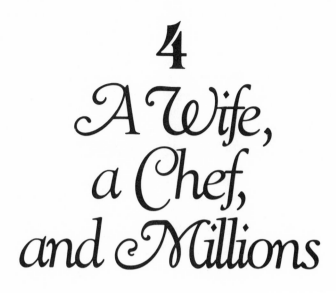

4

A Wife, a Chef, and Millions

As striking as "a sketch by Rembrandt . . . with the profile of an intelligent monkey," according to Michelet[1]; "short, ugly, and proud," in the opinion of Castellane[2]; and for Heine,[3] a "distinguished and casual" man whose eye disclosed "something so solid, so positive, and so absolute that one could believe he carried all the money in the world in his pocket"[4]—so did James appear after several years of Parisian life.

Evidently James took great care to conceal the bouts of anxiety that often left him despondent. After all, his financial empire had the fragility of paper. And he knew this, which explains his conscientious handling of all his affairs, the attention he paid to the smallest details, his fears and hesitations, the risks he calculated to the nth degree. Sometimes James got carried away by an overactive imagination—what his brother Amschel, in his inimitable style, called "an unfortunate tendency to concentrate on general ideas"[5]—and then it took Nathan's good sense and Salomon's realism to console him. The caricatures that began to circulate cut James to the quick, whereas his brothers pinned them to the wall, as signs of Rothschild success. "I hope that our beloved children, my Anselm and [your] Lionel, will find themselves so caricatured when,

73

with God's help, they have achieved some position in society," Salomon wrote to Nathan.[6] But James lacked the reassuring, disciplined family that surrounded Nathan and gave him his remarkable aplomb. "Have a chair," said the English Rothschild, all the while continuing to read a paper, as a Prince was being introduced into his office. "Do you know who I am?" exclaimed the nobleman, shocked by such off-handedness. "Take two chairs," Nathan then suggested, turning the page, his eye glued to it.

James could not match his brother in self-confidence. Caught up in a mixture of success and solitude, he began thinking about marriage in 1824.

At thirty-two, James de Rothschild had exhausted the pleasures of bachelorhood. He was seen at the Opéra in the company of a lady the *Gazette* described as "highly decorated." Indeed, his liaisons generated so much gossip that the Rothschild family began to worry. James found himself called upon to explain his behavior and assure his brothers that he was leading a life of perfect virtue! But then there were the horses and carriages, an area in which James had assumed an unprecedented elegance. His *daumont*, a barouche with four dapple-gray horses and two postilions liveried in blue and gold, created a sensation at Longchamps. The satisfactions of self-respect no longer sufficed for James. He wanted to change his style.

In Paris, anyone wishing to break into society is better off alone than burdened with a companion unversed in the refinements of aristocratic manners. By now, however, James had attained a level where it became essential that he have a real household—and thus someone to be mistress of it. Naturally, he wanted children. And there could be no question, despite all the liberties he took with religion, of giving his progeny a mother who was not Jewish. James knew how much he owed his family and recognized, along with his brothers, that "their family [was] admired precisely because of its Jewish character. In this it is unique since, when it comes to wealth, many Gentiles surpass [us].'"[7] But in his search for a wife James did not turn to the Jewish milieu in France, where at the end of the Revolution an *haute bourgeoisie* had emerged, a small but powerful group, recruited essentially from financial circles and composed of such families as the Worms de Romilly, the Halphens, the Furtados, the Goudchaux, the Ratisbonnes, many of them with ancient roots in the French provinces. This environment held no allure for James, who preferred not to become too closely indentified with French Judaism. He refused to participate in the activities of the Consistory and maintained a general aloofness, thereby easing his way into the salons of the Faubourg Saint-Germain. This world became his "speciality,"[8] and he wanted to keep it so.

Among the Rothschilds, moreover, marriage was not a matter of individual preference, a fact that became evident to James during the four years of discussion leading up to Karl's marriage. It was indispensable, first of all, that the union be approved by all four brothers and their mother. As early as 1814 James, despite his young age, had been invited to observe and evaluate a bridal candidate. "Examine her closely and tell me what you think," Amschel instructed.[9] The young woman had to be from an irreproachable family, Jewish and proud of it. The proposed alliance had also to promise something worthwhile for the Rothschild's business interest. The first condition could not be so easily satisfied in Germany, where conversions were becoming more and more numerous. "I could marry," reported Karl in the course of his search, "the most beautiful and the richest girl in Berlin, which I would not do for all the treasures in the world, because here in Berlin, if she herself has not been converted, then a brother or a sister-in-law has. . . . We ourselves have made our fortune as Jews, and we want nothing to do with such people."[10] Karl would have happily wed Fräulein Heine, the daughter of the most important banker in Hamburg (and coincidentally the first love of her cousin, the poet Heinrich Heine), even though she was delicate and subject to migraines, if only his brothers had wanted to establish a branch of their firm in Hamburg. But the Rothschilds decided against the idea, and Fräulein Heine was abandoned. Finally, Karl cast his eye upon Fräulein Herz, a pretty young thing, recently arrived in the city, who had "the advantage of being socially acceptable in Frankfurt as well as elsewhere."[11] "The negotiation, to Karl's great joy, progressed to the verge of conclusion, only to be checked when Amschel and his dear mother learned that Frau Herz "knew nothing about the Day of Atonement, Passover rites, or kosher meat."[12] How, given these conditions, could the little one be expected to keep an Orthodox house? But Karl held his ground. Amschel and Gudule had given their approval, and they could not take it back. Moreover, his piety was well known, and he would do everything necessary to assure respect for tradition in his household. "It's a good husband who makes a good wife,"[13] Karl declared when, at last, he married in 1818.[14]

As for James, he had become all too aware of the liabilities presented by most of the prospective brides, since scarcely a month passed without Amschel and Karl evaluating Jewish bankers with daughters to propose for the last and youngest of the Rothschild brothers. Finally. the man himself discovered a solution to the problem: marry within the family. Thus he chose a pretty niece thirteen years his junior, the daughter of Salomon who had shown enough affection to be irritated that he had not kept his promise, given the day of his departure for Paris, to answer her letters regularly.

This solution suited everyone. Since his daughter would have to be dowered, Salomon felt it less onerous to pay the sum to his brother and partner, than to a stranger, and thus settled on her a full 1,500,000 francs.[15] The marriage contract stipulated that the fiancé would offer presents in keeping with his position and provide the wedding clothes, the nuptial belt, and the ring. There would be no joint estate between the spouses. And what a relief not to endure the process of instructing an outsider in the ways of a family that placed such emphasis on the secrecy of their communications with one another and that staged a gathering of the clan so frequently. Furthermore, it was a pleasure to be able to continue expressing themselves in their Frankfurt dialect and writing in Yiddish, the language that the first generation of Rothschilds preferred to all others.

With everything falling rapidly into place, the marriage provided the occasion for a grand family festival, celebrated in a spirit of general rejoicing at Frankfurt, still the family's home base. Quickly the Rothschilds came to appreciate the advantages of such an alliance and began transforming it into policy. Two years later, Nathan married his daughter to Salomon's son. Of the eighteen matches made by the grandchildren of Mayer Amschel, sixteen were contracted between first cousins.

Such a custom had in no way been unusual in the eighteenth century. Aristocrats and bourgeois alike tended toward endogamy, and the Jews naturally, given their membership in tight little communities, married within narrow circles. No one, however, carried this propensity to such lengths as the Rothschilds, which in turn served to reinforce the unique situation that they had created for themselves. Jews, but without becoming too intimately involved with other Jews, habitués of the salons held by the finest flower of the aristocracy and snobs of legendary proportions,[16] yet refusing to sell their daughters in order to pay for admission to such exclusive circles, the Rothschilds maintained throughout their social ascent a certain distrust of alliances outside the family.

Betty, James' bride, was nineteen years old. An adolescence spent in Frankfurt, Paris, and Vienna and numerous journeys, during which her father always made certain that she met as many distinguished people as possible, had left the new Mme de Rothschild sufficiently polished not to seem out of place in Paris. Evidence of her superior education is the fact that she always corresponded in French with her English cousin, Charlotte, who would become her sister-in-law. Not bereft of a sense of humor, she wrote brightly to London about her first evenings *chez* Uncle James: ". . . after having tasted the fine cuisine offered by Uncle, the ladies, having vainly attempted to sing a little air, decided upon a quadrille, which soon ended seeing that all the dancers had forgot the turns. It was very amusing to observe, one by one, another couple begin but fail to finish. . . . the dance gave way to bursts of laughter . . . ."[17]

Betty wasted no time in learning the necessary dance steps or in gaining control of her girlish giggles. With a German accent much less noticeable than that of James, with her classic elegance, regular features, somewhat sober expression, and her touch of pedantry, a quality criticized by Rémusat,[18] Betty provided a good balance for her singular husband. She was also very well organized, serious in everything she did, an excellent mistress of her household, and sufficiently aware of the value of money to take a careful, daily look at the domestic account book and sign it after her inspection. She never allowed herself an impulsive gesture, nor did she ever provoke ridicule or slander. Even a wicked tongue like Castellane's could pronounce that Betty de Rothschild was "rather pretty and very polite." Bocher went so far as to grant her "great distinction." Most of all, the opulence in which she had been brought up endowed her with "that noble indifference which gives the most sumptuous luxury an air of everyday habit."[19] In Paris, where she displayed a studied courtesy without ever overdoing it, Betty set herself to maintain her position with dignity. Rather more subservient in Austria, she discovered how to win the friendship of Princess Metternich, doing so with gifts, much attention, and kindness. She never failed to send her exalted friend the latest novelties—by the Rothschild courier, of course. Finally, she managed to make her husband somewhat more observant in religion, while avoiding an excess of Orthodoxy. James even claimed that his wife kept him from going out on Saturday. Thanks to Mme de Rothschild, gifts to the Jewish community became more regular and more substantial. Fortified by this sensible, determined, and energetic companion, James threw his doors open to *le Tout-Paris*.

"After the decline of the dignity of nobility and noble birth, money has remained the only thing, and money without anxiety is the most beautiful of all beautiful things," remarked Stendhal.[20] James would not have contradicted him. This Rothschild embraced ostentation with an abandon and an excess that were prodigious, suggesting a fierce desire for retaliation, a resolve to outstrip everyone so as to forge a place for himself apart, and a determination to beat the aristocracy at their own game, that of luxury, taste, and refinement. "Madame Grandet was as rich as a Rothschild and wanted to be a Montmorency," wrote Stendhal in 1821, without any need to elaborate.[21] In ten years the name had become synonymous with wealth—modern wealth.

In nineteenth-century France there was a fundamental difference between wealth based on land, like that held by the former governing classes, and wealth of the kind possessed by the Rothschilds and their colleagues, which derived from commerce and existed on paper, in the form of stocks and bonds. No less striking was the difference between the prodigality of James de Rothschild and the caution exercised by his bourgeois counterparts, who associated unchecked luxury with the ostentation of a decadent aristocracy and, through innate prudence, refused to increase the opulence of their lives. This reserve can be explained by the fact that the rich bourgeois of the period—Delesserts, Périers, Davilliers, Mallets, Hottinguers—were rising steadily in a society from which they had never been excluded. They felt at home precisely where they were. They had never known ostracism reinforced by the constant violence and hostility that had pursued the Jews wherever they went before the Revolution. Consequently, the *grande bourgeoisie* enjoyed a surer perspective and a keener sense of social reality than James, the outsider *par excellence,* the man in a hurry, always covering his tracks and forever spurred on by ambitions that no middleclass, native, Gentile Frenchman could imagine.

The approach adopted by James was that of someone determined to avenge himself upon the very society to which he yearned to belong. Small steps, taken cautiously so as to guarantee further progress, did not interest him. Half-measures were out of the question. Only the sensational would do. James hoped to capture everyone's imagination with one grand stroke; when the moment seemed propitious, he would display without restraint the full power of his gold. His exhibitionism was to be so blatant that it would transcend all considerations of good or bad taste. He was never to be a typical parvenu, breathless from the tremendous effort to make his way and surprised at his own success. Hardly had he begun than he had arrived. How did this Rothschild—who had spent his entire life running from one business affair to another, calculating, wheeling, dealing, a man who never had a Mme de Beauséant[22] to explain the ways of the world—succeed in gaining the respect of those Parisians among the mine fields of salon society?

James won his battle for the very good reason that he knew how to surround himself with the right people. This facility for choosing the man most capable of advising him in areas where he had no particular knowledge was one that Heinrich Heine admired in James. Thus the first receptions given by this Rothschild were organized by an architect, Berthault, a survivor of the *ancien régime* who had designed the parks at Stains and Pontchartrain and staged *fêtes* for the Comte d'Artois, Louis XVI's youngest brother, at Bagatelle. James, no longer loath to spend money he had so much pleasure earning, placed Berthault in charge of everything. He gave him complete liberty, whether it had to do with the splendor of the antechambers flowering like greenhouses or the brilliance of the ballroom constructed in the garden, illuminated by chandeliers and candelabra, furnished with bronze consoles, blue-and-gold stools, and a stage large enough to hold an orchestra of forty, the whole scene festooned with swags and garlands. Also from Berthault's creative hand came the surprise of the grand staircase, each step of which bore a vase filled with rare plants; the sumptuousness of the salon displaying quantities of pictures and objets d'art, but also enlivened by marvelous toys and automatons for the diversion of nondancing guests; and, finally, the imposing solemnity of the maîtres d'hôtel in their black dresscoats and epaulets. The buffets, built in tiers and loaded with the most fashionable delicacies, including spun sugar formed into Palladian villas, Gothic ruins, or windmills, were the work of the famous Carême. Formerly chef to Talleyrand, Carême was an artist who had left England's Prince Regent because he did not like "that bourgeois ménage,"[23] and who could tolerate no more than a few months in service to Tsar Alexander in Saint Petersburg, a place "rendered vile by humiliating surveillance following on abuse."[24] He was to finish his career in "the good family of Monsieur le Baron," where he appreciated the great "understanding, a product of proper respect and the absence of familiarity."[25] James, who esteemed his artist-chef, rejoiced in the extraordinary refinements that characterized his table and soon began playing the role of gastronomic counselor to all his nephews.

Thereafter, James gave one gala after another, all of which received a good press. Lady Morgan, an indefatigable traveler, tells in her memoirs of the excitement she felt at the prospect of being invited "to the best table in France, in Europe," and her delighted confusion upon seeing the dessert, a daring structure of sugar columns on which Carême had inscribed her name.[26] Journalists, cordially received *chez* Rothschild, published glowing accounts. *La Gazette de France* and *La Quotidienne*, both aristocratic and rather stuffy publications, set the tone by expressing appreciation of "what the court and the city offered in the way of distinguished society." More surprising yet, no one refused James' invitations. Needless to say, the diplomatic corps and officialdom, always present as part of their duty, lent an air of dignity and seriousness to every Rothschild reception. The Ambassadors of Prussia, Austria, Russia, or Great Britain, and, of course, Metternich whenever he was in Paris, all men of power and of the most noble blood, served as social guarantees, and thus held the door open for the more reluctant inhabitants of the Faubourg Saint-Germain. Having first accepted an invitation out of curiosity to see a house that was said to be like no other, the Noailles soon became habitués, along with the Montmorencys, the Princesse de Ligne, and the Orléans Princes. In their diaries, where they were happy to note *fête éblouissante* after each Rothschild reception, these guests found nothing to criticize, unlike the Goncourts who considered James, under the Second Empire, guilty of "idiotic and ridiculous extravagance."[27]

James, reputedly an arrogant man, managed to make himself respected among the elegant of Paris who clocked in, day after day, at the factory for receptions that developed at the mansion in the Rue Laffitte, a house recently reconstructed in the style of the moment and equipped with every possible comfort. Contemporary taste ran to heaviness, and that of James to gold, if one is to believe the description left by Vicomte de Launay: "The mantels are covered in gold-fringed velvet. The armchairs have lace antimacassars; the walls are concealed under marvelous embroidered, brocaded, spangled fabrics of such thickness and strength they could stand alone and, if needed, actually support what they cover, should the walls give way. The curtains are fabulously beautiful; they are hung double, triple, and all over the place. . . . Every piece of furniture is gilded; the walls too are gilded. . . . . ."[28] The collection of paintings, eclectic in character but dominated by Dutch works, generally of good quality, did not yet contain the extraordinary pictures that James would acquire in the 1840s.

James gave an average of four soirées a week. Dinners for no more than twelve were rare, intimate occasions. To gain some impression of the grand scale on which life proceeded in the Rothschild household, we have only to take a random look at the account books. They show that on a normal day thirty persons came for lunch and sixty for dinner—throughout the year, since the pace did not slacken even when James and Betty sojourned in the country, at their Château de Boulogne-sur-Seine. Silver would be sent by ferry, if more were needed. Even Salomon, who had purchased a mansion in the Rue Pillet-Will round the corner from James, had to help hold it all together, dispatching his own servants to reinforce the Rue Laffitte staff, on condition that the favor be returned. And then to the next round. Entries in the account books fall off only to reflect revolution, as in 1830 and 1848, the sole occasions when the Parisian Rothschilds ceased to entertain. No letup can be discerned even for deaths and births. On May 7, 1835, the day before his eldest, a daughter, was born, James had eighteen guests for dinner; twenty-six came on the day of the event. James was relentless in his pursuit of social acceptance, which meant more for his peace of mind than for his career. In 1829, he snapped up a spectacular social prize by getting himself elected to the Union Club, the most elegant of all the *cercles* within exclusive Paris. Modeled upon London's clubs, the "circles" first came into being at the outset of the Restoration. The Union was founded in 1828 by the Duc de Guise, with a very restricted membership. All general discussion of politics was forbidden, but, according to Castellane, "nothing prevented the individual from expressing his point of view and no one failed to do so. Here one heard the latest news."[29] James had unmistakably penetrated the most closed of all Parisian sanctums, "the fashionable clubs where many are called but few chosen,"[29a] where the purest and most aloof aristocracy make up the majority. Just as he avoided socializing with French Jews, James also strove to set himself apart from his own natural class, that of the great commercial bourgeoisie, of stockbrokers and bankers. The Périers, the Seillières, the Foulds—the flower of the Chaussée-d'Antin—belonged to the Cercle de la Rue de Gramont, a club catering to "deputies, merchants, and bankers."[30] James aimed higher. He wanted to be the only one of his kind and to arrive all at once, not by degrees. Here again, it should be remembered how well his consular title served him. Famous banker though he may have been, it was his diplomatic credentials that permitted James de Rothschild to be elected to the Union Club.

Still, the social whirl did not cause James to lose his head. Always on the alert for the best and most diverse information, he emerged as the brother with the broadest range of interests, this breadth encouraged by Betty, who understood that a salon could succeed only to the degree that it was varied. Nathan cultivated no interests outside his work: "After dinner, I usually have nothing to do. I don't read books; I don't play cards; I don't go to the theatre; my sole pleasure is my business."[31] James, on the other hand, was not content simply to *recevoir utile*—entertain for business reasons—but sought out wit and charm. Nathan, in a teasing mood, had declared to Ludwig Spohr, formerly director of the Frankfurt Opera and the best violinist of his time, that his favorite music was the sound of several coins jangling in his pocket. James took pride in having Rossini as a regular guest in his house. No dinner took place in the Rue Laffitte without a Gérard or a Heine at the table, and James felt "the most fraternal affection"[32] for Dupuytren, the celebrated doctor who had saved his life in the aftermath of a fall from a horse. Learned men fascinated him, and Letronne, the most respected Hellenist of his time, often came to the Rothschilds'. Then there was his membership in the Grand-Orient Lodge, further proof of intellectual openness and curiosity. And whereas his brothers appeared not to appreciate the importance of the century's scientific discoveries—with Nathan refusing to invest in British railways—James stayed abreast of all industrial progress and formed close ties with members of the École Polytechnique.

As for his brothers in Germany, even if they had wanted to share in excitements beyond those caused by the fluctuations of interest rates, they could not easily have done so. When Metternich, motivated by higher considerations, accepted an invitation to Amschel's house in Frankfurt, it caused such a commotion in good society that his example could not be followed. Salomon never had the right to own property, despite his loyalty and immense services to Austria. It bothered him all the more because he knew well how real estate would have helped consolidate his fortune. Salomon even asked Metternich to waive the prohibition, doing so in his most flowery style: "Dare I venture to ask Your Highness on behalf of my brothers and myself for the right to buy properties and other real estate within the frontiers of Austria? I am fully conscious of the fact that the law forbids such transactions. His Majesty can, however, make exceptions for individual cases, and I have a feeling that if Your Highness wished to present my request to His Majesty in a favorable light, your most kind intervention would not fail to influence the most benevolent and just of monarchs in favor of this humble petition."[33] For all its flourishes, the letter produced no results. In Vienna the Rothschilds were not spared the ridicule of society. There was general astonishment, for instance, when Count Kolowrat, one of the great lords at court and a man of political importance, lent his presence to Salomon's table. Kolowrat hastened to explain himself: "What would you have me do? Rothschild attaches such importance to my going there that I sacrifice myself to the state, because the state needs him. Moreover, I took advantage of the occasion to obtain a donation of a thousand florins for the poor. The Jew agreed to this when I asked him, in exchange for the simple pleasure of seeing me."[34]

Nothing of the sort happened in Paris. Baroness de Rothschild gave only moderate amounts when her elegant titled friends sought contributions. In 1826 she parted with only twenty francs for the charities of the Comtesse d'Étampes, the Marquise de Puységur, or the Princesse de Ligne, while contributing a thousand francs every year to the township of Boulogne. Still more substantial were her gifts to the Jewish community, gifts that she augmented regularly. James too began extending much greater largesse to Jews than to Gentiles, which shows the formidable self-assurance he had gained. His gifts were not expressions of gratitude towards a society that had accepted him, like those of his brothers in Vienna or his Jewish colleague Bleichröder in Berlin. James preferred giving to the little Jewish community out of a growing sense of responsibility, though this loyalty to his own kind in no way prevented his taking a stand on political problems of national scope.

In the domestic politics of France, James supported the conservatives, opening his coffers wide to Villèle[35] in support of the Spanish expedition, sent to sustain King Ferdinand VII against an uprising of liberal officers. "Your Highness may use the money from the House of Rothschild for all his financial needs, whether these arise from the army or from the negotiations," Villèle wrote to the Duc d'Angoulême, the son of

Charles X, who was in charge of the operations. James even backed Villèle, although without enthusiasm, in his attempt to convert government bonds into issues offering lower yields as a means of finding the thousand million francs demanded by the émigrés, a drastic, ultraroyalist measure that appeared to bring into question the whole social purpose of the Revolution.

The nobility had not resigned themselves to the loss of their estates, confiscated during the Revolution, and their claims began to alarm the holders of the properties, called *biens nationaux* ("nationalized estates"). Nevertheless, following a year-long discussion, a law was passed granting the dispossessed émigrés—the aristocrats, now returned to France, who had forfeited their lands once they fled abroad during the Revolution—an indemnity equal to their revenues in 1790 multiplied by twenty, up to a maximum total of a thousand million francs. The indemnity would be paid in annual installments of 30 million francs. To raise the money—which in fact amounted only to 625 million—the government lowered interest rates from five to four percent, a measure that could not but generate bitterness among bondholders, most of them members of the bourgeoisie.

While James made periodic incursions into French internal politics, the experience did not enchant him. He understood the dangers only too well. To begin with, it exposed him to criticism on the grounds that he was a foreigner. In the heat of the émigré debate the Rothschilds found themselves labeled as a "European pawnshop that raises and lowers prices to suit itself." Villèle's program brought a violent attack from Casimir Périer: "For four months you have been scheming with foreigners, signing secret treaties with them, keeping them in the know, while the whole of France remained ignorant of your plotting."[36] Finally, James began to doubt the opportuneness of the program and said so to Metternich: "A transaction of this nature can recommend itself at one moment, whereas it becomes doubtful at another."[37] A true Rothschild, he preferred to carry out his operations within the confines of his family, timing them by their own natural rhythm.

During those last days of the Restoration James seemed to be adding the final touches to his image. Aspiring to total dignity, he made certain that his private life gave no cause for comment. No one could have been more conscious of the moral guarantee that a banker had to give clients who were often ignorant and thus easily frightened away. James also knew that when it came to foreign loans, investors counted on his name more than anything else. Buyers would pick up a Rothschild loan with greater alacrity than notes issued against the credit of Russia, Prussia, or Hesse. Moreover, James understood that he was functioning in an environment of increasing public scrutiny. At a time when news agencies did not exist and papers remained small, the Bourse served as the main forum for the exchange of information, true or false. In the late 1820s, even the least credible rumors could create devastating confusion. For M. de Rothschild to appear nervous was to risk setting off a panic. Consequently, James drilled himself into a regular routine.

At the Bourse James made his entrance at the same time every day, just before the exchange closed, always dressed in black and usually accompanied by a nephew, Anselm, Betty's brother, or one of Nathan's sons. Immediately a crowd would surround him. In this period James still showed the greatest courtesy. He would bow and approach the first of his colleagues, making certain the conversation remained relatively short and never giving any hint of his intentions. "Heavy as a sack, as immobile as a diplomat"[38] was how Balzac characterized James, who had to make every effort to deceive the curious who were watching him. "To decipher" the Baron became a popular game in these purlieus, one that could be highly beneficial for any player who won. It could also entail considerable risk. Nathan, even more than James, was a past master in the art of dissembling. "Eyes are usually denominated the windows of the soul; but here you would conclude that the windows are false ones, or that there was no soul to look out of them. There comes not one ray of light from the interior, neither is there one scintillation of that which comes from without, reflected in any direction. The whole puts you in mind of a skin to let, and you wonder why it stands upright without at least something in it. By and by another figure comes up to it. It then steps two paces aside, and a glance more inquisitive than you would ever have thought of is drawn out of the erewhile fixed and leaden eye, as if one were drawing a sword from a scabbard."[39]

Contemporaries admitted that the complexity of the Rothschild operations was too much for them, due to the location of the five brothers in Naples (where Karl established himself at the request of Metternich, after the restoration of the Bourbons in 1821), Vienna, Frankfurt, London, and Paris. In addition to their dispersal, the family profited from a network of correspondents all but unique in Europe. Everywhere the best bankers vied with one another to represent the Rothschilds, even going so far as to work for them at a loss, on condition that they be given access to the brothers' information service. "Even the shrewdest bankers cannot find their way through the Rothschild maze," conceded one financier, Sartoris, the Neapolitan agent for a Parisian banker.[40] In another letter he observed: "You say that Rothschild is bullish? He is rarely wrong about the market's direction."[41] To know what the Rothschilds were doing could be very advantageous. But how was one to achieve this when so often the brothers' activities "seem to indicate a view of things no one can grasp"? Thus the relentless surveillance of James every minute that he was in public.

The brothers usually managed to frustrate even their closest observers, thanks to the effectiveness of their couriers, for while willing to handle the diplomatic or commercial dispatches of others, they would entrust their own to no one else. Meanwhile, of course, they reserved the fastest transport for themselves. No precaution appeared too great for the Rothschilds. They used Hebrew characters laced with passwords for the most sensitive letters, omitting signatures in case an accident should make disavowal necessary. In order to meet in person ever more frequently, they traveled constantly. *Le Moniteur* for September 6, 1829, noted the possibility of a big financial undertaking, "expected because all the Rothschild brothers are about to gather in Paris." Their competitors found themselves reduced to spying on the couriers. In April 1822, when more than the usual number of Rothschilds met in Frankfurt it created a small panic. At Naples the firm's employees had to change clothes and carriages before entering the city, so great was the excitement generated by their appearance. "Interest rates," joked Heine, "tumbled another two percent. M. de Rothschild, it is reported, had a toothache; others say it was colic."[42]

Not only did the financiers make a practice of studying the Baron and analyzing his every gesture, the political world too, aware of the connection between the strength of the Bourse and the stability of the region, followed him with sharp eyes. Thus in 1830, Mme de Boigne, a careful observer of the diplomatic scene, noted that M. de Rothschild, by visiting the ministry and then going on peacefully to dine in the country with Mme Thuret, the wife of an important banker, "put all minds at rest."[43] But just how far off the mark such close observation could lead one became evident when M. de Rothschild, like many others, allowed himself to be caught unaware by the events of July!

5
The Revolution of 1830

Carried away by power, pleasure, and success, James failed to note that storm clouds were gathering. He was a happy man, having profited enormously from the freedom to do business and do well in it. No one could have derived greater satisfaction from the peace and order of post-Napoleonic France, nor have had less reason to want change. As a consequence, James paid no attention to the first signs of disquiet within the political sector.

The world seemed to smile for James de Rothschild. Success and the universal recognition of it had eased relations between the brothers and put an end to their eternal quarrels. James relished the calm. For years Karl had counseled him against displaying his wealth "to the point of generating anti-Semitism," but now that every visiting celebrity in Naples was accepting invitations to his palace on the Posilippo, Karl had ceased predicting doom. Amschel, at last moved from the Frankfurt ghetto to a beautiful house hidden away in a park filled with tame deer, no longer bombarded his youngest brother with direful letters; he was too caught up in his passion for horticulture. As for marriage, it brought James nothing but joy, symbolized by his admirably run mansion and, most of all, by the birth of a daughter, Charlotte, in 1825 and two sons, Alphonse and Gustave, in 1827 and 1829.

The unified solidarity of the family, still as intimate and productive as ever, survived the dispersal of the brothers and the distractions of wealth. Soon, however, the brothers began worrying about the effects of opulence on their progeny. The immediate cause of the anxiety was Anselm, Salomon's son and the eldest of his generation. At fifteen he had to give up the idea of a trip to Paris, since his father feared the boy might develop a taste for pleasure and frivolity and thus lose "all interest in practical things."[1] "He should not be made to engage in extended studies," his Uncle Karl advised; instead "he should enter business as early as possible, otherwise he will never take to it."[2] And so the five sons of Mayer Amschel kept a tight rein on their children, who, having known nothing of the hard school in which their parents grew up, evinced greater personal refinement but less ardor for competition and less thirst for gain. "It takes ten times more cunning to preserve a fortune than it does to make it, and the task requires sacrificing body and soul, heart and mind,"[3] Nathan kept telling his sons, who were already turning to sports, especially horse racing, as well as to the arts and the other pleasures of life. Meanwhile, however, they continued to display great docility toward their elders.

Financially, the fifteen years since his arrival had made James the preeminent figure in the Place de Paris. Laffitte, once so impressive to the young Frankfurt Jew, had been left far behind. The capital now invested in the Paris branch of the Rothschild firm was three times that of the Laffitte bank. James had all but crushed his competitors. As a result, the house at Boulogne no longer seemed adequate. In preparation for better things, James in 1829 acquired Fouché's estate at Ferrières. Still more surprising was his success in making a place for himself in the Faubourg Saint-Germain. When Victor Balabine, a young attaché at the Russian Embassy and a leading member of society, enumerated the festivities brightening the Paris season, he cited a Rothschild ball alongside a Montmorency reception and a Damas *matinée*. Very likely it was this intimate involvement with the nobility that distorted James' assessment of the forces active in France at the time. Greater familiarity with the commercial bourgeoisie, seething with ambition yet frustrated in their desire for political power, would have given him a more accurate view of things. He did pick up an alarm signal, set off by the collapse of the Bourse in June 1830, but then disregarded it, thereby causing Salomon to send an optimistic report to Metternich: "It appears that the mood of opposition which has grown so much these last months is not directed against the sacred person of the King and the Bourbon dynasty but against the ministers."[4]

Clearly James had failed to take full account of the bitterness felt by the leading bourgeois, chafing at their exclusion from important office, whether political or administrative. The only ministers in the Restoration government who did not belong to the old aristocracy were Villèle and Decazes, and they, in the purest tradition of the *ancien régime*, owed their positions to royal favor. Thus James was surprised by the alliance between the wealthy bourgeoisie and the lower classes, a relationship that struck him as contrary to nature. Nevertheless, the determination of certain bankers—Laffitte, Casimir Périer, Auguste-Simon Bérard (son of the last director of the Compagnie des Indes, Benjamin Delessert)[5]—not to be excluded from power emboldened them to take advantage of Charles X's political ineptitude. They set about to exploit the discontent of the Parisian proletariat, the Faubourg Saint-Antoine, "swarming like an anthill, hardworking, courageous, and as irascible as a beehive [that] was quivering in expectation of and desire for a disturbance."[6]

It was the King, in fact, who precipitated the crisis by issuing four orders whose effect was to suspend the constitution. Parisian journalists immediately assembled to protest. By the next morning, the 27th of July, the demonstration had grown into an insurrection. Barricades were quickly thrown up in streets throughout the working-class quarters. Next, the insurgents marched from the eastern sector of the capital towards the center, which the royal troops could not defend. By the 29th, Paris counted one thousand of its citizens dead, eight hundred of them revolutionaries. The authorities hastened to flee the city. A municipal commission, appointed by the Chamber of Deputies, took charge at the Hôtel de Ville. The next morning Charles X abdicated in favor of his infant grandson and left

France the same day, after stopping at James' house in Boulogne to pick up some money. On the 31st the commission named the Duc d'Orléans Lieutenant-General of the kingdom. Lafayette, the old hero of the first days of the Revolution, embraced him on a balcony before the assembled populace, thereby crowning Louis-Philippe "King of the French."

Had the French at last found someone complex enough to govern them and yet satisfy all their contradictory impulses? His activity in the Jacobin Club, his courageous conduct at Valmy and Jemappes, where he had "carried the tricolor under fire,"[7] his father who had voted for the death of Louis XVI, endowed Louis-Philippe with an authentically revolutionary past. He could also lay claim to an impeccable record as an émigré. Having left France only at the height of the Terror, he could not be criticized for his departure, and once abroad he had refused to join in battle against the French national armies. Nor did he participate in the petty quarrels of the court in exile. Indeed, he led an existence which combined dignity with adventure, first earning his way as a mathematics teacher and then launching out to discover the New World. Finally, after 1815, irreproachable loyalty towards his Bourbon cousins and a traditional marriage to a Neapolitan Princess, Marie-Amélie, Marie-Antoinette's niece, made his introduction into the Restoration world relatively easy. Extremely popular, thanks to discreet behavior seasoned by liberal friendships, Louis-Philippe could stand as the very symbol of reconciliation.

Such was the great hope, but not everyone shared it. "This will last fifteen years," declared Chateaubriand, "then the deluge. . . . Our nephews are going to witness a great uproar."[8]

James did not like revolutions. To begin with, all that commotion was bad for interest rates. Then, he knew he was too thoroughly identified with the Holy Alliance and the Faubourg Saint-Germain to have any illusions about the view that the liberal left held of him. But a revolution that resolved itself in three days and ended with the rise to power of a serious, responsible man, whose colossal fortune the Rothschilds had been managing for several years, was a revolution which promised better days. James wasted no time making up his mind about it. Courageous and courteous enough to offer hospitality and refuge at Ferrières to Baron de Vitrolles,[9] an Ambassador too marked by his ultraright opinions to risk remaining in Paris, he was nonetheless relieved to observe that nowhere had property been threatened by the mob, even a mob "beside itself with rage, that would have preferred to be cut to pieces rather than to submit to the Bourbons."[10] Thus he chose sides openly, doing so all the more easily since he considered that Charles X and his chief minister had proved themselves treacherous by not keeping him abreast of their plans and by giving him false assurances. Taking care that the press publicized his gesture, James gave the Municipal Commission 15,000 francs "intended for the pitifully wounded and the widows and children of those who had fallen in the last days of July."[11] In this way he put his family back on the right path, including three-year-old Alphonse, who found himself dressed like "a little man" in the uniform of the National Guard.[12]

Professionally James continued to be as effective as ever, political events having in no way impeded the House's information services. Nathan in London and Amschel in Frankfurt received the news earlier than did their respective governments, which they immediately alerted. At first, Metternich refused to believe what he heard. The Rothschilds had panicked, he told Gentz. They had been afraid to put the details in writing and the courier to whom they had entrusted an oral message delivered it in exaggerated form. It was the Chancellor, of course, who misjudged. The Rothschilds knew only too well what they were talking about; moreover, they understood that quick action would be necessary if they were to avoid losing everything. There was no time for havering. Nathan, Salomon, Amschel, and Karl fell into line with James, who had come to believe that the Bourbons were gone for good. The only thing to do therefore was to support the new regime and use all their influence to calm the absolutist powers, which were threatening to declare war on those murderous agitators, the French.

Metternich, once fully aware of the true nature of the events, interpreted them as an explosion of anarchic passion against authority. Russia, in its distrust of the new French monarch, became almost insulting. In these circumstances, the Rothschilds gave absolute priority to the task of preserving peace for the sake of maintaining steady, fruitful commerce between Paris, London, Naples, Vienna, and Frankfurt. Fortunately, as soon as Louis-Philippe had been installed, the drop in market values slowed. With the financial world breathing a sigh of relief, the optimistic Laffitte declared: "The reign of the bankers begins."

James was only partially convinced. Too well informed to underestimate the dangers of the international situation, he also worried about the volatile nature of the French. "I assure you that this country is enough to drive one mad, for while sanity and reason favor peace, it's the bellicose notions that come to the fore,"[13] he wrote to Salomon. Three days later he warned Metternich, again by way of Salomon: "The people [of France] are lions, and one should not arouse such a strong and powerful nation."[14]

What became apparent in the letters exchanged by the brothers at this time were the beginnings of national sentiment. Writing to Salomon, James would refer to Metternich as "your Prince," and when he wrote that "the powers are arming and we are obliged to do the same," "we" meant France. In Nathan's correspondence, this phenomenon became still more pronounced. He spoke for the whole country when he declared: "England has no confidence in your ministers, who dream only of revolution, urged on by old Lafayette. . . . Go see *your* King and tell him. . . ." Here, then, were the first stirrings of the nationalism, unconscious yet symptomatic, felt by James and Nathan, who alone of the five brothers, began to identify with their respective countries. But this nascent assimilation should not be taken to mean a disagreement among the Rothschilds. The family still came before all other interests.

The rapidity with which James had abandoned Legitimism—monarchy based upon the main Bourbon line descended from Louis XIV through Louis XVI, Charles X, and the latter's progeny—was to serve him well in regard to King Louis-Philippe, the head of the Orleanist branch of the Bourbon line descended from Louis XIV's brother, Philippe, Duc d'Orléans. In fact, however, it would be difficult to tell which of these two realists had greater need of the other. James could never have imagined playing the role of state banker in a country that was not legally his own without his having the most direct access possible to the center of power. Meanwhile, Louis-Philippe had every reason to want this banker—and what a banker!—behind his program. He needed him to help reestablish the government's credit and also to provide a supplementary, even privileged means of access to Metternich. Louis-Philippe, in fact, had no intention of imposing himself on Europe as a monarch ruling by Divine Right. Almost humbly, he chose to present himself as a conciliator, struggling to check the incipient anarchy that had brought him to power. Conservative Europe had to be persuaded that he sought only to preserve peace and entertained no thought of meddling in the affairs of his neighbors. It is no small irony of history to find a German-born Jew serving as guarantor of the French King before the Holy Alliance. It seems that Louis-Philippe was deeply wounded by the attitude of his "colleagues." "All of you treat me like a pariah and a revolutionary," he blurted in rage to Count Apponyi, Austria's Ambassador in Paris. Had he been treated with greater consideration, Louis-Philippe would certainly not have felt it so imperative to keep James at his side, but circumstances were such that he immediately sought James' support. In fifteen years the Rothschilds had become the keystone of power.

There had been no personal rapport between James and Louis XVIII or Charles X, who took great pains to stand apart from mere mortals. By contrast, Louis-Philippe, as early as August 1830, placed his relations with the Baron on a friendly plane. Oddly enough, it was as a member of the Antiquarian Society that James appeared before the King to congratulate him on his accession. After the reception the monarch detained James to explain his views. "You have seen," he said, "how much happiness I enjoyed in the bosom of my family, happiness that accords with my temperament, which is peaceful and entirely devoid of ambition, and you know me too well not to understand the state of mind in which I undertake my task. . . . By renouncing such an agreeable and carefree existence in order to mount a throne fraught with danger, I have made an enormous sacrifice for my country. . . ."[15] Louis-Philippe seemed anxious to justify the crowning moment of his career. Between James and the King of the French there was to be a meeting of minds.

Louis-Philippe made his approach at a time when James, all pliancy and politeness, was still on the rise and susceptible to flattery. Here was the King treating him like an equal! Louis-Philippe behaved with "extreme courtesy but indiscriminately and without grandeur, the courtesy of a merchant rather than a Prince," according to Tocqueville.[16] Whereas if Charles X had Prince Metternich or the Duke of Wellington to dinner, he "thought that royal favor could go no further and was surprised that he had granted it,"[17] Louis-Philippe understood how to put his interlocutors at ease. Such familiarity might shock a Tocqueville, who criticized the July Monarch's "lack of refinement and noble bearing,"[18] but it struck James as just right. Fully aware of his aristocratic blood[19] and refusing to believe himself "the equal of any other man,"[20] Louis-Philippe felt compelled to suppress the hereditary pride of his race. Thus, by playing upon his bland appearance, he managed to pass for the quintessential bourgeois. The image, however, was more contrived than natural. Heinrich Heine suspected him of hiding a crown under his gray hat and of concealing the scepter of absolutism inside his umbrella! Among less shrewd observers, Louis-Philippe had the reputation of a family man—steady, simple, level-headed, careful—and he chose an entourage in keeping with this. He reigned over his children with imperious authority, allowing his sons no financial independence whatever. Only his eldest son dared stand up to him. Such docility was fortunate, because the King would never have tolerated the least sign of family dissension. That "greedy and pleasant," flexible and tenacious man possessed of an "ambition that only prudence contained,"[21] a passionate concern for industry, and a totally pragmatic mind—this man who gave way to excitement (again according to Heine) only when it came to his most cherished interest, money, would suit James perfectly.

Not only did Louis-Philippe make James feel at home in France, he also seemed to endow him with an ancient and honorable past. Whenever he used James as the means of semiofficially transmitting his opinions or intentions to Metternich, the King took care to emphasize that he and James shared the same interests. You are one of us, he seemed to say to Baron de Rothschild, and our aims are identical: preserving the peace and protecting private property. This question of private property was fundamental to any judgment bearing on the loyalty of individuals. James, during a conversation with the King, stated quite candidly: "My family and my assets are in France; therefore, I cannot be suspected of treachery toward Your Majesty."[22] Convinced, Louis-Philippe never misled him, but, of course, it would have been absurd to betray a man who continued to manage the sovereign's personal fortune.

The Rothschild brothers derived great satisfaction from these connections and never ceased to stress them. "My brother," Salomon reported to Gentz, "had occasion to see His Majesty quite casually. He goes to the palace whenever he wishes."[23] James was penetrating deep into French political life, especially after the ruin of Laffitte. He used all his influence to have "his friend" Casimir Périer named to head the government. A *grand bourgeois* so authoritarian that Louis-Philippe had punned on his name, calling him *Casimir Premier*, Périer inspired confidence in James, for the very good reason that "if war broke out, [Périer] would lose all his properties and all his factories. . . . This is why I believe peace possible," James concluded in a letter circulated to his brothers.[24] Although classic, and irrefutable, the argument hardly did justice to Périer. The Premier, in addition to being a prudent man of property, was a true statesman who devoted the whole of his energy to stabilizing the monarchy within the framework of the new constitution and to infusing the bourgeoisie with the courage to govern, come riot or reaction.

To mark his satisfaction and faith in the new order of things, James decided to give a grand Mardi Gras ball on February 15, 1831. All the usual high society gathered in the Rue Laffitte, but the spirit of rejoicing had yet to return. Paris still seethed with anger, and, as Count Apponyi noted in his journal, "at 3 a.m. we heard the bugles calling up a battalion to arms. That caused a number of people to leave. The mixture of party masks and mob makes an odd spectacle,"[25] and a spectacle, one might add, characteristic of the period. The Prince de Joinville, one of the King's sons, described a large diplomatic dinner at the Tuileries during which the conversation was repeatedly drowned by a great uproar in the street below. The guests simply looked at their plates every time the clanking of iron and the clatter of horses' hooves was heard, signifying another cavalry charge. The company barely managed to choke down their meal, conscious as they were that this monarchy, born of riot, would not find it easy to overcome its lack of constitutional legitimacy. The regime would have to persuade some to accept the revolution and others to be content with their gains, instead of continuing to foment popular unrest. "It's madness," wrote Heinrich Heine, "to revive the rhetoric of 1793. . . . The man who gathers up the fallen red blossoms of spring and sticks them back on the trees is as silly as the one who replants faded lily branches in shifting sands."[26] Périer, convinced "that there was more glory for those who finish revolutions than those who begin them,"[27] was on the verge of achieving some balance among the divergent forces when cholera broke out.

Originating in India, the epidemic had ravaged Russia and Central Europe throughout 1831. By February 1832 cases were being reported in London. A month later the disease struck Paris and spread with terrifying speed. The first areas to succumb were the poorer ones in the eastern part of the city, with their dark, dank streets, but not even the new, airy districts, populated by well-to-do bourgeois, would be spared for long. From two hundred victims a day, the death rate rose, at the climax of the siege on April 11, 1832, to twelve hundred a day, a toll so terrible that newspapers refused to publish it for fear of aggravating the general panic. "It was a horrible sight," recalled George Sand thirty years later. "On certain days large removal vans . . . converted into hearses for the poor, rolled by in endless succession. The most frightful part was not so much the bodies heaped up pell-mell like so many bundles, but rather the absence of relatives and friends in the wake of these funeral wagons; the drivers quickening their pace, swearing and whipping the horses; the passersby drawing away in fear of the hideous cortège; the enraged workers who imagined some fantastic scheme to poison the populace, raising their fists against Heaven. Once the threatening groups had moved on, it was frightful to see the dejected or indifferent expressions that rendered them all either irritating or stupid."[28] If in Central Europe the plague hysteria had caused a renewal of violence and hostility towards the Jews, accused of polluting the wells, in France the terror almost set off a class war. Rumor running through the slums held that the cholera was an invention of the bourgeois eager to rid themselves of the people, that villains skulked along streets at night poisoning all the fountains. A young man who made the mistake of being well dressed was "murdered because he had been seen looking through the door of a wine merchant,"[29] while another dandy was struck down simply because he had paused near a fountain in the Faubourg Saint-Germain. Meanwhile, angry crowds gathered at the Hôtel-Dieu, the largest hospital in Paris, shouting: "Down with the doctors! Down with the poisoners!"

How could anyone not be shaken by such events? Everything conspired to threaten the stability and even the feasibility of life: the mounting unrest in the streets and the horror of a disease that, after centuries of dormancy, seemed to surge up from the depths of time. Casimir Périer succumbed following a tour of the hospitals. The rich prepared to leave, and at the height of the epidemic the government was issuing seven hundred passports a day. The summer before, Salomon had fled plague-ridden Vienna so hastily that he did not even take time to alert his friend Gentz, who was surprised to find the door bolted when he arrived for his daily visit at the Römischer Kaiser Palace. Then, as the disease caught up with him several months later, Salomon retired to Ferrières along with the women and children, leaving James to assume responsibility for everything. The latter took the elementary precaution of having his walls washed down with lime, avoided all unnecessary meetings, and, never one to leave a penny on the floor, demanded the cancellation and reimbursement of his Opéra subscription. The siege held until June. But with tens of thousands dead and a workers' revolt brutally repressed at Saint-Mérri Cloister, the winter of 1832 proved a cruel season. During this somber, disquieting period of his life, James began reflecting upon what was then called Charity.

If the Revolution ended happily for the well-off, it was not without a nagging awareness that the impoverished masses, disenfranchised, weak, and defenseless, had no hope of escaping their humiliation and distress except through violence and beggary. Paris hummed with socialist sects, whose activity created an atmosphere in which the ideas and aspirations of the liberals, influenced by Saint-Simon and Fourier, could find a receptive audience. James lent an attentive ear to certain of these innovators, all impatient to explore every modern industrial possibility. But the most urgent challenge was to deal with the misery then pressing against the very doors of the Rothschild bank.

Paris at this time was home to an organized population of beggars who allowed no respite to any celebrity. George Sand tells how, along with "her first little success," came a throng of "unemployed artisans, mothers who had pawned everything in order to give their children daily bread . . . would-be ladies of charity . . . and the incessant, awful struggle between the doorbell, the haggling, and work ten times interrupted."[30] She found herself obliged to pay "a small salary to people charged with the responsibility of making inquiries," since she did not have the time to do it herself. If George Sand was assailed to such a degree, one can imagine what the Baron had to endure! Too sensitive not to understand that for a man possessed of a colossal fortune, one that by its own impetus grew larger every day, indifference was out of the question, but also too intelligent not to want the good he did to be effective, James approached the problem on several different fronts. First, he acted within his own area, across the street from the Rothschild mansion at the corner of the present-day Rue Rossini, and there arranged for soup to be distributed daily at noon to the needy of the neighborhood. Since he had regular habits, the great banker invariably found a crowd of beggars waiting at the door when each day at the same hour he left to go by foot to the Bourse. Ernest Feydeau, the father of the dramatist, who delighted in observing James during his apprentice years at the Bourse, claimed that the Baron tossed twenty-franc pieces at any mendicant he recognized by sight. In this way James was acting out a form of folklore widespread among the Rothschilds. The *Schnorrer*—or beggar—was a respected figure in Jewish tradition, and the gift from hand to hand a well-established custom in the ghetto world. At Frankfurt, Amschel too threw coins every time he went out. He even refined the system and gave it a sporting twist. At mealtimes his suppliants launched their petitions through the window, and whenever one of the pebble-weighted bits of paper landed near his plate, the banker would unfold it and respond by flipping a coin back through the air.

Meanwhile, more method was required to deal with the tidal wave of requests that inundated the Rothschild offices.

Irresponsible or imprudent fathers, bankrupt tradesmen, society women overwhelmed with unacknowledged debts, inventors seeking a subsidy—all turned towards James. Nothing could be done with this avalanche of petitions without sorting through them to select the genuine from the fraudulent. Thus James set up a special office with a staff of three men, one of whom analyzed the appeals, while another undertook investigations, and a third made the eventual payments. The requests were all filed in perfect order so that, for instance, one enormous dossier bore the label "Blushing Brows." This recorded the overtures of the poor whose sense of shame caused them to begin their letters with "Monsieur le Baron, it's with blushing brow. . . ." Then there was a box filled with the honest failures; also one for potential suicides, whose messages usually began: "When you receive this letter, I shall be no more, unless your inexhaustible kindness. . . ." Another substantial category consisted of pregnant women. One case that stood apart was the sponger who had the charming idea of offering to tell the Baron, for a trifling fee of fifty thousand francs, how he could prolong his life to age one hundred and fifty. James replied thus: "Sir, I have often been threatened with death if I did not give a certain sum. You are certainly the first to ask me for money while proposing to prolong my life. Your offer is unquestionably far superior to and more humane than the others, but my religion teaches me that we are all under the hand of God, and I want to do nothing to shield myself from His will. By refusing, however, I do not in any way impugn your discovery, which I urge you to use for your own benefit. With regrets that I cannot accommodate you, I congratulate you upon the hundred and fifty years that you are called upon to live in this world."[31]

James now occupied his position with both satisfaction and good humor. From the time he first arrived in France, he had set himself to achieve power and fame. The July Monarchy would grant him an abundance of both.

6
A Public Figure

"Do you know who is Viceroy or even King in France?" Mme de Nesselrode wrote to her husband, the Tsar's Foreign Minister and soon to be Chancellor of all Russia. "It is Rothschild."[1] If Parisians had long been dazzled by the luxury of James' style, they were now impressed by the extent of his political power. Under the July Monarchy, bankers often had more influence over the sovereign than his own ministers did, and, of course, the banker *par excellence* was James. "M. de Rothschild knows Europe Prince by Prince and the Bourse broker by broker. He keeps all their accounts in his head, those of brokers and those of Kings, and he advises them without even consulting his books. He says to so and so: 'Your account will not balance if you take such a minister.' "[2] But had the banker truly become somebody who with a single gesture could change the course of history?

James, whose chief virtue could not be said to have been modesty, was not above making an overt display of his power. Indeed, he loved to let it be known that he had influence over Louis-Philippe. During dinner the Baron felt called upon to clarify things for Mme de Nesselrode: "I know all the ministers;

I see them daily; and as soon as I perceive that the trend they are following is contrary to the interests of the government, I call on the King, whom I see whenever I wish. . . . Since he knows that I have much to lose, and that my sole aim is stability, he has every confidence in me, listens to what I have to say, and takes account of what I tell him."[3] This simplicity and self-satisfaction masked a fierce and elemental determination, a quality that emerges quite clearly in the letters James wrote to his brothers. It also becomes rather crudely apparent at the conclusion of agreements reached with Belgium and The Netherlands: "Now is the moment of which we should take advantage to make ourselves absolute masters of that country's finances. The first step will be to establish ourselves on an intimate footing with Belgium's new Finance Minister, to gain his confidence . . . and to take all the treasury bonds that he may offer us."[4] Should the Minister prove insufficiently submissive, should he have the effrontery to declare, "I do not need the Rothschilds," if he should be "disloyal to us," James wrote in a subsequent letter, "I will show him how his credit can suffer."[5]

Preserving the peace in Europe remained the overriding preoccupation of the Rothschild brothers throughout this period. Such was their concern that they attempted to control the use of the funds their bank placed at the disposal of governments, and they made no secret about it. "Rothschild provides no money for war," asserted an Austrian diplomat, von Prokesch, on December 7, 1830.[6] Belgium, then tempted to take up arms as a means of settling its differences with The Netherlands, found itself financially too dependent on the Rothschilds to give in to its bellicose urges. This was because Salomon had made his views known to the Belgian government through the Rothschild correspondent in Brussels, Richtenberger: "These gentlemen should not count on us unless they decide to follow a line of prudence and moderation. . . . Our goodwill does not yet extend to the point of putting clubs into hands that would beat us, that is, lending money to make war and ruin the credit that we sustain with all our efforts and all our means."[7] Pacificism would become a fixed policy of the Rothschilds. Thirty years later, while writing to his Prussian colleague, Gerson Bleichröder, James declared: "It is a principle of our house not to advance money to make war, and even if it is not in our power to prevent war, the fact that we have not contributed to it puts our minds at rest."[8]

The brothers enjoyed an enormous competitive advantage in the handling of what they called the *nervus rerum*, in that they held a quasi-monopoly when it came to state loans. Moreover, they extended the range of their activity once the revolutionary fervor of 1830 had settled down. Working out of Naples, they gained access to Spain, Portugal, Greece, and the Papal States, all of which became clients of the Rothschilds. Belgium had already fallen into their hands. It was also reported that two Rothschild representatives had arrived in Constantinople "with the intention, it is believed, of entering into negotiation with the Grand Vizier."[9] And despite the chronic troubles disrupting the credit of Brazil, Nathan participated there in the financing of various loans. The Rothschilds did business everywhere, and when the Duc de Broglie remarked that "the finances of Europe . . . now formed a sort of republic, a kind of federation, and were to a certain extent interdependent and each supporting the other,"[10] he did not have to be specific about which banking house filled the office of president of that "République des Finances."

The Rothschilds did not fail to acknowledge the need to work with their colleagues. Indeed, Nathan went so far as to organize and preside over a conference of French and English bankers at Calais, for the purpose of formulating a common policy designed to limit the effects of a competition that could have been disastrous. In general, however, the Rothschilds preferred to maneuver alone and contrived to give their competitors an inferiority complex. "Wouldn't you agree," remarked a banker from Geneva, "that a large financial undertaking in which the House of Rothschild played no part would have twice as much difficulty making any headway? This last observation did not originate with me, but several months ago I found myself at a meeting of bankers, among whom several commented that only rarely had major [financial] operations conducted without the Rothschilds actually succeeded."[11] If professionals expressed themselves in this way, little wonder that a legend began to form in the public mind.

The success of the five brothers, who seemed to share Europe among themselves without ever dividing their forces, fired the imagination. The best writers of the time gave credence to the notion of the all-powerful bankers. "The Jewish banker says: '[God] has given me the royalty of wealth and the understanding of opulence, which is the scepter of society. . . .' A Jew now reigns over the Pope and Christianity. He pays monarchs and buys nations," stated Alfred de Vigny.[12] Jewish polemists joined in and declared: "There is only one power in Europe, and that is Rothschild . . . and speculation is his sword. . . . Rothschild needed states in order to become Rothschild. . . . However, today he no longer needs the state, but the state needs him."[13] Heine put it more humorously, recalling olden times when the King would have had the teeth of M. de Rothschild pulled out had he refused a loan. Today, "Rothschild, Baron and Knight of the Order of Isabella the Catholic, may stroll over to the Tuileries whenever it strikes his fancy, without fear of losing even one tooth to a cash-hungry King."[14] Metternich's spies took the same line and in their reports feigned surprise at the presence in James' office of General Rumigny, whom Louis-Philippe had put in charge of everything related to the Bourse. Rothschild, wrote a certain Klindworth to Count Apponyi, the Austrian Ambassador, "places in each ministry, in every department at all levels, his own creatures who feed him the greatest variety of information."[15]

While the European press devoted long articles to the Rothschild triumphs, American newspapers, often influenced by a group of German Jews to whom the image of an all-powerful Court Jew was familiar, portrayed Rothschild as fabulous and fantastical: "The Rothschilds govern a Christian world. Not a cabinet moves without their advice. They stretch their hand, with equal ease, from Petersburg to Vienna, from Vienna to Paris, from Paris to London, from London to Washington. Baron Rothschild, the head of the house, is the true king of Judah, the prince of the captivity, the Messiah so long looked for by this extraordinary people. . . . The lion of the tribe of Judah, Baron Rothschild, possesses more real force than David—more wisdom than Solomon."[16] Even the wildest rumors came to seem credible. In 1830 an American weekly reported on its front page that the Rothschilds had purchased Jerusalem: "We see nothing improbable that in the pecuniary distress of the sultan, he should sell some parts of his dominions to preserve the rest; or that the Rothschilds should purchase the old capital of their nation. They are wealthy beyond desire, perhaps even avarice; and so situated, it is quite reasonable to suppose that they may seek something else to gratify their ambition, that shall produce most important effects. If secured in the possession, which may be brought about by money, they might instantly, as it were, gather a large nation together, soon to become capable of defending itself, and having a wonderful influence over the commerce and condition of the east—rendering Judah again the place of deposit of a large portion of the wealth of the 'ancient world.' To the sultan the country is of no great value; but, in the hands of the Jews, directed by such men as the Rothschilds, what might it not become, and in a short period of time?"[17]

Such articles, of course, contained many absurdities. Certainly, Jewish communities everywhere made grateful acknowledgment of all they owed to the generosity of the Rothschilds, but it was insulting to insinuate that money could make the Messiah. Throughout the nineteenth century a certain element within Jewish opinion opposed the excessive influence of the wealthy on their community, and nothing could have been more remote from the aspirations of Jews in general, or from those of the Rothschilds in particular, than the creation of a Jewish state. On the contrary, all efforts towards assimilation tended to deny the irreducible peculiarity of the Jewish people. "Everywhere, even in countries that still dispute their claim to the rights of man and citizenship, the Jews strive to prove that they belong to the same nation as those with whom they share the earth, and that they are Jews only before God."[18] Jews who had savored the sweet taste of living in liberal countries liked to believe that they had only to acquire an occidental education in order to meld quickly into the surrounding society. They visualized being Jewish as others were Protestant in France, or Catholic in Great Britain. They entertained no desire whatever to live again as Jews among Jews. The idea of departing from the path of assimilation so as to create a homeland for themselves was inconceivable at this time.

Finally, only the ill-informed could imagine that the first generation of Rothschilds would have been content merely to open their coffers and let them collect manna falling from Heaven. Their princely receptions, their salons filled with elegant society, their hunting parties and cures, masked the reality of an existence devoted totally to work, constantly alert to snatch the least opportunity to make a good deal or to oversee the tiniest detail of its execution. The Rothschilds spent their lives calculating endlessly. Never would they give up their powerful work habits, and never would they weaken in their singleminded determination to neglect nothing that would bring them so much as a sou. The folklore of the family abounds in anecdotes that stress this feeling among the older Rothschilds. When a cabman, for instance, complained of the meager tip given him by Salomon, remarking that the latter's son was always more generous, the elder Rothschild replied: "It's because he has a rich father." Then there was James' reaction to the decision to install pay turnstiles at each of the Bourse's doors. Annoyed professionals claimed that the device would bring down stock prices. Asked what he thought, James replied: "I zay it vill gost me tventy zous a day."[19]

James would never have that birthright of the aristocrat—a light, carefree touch. "The Baron works from morning to night—he has nothing else to do but work,"[20] deplored the ever-ironic Heine. Mayer de Rothschild, Nathan's youngest son, who would adopt an easier way of life, sent his brothers the most piteous accounts of a tour he was then making with Uncle James: "He is in very good spirits, although we are travelling like couriers."[21] James refused to let himself be put off by effort or ennui. "I would not do it for all the world," swore Nathaniel,[22] "receiving rail-road folks from seven in the morning til past five every day, and moving about from the North to Lyons and then to Strasbourg."[23] Only their intimates knew the unremitting pains taken by James and his brothers. Outsiders attributed their success to a mysterious and constant luck. In reality, however, the Rothschilds found themselves obliged to make a considerable effort just to keep up with the times.

The Rothschilds had made a fortune by following a classic eighteenth-century tradition. Money changers at the outset, they gradually expanded their activities to include those of tradesmen, stocking up to sell at a higher price a combination of goods, such as cloth, wine, or colonial commodities. Then, as soon as their accumulated capital permitted, they discovered the profitable world of debt financing. None of these ventures—not even lending—entailed the prolonged commitment of capital. Money turned over and therefore yielded interest very quickly. Under the *ancien régime*, no banker believed that the function of money was to remain tied up for long periods. This explains the Rothschilds' reluctance to invest in industry, a domain requiring a long gamble on the future. Nathan, who blazed so many trails for his brothers, decided against participating in the construction of British railways. Why should he lock up funds when he could earn so much money by concentrating on government loans? After 1830, however, thanks to economic development, these large operations became less frequent. Soon they would even seem a bit archaic in advanced countries like France and Great Britain, where the regularity of tax returns made credit financing less essential. The state still did not protect its interests by placing its own bonds with the public; even so, bankers could no longer count on the easy profits from government financing that they had enjoyed in the preceding period. France did not borrow from the public between 1832 and 1839. In Great Britain during the same period, the government offered only one debt issue—altogether exceptional—designed to indemnify West Indian property holders whose slaves had recently been emancipated. Certainly, as we have seen, there were loans to be underwritten elsewhere, in the less wealthy countries of southern Europe, but here the absence of political stability required that the underwriter take a thousand precautions only to obtain modest results. Given these circumstances, financiers began preparing to modify their policy, and the shrewdest of them perceived that industry would produce the solutions of the future. For someone as circumspect and reflective as James, venturing into a domain where he knew nothing could ever be easy. Who would advise him? Who would help him discover the broad horizons of the modern world?

It so happened that in 1822 James had engaged a young Jew from Bordeaux to serve as a broker of foreign commercial paper. A descendant of one of the oldest and most remarkable families in France's Portuguese colony, Émile Péreire was also a lively and enterprising character whose views extended well beyond the bank. Indeed, they carried him into the realm of political economy, where his passion for social questions led quite naturally towards Saint-Simonianism. Saint-Simon had predicted the advent of a new society managed by industrialists—that is, the producers of wealth—a society where the interests of management and those of labor would be harmonized. For a while, when the model communities were being organized, the movement suffered considerable ridicule. There ensued, however, a period of intellectual renewal spearheaded by a group of young people who combined a scientific education—many of them were graduates of the École Polytechnique—with professional experience. Engineers, bankers, merchants, manufacturers—all were idealists who brought an admirable sense of reality to their attack upon contemporary economic problems. One of the solutions they favored was the creation of railways.

Despite their prolific production of articles for the Saint-Simonian press, first *Le Globe* and then *La Nation*, the group failed to generate the financial support they needed. Finally, James could not resist the enthusiasm and confidence of the young man he affectionately called *le petit Péreire* and agreed to take on the railway venture. It became one of the great concerns of his life; moreover, his personal participation in the enterprise transformed him in the public eye. Until then, James had never exposed his operations to general scrutiny or been accountable to anyone. Now he would find himself compelled to leave his private enclosure and be catapulted into the forefront of events. For the first time in his career, he would have to perform in full public view.

From the discussions that James held with Émile Péreire and his brother Isaac emerged a tiny railway of only 11 miles linking Paris to Saint-Germain. For the Péreires it was a publicity stunt, designed to attract further financing and to overcome the hostility of a public still largely unconvinced, despite the British example, of the advantages to be gained from this mode of transport. Had not Thiers disdainfully declared that "Parisians must have railways as a toy, but no passenger or suitcase will ever be transported by this means"? Even serious people remained persuaded that passengers would be asphyxiated the minute the train entered the shortest tunnel.

Construction got underway as soon as James gave his approval. For the next two years Émile Péreire never left the building site. When not supervising the workers, he withdrew into his small temporary office on the Place de l'Europe, the line's point of departure, and there made plans for future services. The line, which extended to the very bottom of the terrace at Saint-Germain, near the Port du Pecq, opened to great pomp and ceremony on August 24, 1837. Aboard the first train to make the journey were Queen Marie-Amélie and her children. Louis-Philippe did not appear, it seeming altogether too much to expose the sovereign's person to a mechanical vehicle capable of attaining a speed of some 19 miles an hour. (Scarcely more brave was Queen Victoria, who waited until 1842 before facing the ordeal of travel by train.)

James turned the inauguration into a personal triumph. For the luncheon on arrival at Pecq he sent his chef, his battalion of butlers and stewards, and his rarest Sèvres. The guests, for all the fear and excitement aroused by the journey, did justice to the meal, especially to the *pommes soufflées*, a gastronomic invention achieved when the chef, advised that the train would be late, retrieved the potatoes half-done from the deep fry and then resubmerged them at the last minute. The Queen, always appreciative of Betty's courtesy, behaved graciously towards the Baronne de Rothschild. An immense crowd had gathered to see the marvelous machine and stayed to applaud the Princes, the financiers, and the first railwaymen. And the occasion set the speculators thinking. Soon the possibility of participating in operations so eminently capable of producing income began to reveal itself. This was because the banker, given the size of the investment, could not undertake all of it and, even if he had been able, would not have wished to do so. To immobilize so much capital for so long would have made him dangerously vulnerable in the event of a crisis. When it came to industrial affairs in general, not only railways, the House of Rothschild would make it a rule to hold in their portfolio enough shares to give the family the right to keep an eye on the management of the company and stress its responsibilities, but to place the remainder of the stock in the hands of the public.

Thus, for the Saint-Germain railway, the 5-million-franc

capitalization was divided up into shares each with a par value of 500 francs. Such a modest price would permit the stock to be distributed among persons of average means. This produced a twofold breakthrough, for while small investors could now dream of getting rich quickly, financiers would henceforth understand how to use their money to attract that of others.

Confident that railways had a future, James began establishing other ventures. After Paris–Saint-Germain came Paris-Versailles on the right bank of the Seine. Before long, parallel tracks were being traced in every direction, often with a wasteful lack of order. The Versailles line, for instance, was duplicated on the left bank, a route awarded by the government to the Fould group. After several years of trial and error, a law was passed in 1842 providing for the construction of a star-shaped network, with Paris at the center, and a precise mode of financing. While the state assumed responsibility for the infrastructure, including the considerable cost of land expropriation, the corporations and companies awarded the rights of exploitation for a given period would take charge of laying the track and providing the rolling stock. Needless to say, the various financial groups launched into bitter competition with one another whenever an award was to be made.

When the time came for the development of a Paris-Lille-Brussels service, James went into such a frenzy that he set tongues wagging. The activities "of that rogue of a Rothschild"[24] were not to everyone's taste, but James ignored public opinion and plotted his own course. He needed support, from the Chamber of Deputies and from the press, in order to gain the votes necessary to float the credit for the construction of lines that interested him as the beginning of what would become the Compagnie du Chemin de Fer du Nord. He procured them. "If the government fails to stand by the right bank," he stated at the time, "I will have it attacked by the entire press. The newspapers, as a general rule, make a strong impression."[25] In 1842, James succeeded in subscribing a quarter of the company's capitalization, equal to 200 million francs, once again divided into shares with a par of 500 francs. Some twenty thousand stockholders would virtually trample one another underfoot for the opportunity to turn their savings over to the bankers.

This was the beginning of the railway craze. The demand for shares exceeded the supply, and James found himself more avidly solicited than any other financier, since his name alone, already a synonym for wealth, seemed a sufficient guarantee of the investment to trigger soaring hopes. But neither impartiality nor anonymity governed the distribution of shares. A somewhat bitter note, drawn from the archives of the Neuflize Bank, asserts that "Messrs. de Rothschild are not in the habit of opening subscriptions to the public. They place shares with their friends and a few privileged firms, among which we are not numbered. They also receive a great many requests to which, arbitrarily, they may or may not reply."[26] Indeed, M. de Rothschild found he had plenty to choose from. "If he has saved all the letters addressed to him at the time of the northern railway award, not only by deputies and public officials, but also by ladies of rank, he should have quite a valuable collection of autographs," observed Duvergier de Hauranne,[27] a liberal Deputy who, according to Tocqueville, distinguished himself by his rare disinterestedness and sincerity.[28]

During this period James' innate arrogance became more pronounced than ever. Lordly and contemptuous, he savored his triumph untroubled by modesty. Ministerial crises struck him as futile convulsions, albeit necessary inasmuch as "our French ministers are like table napkins: after a while they must be laundered and left to lie a bit; it improves them."[29] He even abandoned the discretion that over the years had endowed him with such dignity. "I have yet to meet the woman who would deny me her favors,"[30] he announced proudly to the Prince de Joinville, one of Louis-Philippe's sons. "He was bragging," asserted the Prince twenty years later when he wrote his memoirs, amusing himself by recalling the short stature of the pot-bellied Baron. But one never knows! In 1842, certainly, James must have enjoyed some unexpected satisfactions. He found himself, in fact, courted shamelessly on all sides. "Just now everyone goes cup in hand to M. de Rothschild," reported Heine. "He stands in a downpour of letters seeking charity, and since the most fashionable socialites lead the way with their worthy example, it is no longer shameful to beg. M. de Rothschild is therefore the man of the hour. . . . M. le Baron is not so warmly enthusiastic about our living poets as about the illustrious dead, for example Homer, Sophocles, Dante, Cervantes, Shakespeare, Goethe, all deceased poets, glorified geniuses who, stripped and purified of their terrestrial dross, have long since been elevated above the earth's poverty and do not seek shares in the northern railway."[31]

Heine held himself aloof. Association with his uncle, the Hamburg banker and a Rothschild correspondent, had taught the poet not to ask too much of the world's great. Balzac, however, could not resist it and roared with triumph when finally he succeeded in obtaining a few shares: "I've got fifteen shares of the Chemin de Fer du Nord—it's gained 400 francs, and it's expected to gain 1,500."[32]

In this feverish atmosphere, what saved James from megalomania was his business sense. Too prudent to get caught up in a fad, as well as too experienced not to take account of the potential dangers of such widespread speculation, he made a good foil for the fiery enthusiasm of the Péreires. Quick but never precipitate, ambitious yet realistic, he played an essential role in the development of French railways. Prosper Enfantin, spiritual heir to Saint-Simon and the great figure of the Saint-Simonian movement, summarized the situation well when he wrote: "Today, one must steal close to de Rothschild, no pun intended . . . and keep on the rails, if one is truly to take part in the great business of the world. . . . To traffic in rumors, with Thiers, Guizot, and Molé, a game that Louis-Philippe plays so well, is for Rothschild an infant's game, which he doesn't even deign to play. He profits from deals, but he plays with railroads, and congratulated me on joining the party, saying, or at least causing me to understand, that here was a big, rough game for strong men."[33]

This excess of deference towards James on the part of everyone touched by the speculation fever had unfortunate consequences. Convinced that no one thought of anything but self-enrichment, he failed once more to detect the discontent that was overtaking the country or the first tremors of the cataclysm that would come in 1848. "Those who have railway shares want to hold them in order to realize as much profit as possible. Those who have none hope to acquire them in the near future. Since these aspirations cannot be realized unless peace and order are maintained, everyone now declares himself to be conservative and pro-government."[34] James oversimplified to an outrageous, even dangerous degree. And his sons' letters are even more symptomatic in their blind optimism: "Everything is calm in France; a strong majority favors the administration. Industry and railroads absorb all thought and turn it away from politics. Please God that we remain in this fortunate state of peace."[35]

Impressed by what he observed round him, James forgot that the advent of large-scale capitalism, the development of the financial markets, and the Industrial Revolution had not eliminated poverty. On the contrary, the interests of the "have-nots" often opposed those of the "haves," and the distress of the unemployed and the hungry, left behind in the race towards progress, was becoming progressively more poignant. The capitalists seemed like great pumps sucking up the money of others. The innovators of the early nineteenth century had evolved into profiteers in the eyes of the proletariat, which had grown much larger, thanks to all the new forms of free enterprise.

James was, as much by his situation as by his personality, the symbol of symbols. Thus, for the first time in his career, he found himself the target of truly virulent attacks. Toussenel, the first anti-Semitic journalist, cited him by name in his pamphlet, *The Jews: The Kings of Our Time*. It came at the very moment when James was openly trying to influence the government and the press in a matter that concerned only the Jews: the Damascus Affair. He was about to discover what it was to be both a capitalist and a Jew.

7
Pariah King

The Damascus Affair was a typical Middle Eastern crisis, brought on in this instance by the revolt of Muhammed-Ali, Pasha of Egypt, against his suzerain, the Sultan of Turkey. It placed France at odds with the rest of Europe, since Muhammed-Ali, with French support, had conquered Syria and was turning towards Arabia. Alarmed, Great Britain convinced its allies, Russia, Austria, and Prussia, of the risks involved in such a development and succeeded in having them sign a treaty, the Quadruple Alliance, defending Turkish interests and throwing France into damaging diplomatic isolation. The fierce reaction in France was that the time had come to avenge the humiliation suffered as a result of the treaties of 1815. A war party, led by Thiers, declared its determination to stand up to the whole of Europe and to wage war on the Rhine. "We have owned your German Rhine. We held it in our glass," exclaimed Alfred de Musset, intoxicated with martial enthusiasm. Jingoists, ever at the ready, indulged in dreams of facile victory.

Now, for the first time, James took sides openly in regard to a diplomatic crisis. By preaching calm and moderation, he placed himself in opposition to, at least, Thiers, the head of the government, if not to Louis-Philippe, who knew deep down that France could not undertake military action against the whole of Europe. The Bourse, which did not share the soaring enthusiasm of the poets, developed a case of the jitters, causing government bonds to plummet. "The public is in a somber mood . . . all of which disturbs the market terribly. . . . And the Rothschilds have withdrawn from a hunting party scheduled for tomorrow, not wanting to be away for a moment," Guizot wrote as a warning to Thiers.[1] James, however, refused to take a strong initiative. He could have countered Thiers by using all his power to bring about a stock-market crash. In these circumstances the King, who was so sensitive to fluctuations in the price of public debt that he viewed them as the best possible barometer of public opinion, would not have supported his Minister. But James held back. Thiers' political existence "rests upon such an inextricable edifice, constituted of so many elements, that it would be almost impossible, meaning dangerous, in any event extremely imprudent, to overturn him," he had Nathaniel write to the rest of the family.[1a] He therefore resigned himself to observe "the manner by which that man, the most arrogant of all the parvenus, progressively encircles this poor country and drags us towards the abyss."[2]

On top of all this came an incident that would have far-reaching repercussions. To put it briefly, however, the affair served to crystallize, for the first time, a conflict that thereafter would often tear at the hearts of the Jewish community, involving the reconciliation of loyalty to one's country and solidarity with oppressed Jews elsewhere in the world. French Jewry was therefore ill prepared to deal with the problem that suddenly confronted them in January 1840, when a Capuchin of Sardinian origin disappeared in Damascus, the capital of Syria, which had just been conquered by Muhammed-Ali with the approval of France. Since the monk practiced medicine and had been especially occupied in propagating vaccination against smallpox, the entire population of Damascus knew him, and his inexplicable absence was causing comment in every quarter of a city divided up among Moslems, Jews, and Christians. The French Government intervened because, as a Catholic, Father Thomas came under the protection of France. Thus it was the French Consul who went to the monastery, confirmed the monk's disappearance, and initiated the investigation. On the way there the crowd accompanying him grew rowdy, accusing the Jews of murder.

The Jews of Damascus had become accustomed to such summary judgments. Moslems and Christians alike were always claiming that Jews made a practice of murdering Christians in order to use their blood as an ingredient in unleavened bread. Moreover, the East seemed regularly to produce more baseless accusations than any other part of the world, and not all of them were directed against Jews. At Adrianople, in the same period, the disappearance of a Moslem sparked off mob action against Christians, and only intervention by the Great Powers saved fifteen Christian notables from being turned over to the executioners.

To arrive at a fair judgment in such an affair required exceptional energy and an unusual degree of impartiality. At Damascus, the investigation was undertaken by the Syrian authorities and the French Consul, Ratti-Menton. The latter proceeded with dispatch. He simply went into the Jewish quarter, arrested a barber who had seen Father Thomas the day he disappeared, and surrendered him to the Syrians. Under torture, the poor man denounced other Jews, some dozen of whom were arrested forthwith. A few of these collapsed in the course of brutal interrogation, while others confessed. One of the accused, however, Isaac Piccioto, a member of one of the most important Jewish families in Damascus, was found to be an Austrian protégé. Once he managed to inform his Consul, the case moved beyond the frontiers of Syria.

It was a matter of public knowledge that James and his brothers felt concern for the lot of their coreligionists. The preeminent position they had attained bore with it a responsibility towards less fortunate Jews. The Rothschilds never doubted this, and even had they tried to do so, the countless letters sent them from Jewish communities everywhere in the world would have made it impossible. The letters all reiterated the same themes: on the one hand, the Rothschilds' success proved that Judaism did not necessarily constitute an obstacle to success; on the other, the family had "a debt of gratitude for the benefits bestowed upon them by Providence and owed it to their glory to show themselves to be the great benefactors of their race." Whenever an incident occurred, the Rothschilds spared themselves no pain and tirelessly used their influence, calling upon every member of the clan, to make certain justice was done. With their Jewish susceptibility, they quickly took offense, for no great effort was required to imagine the reality of the persecutions. "I think it will do good when once over [we] show people generally that the day is gone by when any religious sect may be molested with impunity," wrote Nathaniel to his brother, Anthony, in London.[3] He then went on to say that the French Premier had informed the Chamber of his belief that the Jews had committed murders in order to obtain Christian blood for ritual use, a calumny that Nathaniel hotly declared could leave no Jew untouched.

The Rothschilds meant what they said. As soon as the affair became known they centralized their operations. The Austrian Consul in Damascus, having concluded his inquiry and satisfied himself that the murder could not be imputed to the Jews, sent his report directly to James, who received it at the very moment that Thiers received the dispatch sent by Ratti-Menton to the Quai d'Orsay. From that moment on the two men confronted one another through the medium of the daily papers.

La Quotidienne fired the first shot by asserting that the case smacked of "influence from an extremely powerful man who protects Jews with his immense credit, and whom cabinet members accommodate because he has considerable funds at his disposal and they often need him." Thiers was even more explicit and had *Le Constitutionnel* print a charge so worded as to inflame French national pride: "For some days now we have heard much about M. de Rothschild and his maneuvers. M. de Rothschild is a man of finance and does not want war. Nothing could be easier to understand. M. de Rothschild is an Austrian subject and the Austrian Consul in Paris, and as such he has little concern for the honor and interests of France. This too is understandable. But what, pray, have you to do, M. de Rothschild, man of the Bourse, M. de Rothschild, agent of Metternich, with our Chambers of Deputies and our majority? By what right and by what authority does this King of Finance meddle in our affairs? Is he the judge of our honor, and should his fiscal interests prevail over our national interests? We speak of fiscal interests, but, surprisingly enough, if one can believe highly accredited reports, it is not just financial grievances that the Jewish banker would lodge against the cabinet. There also seems to be wounded vanity to satisfy. M. de Rothschild had promised his coreligionists to have our Consul General in Damascus dismissed for the position he took in the trial of Jews being held in that city. The steadfastness of the Premier has resisted the mighty banker's demands. Hence, the irritation of the mighty banker and the fervor with which he throws himself into intrigues where he has no business."[4]

James did not allow himself to be drawn into an argument with Thiers. He was content merely to have a short notice inserted in the next morning's *Constitutionnel*: "If I desire peace, I desire a peace honorable for France and for Europe. In these circumstances there is a service that men of finance can render to the country, and I believe I have never held back. If France is not my country, it is the country of my children. I have lived here for twenty years, here I have my family, my affections, and all my interests."[5]

James ignored the reference to his Jewish loyalties. Futile discretion! *L'Univers*, a Catholic sheet, cruelly heaped blame on Jews in general: "It is the Jews who betray both the victim and his defender in the person of our Consul; it is the Jews who find influence here, credit, authority, and publicity even among certain Catholics."[6] The bitterness of these remarks can be explained by the tactic adopted by James. Since some newspapers had refused to publish the material he provided, James began buying space for their insertion in sections reserved for paid announcements. "Given these circumstances," he declared, "we have only one means left to us, which is very effective in this case, and that is to turn to the newspapers. Today we have arranged for *Les Débats*, as well as other papers, to print a detailed exposé based upon a report made by the Austrian Consul, and we have also arranged for the same article, with all its details, to be published in the *Augsburger Allgemeine Zeitung*."[7] It was this step which gave rise to gossip about the press being bribed by leading Jews, most particularly by the Rothschilds.

In reality, most Jews did not enter into the quarrel quite so vigorously. "The Jews in France," remarked Heine, "have already been emancipated too long for racial ties not to have considerably loosened. They have all but lost themselves, or rather they have been absorbed into the French nation. These Jews are Frenchmen just like any other. . . ."[8] They thought so, anyway.

Thanks to the genuine intellectual and moral freedom that had flourished since the Restoration, the Jews of France felt no pressure to choose between their religion and their new homeland, unlike the situation in Germany or even in Great Britain. Central European Jews still could not obtain employment other than in banking or trade without first undergoing conversion. And in England the schools and universities most adept at producing true gentlemen—the prestigious institutions of Eton, Rugby, Oxford, and Cambridge—closed their doors to Jews by requiring that all students take a Christian oath.[9] A Jew had the right to vote but not to be elected, or at least he could not sit in Parliament since there too a Christian oath was mandatory before any member could take his seat. Thus conversion provided the only means by which a Jew might enter public life. No such impediments existed in France. The transition whereby the Jews of France became French was a smooth one. Young Jews could take part in national activities without cutting themselves off from their traditional milieu. As a result, conversions were negligible,[10] changes of name almost nonexistent,[11] and mixed marriage extremely rare. Furthermore, young French Jews could develop along parallel lines, engaging in political activity while also participating in the life of the Jewish community.

The 1830 revolution highlighted this development by providing an opportunity for young Jews to distinguish themselves. Michel Goudchaux, for example, the son of a Nancy banker sent to Paris to direct a branch of the family business, found it possible to extend himself well beyond the task of making money. He helped found a liberal and republican newspaper, *Le National*, and was wounded during the invasion of the Tuileries on July 29, 1830. After calm had returned, he was simultaneously elected mayor of a Paris *arrondissement* and vicepresident of the Consistory. Another active member of the Central Consistory, the engineer Michel Alcan, was elected to the Chamber of Deputies in 1830. Philippe Anspach, a lawyer from Metz and a committed partisan of the revolution, achieved a distinguished judicial career that led all the way to the Supreme Court of Appeals (the first Jew to attain such heights in this profession), at the same time that he remained continuously involved in the affairs of his religious community. Far from suppressing his religious affiliation, Judge Anspach stressed it by always attending official receptions at court as a member of the Consistory rather than as a magistrate.

The best example of how the assimilation process functioned in France is to be found in the brilliant career of Adolph Crémieux. Born at Nîmes in 1796, he qualified for a scholarship that permitted him to study at the Lycée Impérial in Paris. There were only seven Jews in the French lycées at this time. Young Crémieux gained great renown by winning a prize in the Concours Général, for which the best students in the lycées competed. It permitted him to take up law. In 1830 Crémieux left Nîmes for the French capital, got himself elected to the Chamber of Deputies, and set about becoming a leader within the Jewish community. This brought him into close collaboration with James for the defense of their coreligionists wherever the need arose. Together they joined the Philanthropic Society for Jewish Emancipation in the World presided over by Lafayette.

The élan that catapulted these young men into the mainstream of French life can be explained by measures that the new regime took in favor of the Jews. In their first assembly, the Deputies voted unanimously for the separation of Church and State, a decision that in effect abolished all discrimination between Jews and Christians. Beginning in November 1830, rabbis would be paid by the government, which placed them on the same footing as ministers of other faiths. At Metz, an overjoyed Chief Rabbi called it, quite simply, "the greatest act of justice ever attained by the Hebrews since the destruction of the second Temple."[12] Transferred from Metz to Paris, the rabbinical training college came to be considered a state institution. Meanwhile, integrated Jews supported a movement designed to make Judaism more modern in its outward manifestations. Ladino and Chuadit, those dialects that French Mediterranean Jews had compounded of Hebrew and Spanish or Provençale, quickly disappeared from everyday use. Yiddish, however, was kept alive, largely as a result of the immigration of Teutonic Jews from Central Europe. Jewish schoolchildren were punished with a fine whenever they lapsed into Yiddish while talking among themselves.

Little by little, the old language of the ghetto would be spoken only by the elderly, who soon found it difficult to recognize their own synagogues. From the raucous, disorderly meeting places they had always been, temples became more peaceful and quiet, in the manner of Christian places of worship, which existed solely for prayer and meditation. More decorum seemed to be what French Jews demanded of the traditionalists. Sermons in French, the unfamiliar sound of an organ, the presentation of the newborn in the temple, boys and girls alike, the dignified demeanor of the congregation—all transformed the atmosphere of Jewish assemblies. A necessary change, insisted the new generations, which sought ever-greater flexibility in the observance of interdicts and ceremonials.

Still, modernization proved slow and laborious, for each new influx of Central European or Oriental Jews served as a restraint. The leading lights among the immigrants—the Rachels, the Meyerbeers, the Offenbachs, all of whom integrated the very day they arrived—were hardly representative of the mass. The new arrivals had to be taught, wherever this was possible and they were willing, to discard their traditional attire, to eat Western food, to speak French. In short, they had to abandon the bizarre appearance that made the established and accepted Jews of France feel ill at ease. The latter had nothing in common with "those Frankfurt money changers, those Russian usurers, those Polish innkeepers, those Galician pawnbrokers."[13] The struggle to bring about the "inner emancipation" of French Judaism, as Salomon Reinach phrased it, was to continue throughout the nineteenth century. In 1900 Reinach recalled that Orthodoxy had been an impediment imposed by the Jews upon themselves: "At a time when the progress of science and conscience has done so much to bring men together, the ritualism of the Jews kept them isolated. They ringed themselves about with a moat deeper than that dug by all the prejudices and hatreds. They gave credence to the false idea that the Jews were aliens among nations."[14] In 1830 no one could have foreseen the immensity of the task to be accomplished.

All the Jewish communities of France joined together in celebrating the accession of the new sovereign, "this King elected by the nation, risen from the barricades, who has enlarged our liberties."[15] At Lille the Rabbi did not hesitate to compare Louis-Philippe to King Samuel.[16]

Thus euphoria reigned among the Jews of France when they were suddenly shaken by the Damascus Affair and placed on the horns of a dilemma. If they attempted to defend their coreligionists, they seemed to oppose France since, paradoxically, it was France—among all nations the one which had done the most for their liberty and dignity—that was now turning against them. The crowning irony was that Austria had come to their defense. Metternich, who accommodated himself so marvelously to the arbitrary treatment suffered by Jews in Austria, made it a point of honor to stand up for the Jews of Damascus. But, of course, the affair provided a perfect opportunity for the Austrian Chancellor to register his hostility towards France's Middle Eastern policy, as well as to render a great service to his friends the Rothschilds, who, with their usual vigor and zeal, had immediately begged him to intervene.

Thiers ruthlessly simplified the matter when he took the floor in the Chamber of Deputies: "You protest in the name of the Jews; well, I protest in the name of the French. And if I may be permitted to say so, something extremely honorable is happening among the Jews. Once the story became public knowledge their disquiet was apparent all over Europe, and they have handled the affair with a zeal and a fervor that profoundly honors them in my eyes. If I may be permitted to say so, they are more powerful in the world than they pretend to be, and at this very moment, they are lodging complaints at every foreign chancellery. And they do it with a zeal, an ardor that exceeds all imagination. A minister must have courage to defend his agent who is attacked in this way."[17]

The polemic went beyond the Chamber of Deputies. The Jews found themselves buffeted by a blast of modish and derisive anti-Semitism. "During the sad Damascus period," recalled *Archives israélites* two years later, "did none of your friends say to you, laughing with that soul-chilling laughter: 'I don't want to lunch with you for fear that you might have me served a cutlet from Father Thomas'?" The Jews, though deeply distressed, did not in fact make quite the fuss that Thiers would have everyone believe. "The interest taken by Parisian Jews in the Damascus tragedy amounted to nothing more than a few insignificant demonstrations. The Jewish Consistory, with all the halfheartedness typical of established bodies, assembled and debated. The sole result of the deliberations was a unanimous resolution to bring the documents in the case to the public's attention."[18] James and Crémieux were practically the only ones who constantly stepped forward and assumed responsibility for the defense. Heine paid homage to Crémieux who, "sacrificing his personal interests, and scorning the traps of spite, challenged the most odious of the insinuations."[18a] Crémieux felt the situation more acutely than James for the simple reason that he was more French. His family had lived on French soil for generations. A pure product of the imperial schools, he identified totally with his homeland. At the same time, however, he felt painfully torn by the Damascus problem, and when he exclaimed "France is against us," he consciously chose to be a Jew before being French. Most French Jews did not want to face up to that choice. They refused to challenge the order of things at the heart of French society. On the one hand, they still did not feel sufficiently secure in their emancipation to adopt an attitude so contrary to the general policy; on the other, they tended, as a consequence of their own assimilation, to disengage themselves from Near Eastern Jews with whom they had nothing in common. To jeopardize advantages so recently acquired for the sake of a few Damascene Jews struck them as absurd. Crémieux, sure of himself, courageous, and capable of maintaining his distance from the government, was an exception.

For James the problem did not present itself in the same terms. First of all, he had never sought naturalization; thus he was not a French citizen. He always cited his holdings in France as a means of establishing his attachment to the country, and this made a persuasive argument, coming as it did from a man like James. But in his own innermost self he remained above all else a Rothschild, which for him constituted a unique species. In his own personal hierarchy he was first a Rothschild, then a Jew, and finally a Frenchman, by feeling if not by passport.

The primacy of the family reveals itself clearly in a letter written to Nathaniel about the marriage of his niece Hannah to an English Protestant, Henry Fitzroy. That the young man was handsome and charming went without saying. He also came from an excellent family, being the youngest son of the Earl of Southampton. But he was not Jewish, and this enraged James. To marry a Christian was an insult. "It's not," he insisted, "that I'm a fanatical admirer of the Jews, although I'm careful to retain my religion . . . [but] in our family we have always tried to keep up the love for, the attachment to the family . . . in this way it was more or less understood from early childhood [that] the children would never think of marrying outside the family. This way the fortune would stay inside the family . . . and Mayer will marry Anselm's daughter and Lionel's daughter will marry another child of our family, in order to keep the name of Rothschild honored."[19]

But being a Rothschild meant taking up the cause of oppressed coreligionists, and James did it, with no crisis of patriotic conscience. Moreover, once the initiative in the defense of the accused of Damascus passed to English Jews, the Rothschilds remained at the head of the movement. "You must exert yourself a little, dear Rabbi, and get up a good subscription to pay the expenses of sending Crémieux thence. Put the house down for £1,000 at once to make a beginning. I am curious to know what Isaac Goldsmid will do," Nathaniel wrote to his brothers in London.[20] It was finally decided that Sir Moses Montefiore,[21] Crémieux, and Salomon Munk[22] would travel to the Middle East in order to negotiate directly with the authorities. The mission ended in complete success, the emissaries obtaining not only the release of the imprisoned Jews but also an acknowledgment of their innocence. Better still, they pushed on to Constantinople and there persuaded the Sultan to issue a firman declaring the absurdity of the allegations of ritual murder.

Simultaneously, the international crisis resolved itself with the dismissal of Thiers, a development in which James must have had a hand. In the course of a long private audience granted by Louis-Philippe, the Baron had argued that government securities stood on the brink of total collapse. Louis-Philippe, who had never been so war-minded as his "little

Minister," named Guizot Premier. The new leader took a far more rational view of France's position in Europe. The Jewish envoys made a triumphant return. Not only had they saved Jewry from dreadful humiliation, but they had also demonstrated the power of the Jews in Western Europe. They had mounted their own defense, and had won their case. An enthusiastic reception awaited Crémieux wherever he stopped, in Corfu, Venice, and Frankfurt. Only French Jewry, reluctant to offend Louis-Philippe and his government, maintained a certain reserve.

The events in Damascus showed that, together, the richest and most influential Jews constituted a network that, while neither official nor institutionalized, was nonetheless extremely effective. They had made publicity their weapon, and they knew how to utilize the press. Damascus was the first incident of Jewish persecution to have such wide newspaper coverage. And it brought to light the strength of the Rothschild group, with all its ramifications, including the capacity to act simultaneously in France, England, and Austria. It was precisely that power of intervention that would provoke violent reactions in the period after 1840.

James was to be attacked both as a Jew and as a capitalist millionaire. The "anti-Semites," who did not yet exist officially since the term would enter the language only in 1889, saw him as the personification of Jewry. For them, the Jew was by nature a capitalist and a crook. "A Jew is a man who demonstrates that two times two equals three."[23] The same circles loved to insist upon the universal opulence of Jews. Their publications would have it believed that the average Parisian had a monthly income of 300 francs, while that of Jews living in the capital went as high as 12,500 francs. Every Jew, it seemed, had been touched by the Midas hand of the Rothschilds. "Since Kings have become the chamberlains of Salomon, Baron de Rothschild, the Jews have tombs of marble in Venice."[24] It hardly mattered that James' coreligionists, who did not themselves make the mistake of imagining the Baron to be representative of the average Jew, wrote vehemently to condemn the gross exaggeration of his power.

Jewish intellectuals had long since rebelled against the excessive respect that the Consistory showed for wealth. "Have money and you become eminent; with gold, you move on to the consistory; with diamonds, you attain the Central Consistory,"[25] commented Olry Terquem, librarian of the Arsenal, celebrated mathematician, and redoutable polemist. *Univers is-raélite*, the Conservative Jewish review, expressed shock at the extent to which religious honors were sold in the synagogue, calling the practice one that "brought humiliation upon the spiritual leaders of the community."[26] The blatant ostentation that gave James the nickname "Chief Rabbi of the Right Bank," or even "High Priest of Judaism,"[27] eventually came to annoy his fellow Jews. Jewish circles liked to congratulate themselves on the successes achieved by their own (the Jewish press published every distinction, whether won at the lycée, the university, in government service or the military), but those of James sometimes seemed a bit too much. Thus when the Baron had the honor of being received at the Vatican, in recognition of a loan negotiated in 1832, the occasion brought sarcastic words from Ludwig Börne[28]: "Rothschild has kissed the hand of the Pope. . . . Order has at last been reestablished. . . . A Christian kisses the feet of the Pope, and a Jew kisses his hand. If Rothschild had been able to obtain his Roman loan at sixty percent, instead of sixty-five, and if he had been able to send the Cardinal Camerlingo more than 10,000 ducats, he would have been permitted to embrace Saint Peter. Wouldn't the world be happier if all Kings were deposed and the Rothschild family placed on their thrones?"[29] Alexandre Weill, an acerbic, passionate, and then widely read Jewish political journalist, had often criticized the Consistory's subservience towards rich bankers, most notably the Rothschilds. In 1844, he published a violent attack on the latter, doing so in Stuttgart since it was easier for a Jew to take on the Rothschilds in Germany than in France. The Jewish communities of Germany, being more numerous as well as more vigorous, had escaped domination by their banking members, whereas the small French community, externally beset with financial difficulties, did not dare gainsay its financial benefactors. By 1840 James had begun to assume a leading role in the financial affairs of the community, largely making up the difference between government grant and actual need.

So conscious were the Rothschilds of the jealousy surrounding them (which Heine defined as the feelings of those who say to themselves, "what we don't have, the Rothschilds possess. When a man has no more money, he becomes the enemy of the Rothschilds"[30]) that Salomon said in regard to a pamphlet directed against him: "Only a Jew could have written that."[31] These anti-Rothschild writings marked the beginning of a general shift in mood. Inasmuch as speculation seemed to have infected every level of a society governed by a King who could have been crowned at "Notre-Dame de la Bourse with Rothschild officiating as Bishop,"[32] the reign of money came in for increasingly virulent criticism. The most violent pamphlets targeted the Rothschilds, whose very name evoked at one and the same time images of millions, Judaism, and cosmopolitanism. Two accidents brought the hostility to a head. When on May 8, 1846, a train on the famous Saint-Germain line was derailed, killing fifty-five people, a shocked public tended to blame the engineers less than the financiers: "Money alone counts; human life is nothing."[33] Then came the devastating harvest of 1846. As France approached a state of famine, James arranged to purchase enormous quantities of wheat, mainly in the United States, in order to establish a system by which bread vouchers would be distributed to needy families. A special bakery designed to supply the poor was set up at Chapelle-Saint-Denis. But this Rothschild philanthropy had the opposite effect to the intended one. "The public didn't want to believe that a Jew could have a heart."[34] James found himself labeled "Hoarder"! *Le National* even accused the Baron of "soaking his flour in the sweat of the people."[35]

These poisoned seeds fell on well-prepared soil. In 1845 Toussenel had brought out a book entitled *The Jews, Kings of Our Time: A History of Financial Feudalism*, in which for the first time socialism and anti-Semitism joined forces to assault Jewish capitalism. Soon after came a torrent of publications with even more pointed and provocative titles, most often signed with the pseudonym "Satan": *Rothschild I, His Servants and His People* (1845); *War Among Thieves: A Secret Chronicle of the Bourse and the Railways* (1846); *You Sleep Rothschild and Shares Fall; The First Side-Splitting Treatment, Translated from the Hebrew. . . . A Radical Cure for the Railway Epidemic*. Since such pamphlets were more often stuffed into mailboxes than actually purchased, the

1. The Frankfurt ghetto, where James was born in 1792, sheltered a population governed by its own laws and isolated from its neighbors by religion, language, and culture.

left: 2. The five Rothschild brothers: at top, the eldest, Amschel, who remained in Frankfurt while his brothers spread all over Europe; below, from left to right: Salomon (Vienna) and Nathan (London), then Karl (Naples) and James (Paris). "We are like the mechanism of a watch; each part is essential."

opposite: 5, 6. James installed his offices and household in the former mansion of Queen Hortense on the Rue Laffitte. In 1834 he transformed it "into a poetic residence that had the air of an artist's palace more than a millionaire's mansion." He would die there in 1868. View from the courtyard (5); view from the garden (6).

3. The arms of the Rothschild family. In 1822 the Austrian Emperor granted each of the five brothers the title of Baron, a rare distinction for Jews.

4. "In Paris only elegance counts," lamented a still largely unpolished James in 1811, the year he arrived in the French capital. The artist represented him as he would have wished to be.

7. Betty married her Uncle James in 1824. The little Frankfurt Jewess transformed herself into an elegant Parisienne. Here she is, grandly attired and posing for Ingres, just before the Revolution of 1848.

8. Gudule, the mother of the Roth-schild brothers, died in 1849 at the age of ninety-six, still faithful to the customs of the ghetto. Here she is portrayed in Sabbath attire, the wide collar, a sign of distinction, and the face set off by the coif required of married women. Sumptuary laws, fallen into disuse, no longer prohibited the wearing of jewels in the synagogue.

above: 9. Baron James.

right: 10. James chose Ary Scheffer for the portrait of his only daughter, Charlotte, Baroness Nathaniel. Talented painter and fine musician, Charlotte was so melancholy that her sisters-in-law noted the occasions when she smiled.

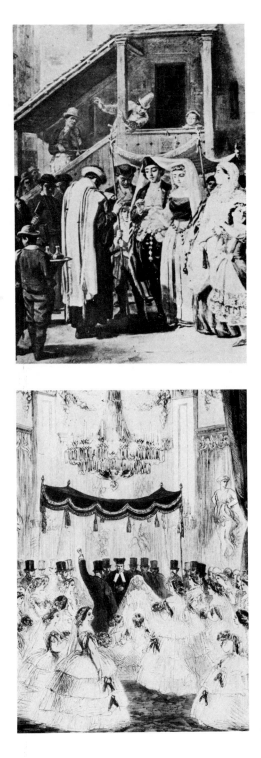

left: 11. In Frankfurt the Rothschilds always observed Jewish ritual. When Lionel and Charlotte married in 1836 the ceremony was Orthodox. The men wore the old costume, the women exchanged the traditional belts, and the bride received, on the index finger of her right hand, a ring shaped like a house.

left: 12. Twenty years later in England: the marriage of Lionel's daughter, Leonora, and James' son, Alphonse. The groom breaks the crystal glass, in keeping with Jewish custom, but the bride's wedding gown and the crinolines of the bridesmaids are more Victorian than Talmudic.

opposite: 13. Gustave was the first Rothschild son not to marry a relative. His marriage to Cécile Anspach was celebrated in the temple on the Rue Notre-Dame-de-Nazareth, an 1822 structure whose light-toned, grandiose décor could hardly be more different from the old synagogues. Only the absence of women on the main floor indicates the religious orientation of the assembly.

left: 14. Eugène Lami's watercolor of the dining room at Ferrières, the Rothschild château in which a Second Empire style was imposed upon a Victorian country house derived from an Elizabethan plan.

y, "the curtains are fabulously beautiful . . . hung
uble, triple, and all over the place." Curtains in Au-
sson tapestry from James' mansion.

ow left: 16. The Paris–Saint-Germain line, financed by
mes, was inaugurated by Queen Marie-Amélie in 1837.
e train ran the 19 kilometer (11-mile) distance at a
eed of 30 kilometers (19 miles) an hour. The govern-
ent refused to allow Louis-Philippe to expose his royal
rson to the potential dangers of the inaugural journey.

17. A private apart-
ment at Ferrières in a
watercolor by Eugène
Lami, the decorator
who succeeded in
adapting "the magnif-
icence of a Veronese to
a grand hotel."

left: 18. The bust portrait of James, benefactor of Paris' Jewish community, presides over the affairs of the retirement home that the Baron founded in the Rue Picpus on May 26, 1852.

below: 19. Ferrières was rebuilt in 1859 by the English architect Joseph Paxton, author of London's Crystal Palace. Romantic, extravagant, and incomparably comfortable (by nineteenth-century standards), the château is an outstanding example of the Second Empire style.

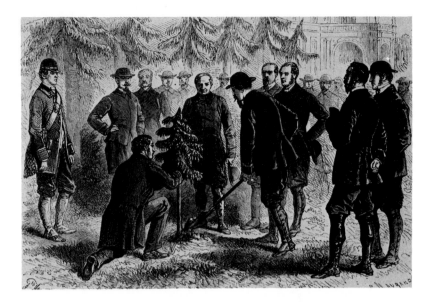

20. The visit of Napoleon III (at center, in profile) to Ferrières in December 1862 constituted an acknowledgment of James' power (at center, full face) by a sovereign who had been hostile to the Baron.

MIS EN BOUTEILLES AU CHÂTEAU

CHATEAU LAFITE-ROTHSCHILD

DÉPOSÉ.

APPELLATION PAUILLAC CONTRÔLÉE

21. James' last important acquisition: Château Lafite, which the Baron purchased in August 1868, thereby realizing an ambition first conceived in 1830.

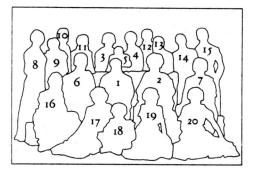

22. "La Gustaverie," the family and descendants of Gustave, James' second son, at the height of the Belle Époque:

1. Baron Gustave
2. Baroness Gustave
3. Baroness Robert
4. Baron Robert
5. Diane de Rothschild (Mme Joseph Benvenuti)
6. Lucie de Rothschild (Baroness Lambert)
7. Aline de Rothschild (Lady Sassoon)
8. Claude Lambert (Mme Jean Stern)
9. Simone Stern (Comtesse Sanjust di Teulada)
10. Jean Stern
11. Baron Emmanuel Leonino
12. Baron Henri Lambert
13. Baron Lambert
14. Sir Edward Sassoon
15. Sir Philip Sassoon
16. Antoinette Leonino (Baroness Antoinette Leonino)
17. Betty Lambert (Baroness de Bonstetten)
18. Renée Lambert (Baroness de Becker)
19. Marguerite Leonino (Mme Hubert de Monbrison)
20. Sybil Sassoon (Marchioness of Cholmondeley)

26. In his youth considered "frightfully ugly" by his contemporaries, James gained with age a genuine authority and learned the discrete art of elegance, evident here in his last portrait.

27. The signature of Baron James.

number of titles caused less concern than their general diffusion. For a while the author was thought to have been the Jew Alexandre Weill. However, he vigorously protested his innocence in a letter to *Archives israélites* and named the author, a certain Georges Dairnvaell.

Opposition within Jewish circles to these attacks upon James tended to be lukewarm.[36] Parisian Jews in general seem to have been somewhat annoyed at having to defend the Baron simply because he was Jewish. "The high position of M. de Rothschild may do us more harm than good," declared *Archives* in 1846, and the notion of a ponderous Rothschild fortune unjustly borne by the entire Jewish community would follow James to the grave. Even his obituary notice recalled that "what had been most unfortunate were the insults that all the Jews suffered on his account and the fact that our religion bore the backlash from a fortune which, naturally, did not benefit each and every one of us."[37] But the condemnation was to shift so quickly and so absurdly from one man to the entire group that something had to be done.

Not only was James constantly referred to as the "King of the Jews," but Toussenel, for example, ended up using "Rothschild" and "Jew" as interchangeable synonyms. Even more disturbing for the Jewish community, already sensitive to the slightest abusive insinuation, was the way "Jew" came to signify not merely Israelite but, more crudely, "a species given over wholly to trafficking, a totally unproductive parasite, living off the substance and the labor of others."[38] Another painful analogy, for Jews who had been French only a short while and were so proud of their newfound nationality, was that made between Jews and foreigners. French Jews found themselves lumped together with "all the readers of the Bible, whether they are called . . . Genevans, Dutch, English, or Americans, who must have found it written in their prayer books that God has granted to the servants of His Law a monopoly on the exploitation of the globe, because all these mercantile peoples bring the fervor of religious fanaticism to the art of holding the human race to ransom."[39]

In the face of such attacks, Jews of all spheres longed to discard a designation as vague, pejorative, and burdensome as "Jew" in favor of "Israelite," which had the merit of being more explicit. But they failed to bring about any change. Pierre Leroux, who had abandoned Saint-Simonianism for a kind of religious socialism, declared: "We speak of Jews as the dictionary would. . . . Jew: the word is considered here not as the name of a nation but as employed figuratively in certain phrases. Thus a man who lends at usurious rates is called a Jew. . . . It is the familiar term for all those who display great greed. . . . We are fighting against the Jewish spirit . . . and not against Jews as a collection of individuals or any Jew in particular."[40] But such subtle distinctions between the Jewish spirit and the individual Jew offered little comfort in the face of the conclusion drawn by Georges Dairnvaell: "This pamphlet does not address itself to the religion of the Jews but rather to their greed, to their insolence, so characteristic of yesterday's slaves who today are free and rich, to their thirst for gold, and to their insatiable need of wealth and power. Today they consent to being protected; tomorrow they will be the protectors and masters, and the despotism of the freedman is the most withering and the most odious of all despotisms."[41]

How were such assertions to be countered? How could the Central Consistory, that "natural guardian of Israelite interests," be compelled to make a response? What course should one adopt? There were no easy answers.

The measures proposed ran from "a good thrashing administered to one of those coffeehouse gentlemen" to bringing before the public prosecutor, under the terms of the Civil Code, "the culpable attempts of men who seek to spread hatred and contempt."[42] Efforts were made to form a committee for the defense of Jewish interests, but they failed. It was as if the Jews preferred not to tackle the problem openly for fear of aggravating it. Now, in the light of subsequent events, their attitude may be hard to understand. We know that before the end of the century the Jews of France would suffer the agony of the Dreyfus Affair; we also know the fate that awaited the Jewish communities among the horrors of World War II. Given this history, the imprecations of the first modern anti-Semites assume a tragic and premonitory quality. But the Jews of 1840 had no reason to depress themselves with such presentiments. Why shouldn't they have trusted the French government? How easy it was to believe that the trend towards liberalism and tolerance was irreversible? Compared to past, yet only too recent, injustices, the new wave of abuse appeared more despicable than threatening. Paris' Jewish community could reasonably believe itself to be on the right and victorious path first pointed out by the French Revolution.

As if to prove it, a bold defense of James came, not from the Jews, but from the Saint-Simonians, in the form of an article published in *Le Globe* and then reprinted in its entirety in *Archives israélites*. Here, James virtually became the heir of Robespierre: "There is no one today who better represents the triumph of equality and work in the nineteenth century than M. le Baron de Rothschild. What is he, in fact? Was he born a Baron? No, he wasn't even born a citizen; he was born a pariah. At the time of his birth, civil liberty, and even less political liberty, did not exist for Jews. To be a Jew was to be less than a lackey; it was to be less than a man; it was to be a dog that children chased in the street, hurling insults and stones. Thanks to the holy principle of equality, the Jew has become a man, the Jew has become a citizen; and once his intelligence, his activity, and his work allowed, he could rise within the social hierarchy. What better or more incontrovertible evidence could there be that the principle of equality has prevailed? Yet, it's democrats who close their minds and eyes to this spectacle! Nominal democrats, no doubt. Sincere democrats would have applauded this Jew who, beginning at the bottom of the social ladder, has arrived by virtue of equality at the highest rung.

"Was this Jew born a millionaire? No, he was born poor, and if only you knew what genius, patience, and hard work were required to construct that European edifice called the House of Rothschild, you would admire rather than insult it. . . . You tactlessly cite Figaro,[43] without understanding that Figaro was one of the privileged by comparison with M. de Rothschild, since Figaro had only to be born in order to see before him the vast and open battlefield of work. At his birth, M. de Rothschild found this battlefield closed to him, and yet he has, aided by freedom, climbed higher than you. To abuse M. de Rothschild is to blaspheme against equality and labor."[44]

The subject of all this discussion remained impassive, his lips sealed. James made no effort to enlist the aid of his political friends, unlike his brothers in Germany, who did everything possible to prevent the spread of such libel. He refused even to acknowledge—that is, to pay—the anonymous opportunists who published pamphlets in his defense.[45] The pride that had done so much to spur James on to ever-greater success permitted him to return his adversaries' contempt a hundred times over, his astonishing arrogance nourished by a sense that he was riding comfortably on the main current of history. As for *Le Globe*'s defense, he approved it without reservation. Heine, in *Lutèce*, explains that, paradoxically, the Rothschilds, "those bankers to Kings, those princely rich men . . . are conscious of their revolutionary mission."[46] One day, in an expansive mood, James took a stroll down the boulevards with Heine, his arm looped over the poet's in a gesture of familial affection, and explained how he, Rothschild, was the destroyer of the old aristocracy and the founder of a new democracy. And Heine, with less irony than might appear, concluded: "I see Rothschild as one of the greatest of the revolutionaries who founded modern democracy. . . . Richelieu, Robespierre, and Rothschild are the three most terrifying levelers in Europe."[47]

But this last "leveler" guarded his preeminence jealously and never hesitated to insist upon being shown respect of the most unlimited kind. "Men of every class and religion, Gentiles as well as Jews, leaned forward, bowed, and prostrated themselves before him. The most accomplished acrobats could not have kowtowed with more skill. I have seen people approach the great Baron shaking as if they had touched one of Volta's batteries."[48] Far from being disgusted by such obsequiousness, James viewed total subordination as the norm. Both in his family and in the bank his authoritarianism had free reign. Add to this his refusal to become a French national, his obvious desire to make a separate place for himself within his religious community, as well as in French society, his stubborn determination to remain himself, and we have some sense of the formidable ego that blazed within James de Rothschild.

8
The Great Mogul

The imperturbable self-assurance of James became all the more of an asset once he emerged as head of the family after the death of Nathan. The latter had collapsed suddenly while in Frankfurt, where the entire Rothschild tribe were gathered for the marriage of his eldest son, Lionel, to Charlotte, Karl's eldest daughter. A neglected abscess, followed by chills and fever, confined him to bed as soon as he arrived in Germany. "Papa has not yet left his bed; his boil has not come to a head and gives him a great deal of pain. . . . He has declared the wedding shall not be postponed," wrote Lionel.[1] Hannah, Nathan's anxious wife, sent for their doctor from London, but it was too late. In a recent study, Lord Rothschild has established that the "boil" was in fact a large abscess that would not heal, thus conceivably the symptom of a serious disease, such as diabetes or cancer.[1a] Nathan died on July 28, 1836, at the age of fifty-nine.

The sons of Nathan Rothschild returned his body to London and there arranged a spectacular funeral. The Lord Mayor, along with high government officials and the diplomatic corps, walked in the funeral procession of a man whose death struck the public as "one of the most important events for the City, and perhaps for Europe, to have happened in a long time."[1b] His will, similar to that of his father, stipulated that the five Rothschild banks should remain a single entity and that his sons, whatever the circumstances, must act in harmony with their uncles. Nathan left four sons and three daughters. Only his eldest girl had married, taking her cousin Anselm, the brother of Betty, as her spouse. Accustomed to opulence, all the young Rothschild men, the eldest of whom was twenty-eight, displayed less enterprise in finance than their fathers and considerably more susceptibility to the good life. The first move made by Lionel was to ask Queen Victoria, who had just succeeded to the throne, for permission to bear the Austrian title of Baron, which his father had treated with such magnificent disdain.

James immediately took these young people in hand and assumed the role of moral leader played until then by Nathan. It was not only that Paris was a more important financial center than Vienna or Frankfurt, and considerably more so than Naples, but also that being the youngest son of Mayer Amschel, James formed a natural link between the first and second generations of Rothschilds. To his nieces and nephews Uncle Amschel, with his Orthodox habits, his lack of social finesse, and his old-fashioned deference toward the world's great (he had invited Bismarck to dinner so far in advance that the latter replied rudely that he would come provided he was still alive), seemed a relic of a bygone age. The poor man looked so elderly that visitors often thought he must be the husband of that alert old lady, his mother! Queen Victoria, in particular, remained convinced all her life that she had been presented to the founder of the House of Rothschild, the spouse of "that wonderful old Frau Rothschild," whom she met once during a passage through Frankfurt, and would never accept the fact that the real founder had died before she was born. Disconcerted by the long Hebrew prayers that began every meal and by the social isolation in which Amschel lived, the young Rothschilds, French and English alike, felt completely out of place in Frankfurt. Bismarck, following one of his visits to Amschel, wrote to his wife that "the old banker was an object of condescension on the part of his nephews, pretentious individuals soaked in French or English fashion who would inherit his wealth with neither love nor gratitude."[2]

Karl, for his part, lacked the intellectual ability of his brothers, and Salomon, vital and enterprising as he was, suffered from having no real base. He would leave Vienna forever in 1848, but well before the revolution of that year he had come to spend most of his time in Paris, without ever managing to cut a particularly vivid figure there. In the opinion of his English nephews, the old Austrian Baron, solitary, grumpy, and often felled by migraines, rheumatism, and stomach cramps, had no style, reigning as he did over a house where only Yiddish or German was spoken, where the master went to bed at eight in the evening so as to rise at five in the morning, where "the cooking has always been wretched and the wines still worse."[3]

Thus the role of model fell to James, whose ostentation had miraculously come to seem natural and even well-bred, and whose influence extended over such diverse fields. Moreover, James willingly opened his arms to his nephews, since it gave him pleasure to train them as bankers, while also introducing them to the good life that he had discovered with such delight himself.

For them, the Machiavellian financier reduced his complex theories to formulas of lucid simplicity: "Follow my advice, work with gold. It will never go bankrupt."[4] He taught them the tricks of the trade: "If someone comes and offers you a deal, receive him politely and avoid, as far as possible, giving a definite refusal. By having an air of acceptance, you give yourself the chance to learn what's afoot, which is always a good thing."[5] And he became concerned at the least sign of diminished effort: "Why does Rabbi Mayer not write? Has he gone hunting? I certainly hope not. A young man should work; it's his duty."[6] He encouraged his nephews to take risks: "Does it make any difference whether you have a few millions more or less in your wallet? We need not be cautious because we have no commitments . . ."[7] On the other hand, useless waste drove him mad. At one point he thought of having manure brought over from Great Britain to fertilize the land at Ferrières, but he recoiled at the price.[8] Asking Nathaniel to reserve a hotel room for him in London, James wrote: "I tell you candidly that I do not want anything splendid, and I know that francs in Paris and guineas in London are spent at the same rate."[9]

At the same time, James could be generous, and even prodigal, when it came to elegance, a fine table, and works of art.

He ordered his brilliantine from London: "I have exactly two hairs left, and I intend to take care of them."[10] When it came to such things, only the best would do, and he was never content until everyone in his entourage had joined him in this. Sojourns in the Rue Laffitte became training courses in gastronomy: "I have at last become a gourmet," proclaimed Anthony after a visit to Paris.

James had a particular predilection for the wine of Château Lafite. He tried to buy the vineyard just before the 1830 revolution, but failed to persuade the owner to sell.[11] He consoled himself by drinking and having others drink barrel after barrel. "My dear Mayer," he announced to his nephew, "you are going to get fifty bottles of good Château Lafite. . . . If you like my choice and are ready to trust me, I will be happy to take charge of stocking your wine cellar."[12] He also discovered the joy and anguish of the collector. No blind follower of specialists' advice, he allowed his search for treasures to become a consuming passion. In the course of a stay in Germany, ostensibly made to take the waters and for a rest, James could not stay put. "We have in the company of Uncle James been making excursions in the neighborhood in search of curiosities," wrote Mayer to his mother. "You have no idea what an interest our good uncle takes in running after the productions of classic antiquity; as soon as he hears of anything that is to be sold he immediately orders a carriage and does not mind in the least the distance or the weather. In this way we went to Constance, which is at least 40 miles from here, and all that was worth seeing consisted of a couple of dozen of cracked painted window-glasses. His fancy or mania has become so known that all the peasants from the surrounding country bring their ornaments; however, he has managed to pick up a very handsome coup and dish, for which he had to pay a good cozy price. . . ."[13] Laugh as they might, the "bric-a-brac" that James took back to Paris won the admiration of connoisseurs. Soon he would find it difficult to sell a picture despite the profit it would bring: "I wrote to you yesterday asking you to dispose of the Rembrandt, if it could be done with advantage, but on reflection I find I had better keep it if you have not bought the Murillo for me."[14]

But there were more than objects. James and Betty drew a

great variety of remarkable people to their home. "What a pity," regretted Anthony, "that our parents don't have more fun in London." A good-natured camaraderie, unusual for the period, characterized the relationship that James developed with artists, providing yet further proof of his originality. Had he been totally Faubourg Saint-Germain, he would never have dreamed of inviting Bohemia to his house, and had he been purely Chaussée-d'Antin, he would have had trouble attracting such circles.

He succeeded—whether by charm, by genuine taste, or out of fear of what could be wrought by a sharp pen or a treacherous brushstroke—in establishing bonds of great freedom and good humor with the writers, painters, and musicians who frequented his salon. There was Heine who, making light of the summits to which James had climbed, tells of the time when, following a succulent meal, the Baron served him a Lacrima-Christi, a much admired sweet Italian wine, and then wondered about its name. "You see," Heine replied, "it's because Christ wept that rich Jews drink such a delicate wine while so many poor Christians are hungry and thirsty." Then there was Delacroix, praising the intensity of the great financier's expression and offering to paint him as a starving beggar. And George Sand, who accosted James at a bazaar organized for the benefit of Polish refugees and asked for five thousand francs for a perfume bottle. "What would I do with it?" protested James. "Give me instead an autograph. I'll sell it, and we can share the proceeds." "Gladly," retorted Sand, handing him a paper on which she had written: "Received 2,000 francs for the impoverished Poles." With a consoling look Heine laid a hand on James' shoulder.

The contacts between James and Balzac proved more complicated, due to the constant intrusion of money. The financier came to know the writer in August 1832 at Aix-les-Bains where he had gone to take the waters. An immediate sympathy developed, with James rendering Balzac a service at their first encounter. Balzac had been dreaming of going to work in Naples, but the problem of how to send his corrected proofs to Paris troubled him. Ever short of cash, he deplored the heavy expense of postage. James offered to handle the matter, and Balzac was able to reassure his mother: "In Naples I shall have the embassy and couriers of Rothschild, whom I have met and who will give every recommendation to his brother there. . . ."[15] The following winter James complained of not seeing his new friend often enough: "You completely forget your friends from Aix, and you don't come to see us. Won't you choose a day to come and dine with us and some habitués of our little Aix circle? I should be truly charmed to see you at my house. . . . Your very devoted. . . ."[16]

Balzac never again made a journey without saying goodbye to the Baron and arming himself against the hazards of travel. "Thanks to the letter of Rothschild, his house has handed over some money . . . clearly an inadequate [amount]," Balzac wrote from Vienna, "because I hadn't counted on the toll-gates, or the extra horses, or the five hundred diabolical expenses that have seized me by the throat."[17] He had worked out one of his schemes, on this occasion taking a supplement of fifteen hundred francs from the Rothschild bank against a ten-day note, according to a letter written to his publisher, Werdet. Actually, the note was payable on demand, and Werdet had to go and ask James for a delay. The off-handedness of Balzac in financial affairs always astonished James, who advised Werdet: "Beware of M. de Balzac; he's a very casual man."[18] For his part, however, James maintained only the most agreeable relations with the great novelist.

They exchanged invitations to balls and to theatre boxes for "the 'by-invitation-only' premieres [where one] is among one's own set." If James was not free, he sent his regrets personally and, in the most ingratiating terms, asked for an alternative date. This rude man could put on a remarkably refined manner when he wished: "As he has an engagement for tomorrow that will deprive him of the greater part of the evening, he would deeply regret having to cede to others a pleasure that he would eagerly retain for himself."[19]

In 1836 Balzac dedicated *L'Enfant maudit* to Betty. Ten years later he would offer James *Un Homme d'affaires*. The title was well chosen for a novel that abounded in letters of credit, debtors' ruses, and illicit amours. James was delighted. To the end of his life, Balzac kept an account at the Rothschild bank, borrowed often from them, and performed endless feats in order to remain more or less solvent. One of his dodges consisted in having himself paid into an account opened in his mother's maiden name, the better to prevent the bank from debiting his account for sums paid. As we have seen, he obtained some of the coveted shares in the Compagnie du Nord. Meanwhile, Balzac never hesitated to consult James on personal matters. But what could be more intertwined than love and money? James, who had been privy to a good many confidences, enjoyed the reputation of being discreet.

During his pursuit of the beautiful Pole, Mme Hanska, Balzac had a live-in housekeeper, the amiable and complaisant Mme de Breugnol. Mme Hanska, during one of her prenuptial visits, could not help but note the housekeeper's attractiveness and demanded that she be dismissed. Balzac, mindful of the years of affection and care that Mme de Breugnol had given him, wanted to set her up in some kind of business. They agreed on the purchase of a tobacco shop, and then a stamp shop, the latter deemed more dignified but also more difficult to acquire. Balzac therefore paid James a visit and gave him a detailed explanation: "Rotschild [sic][20] displayed his usual sly decadence. He asked me whether she was pretty, whether I had had her? 'A hundred and more times,' I told him, 'and, if you want, I'll give her to you.' 'Does she have any children?' he inquired. 'No, but give her some.' 'I'm sorry, but I protect only women with children.' This was his way of escaping. Had she had children, he would have said he never protected immorality. 'Well now, do you actually believe, Baron, that you can split hairs with me? I'm a stockholder in the Nord! I want to sign a note, and you'll take care of my business as if it were a 400,000 franc railway.' 'How's that?' he said. 'If you make me go ahead, I'll admire you all the more.' 'And you'll go ahead,' I told him, 'otherwise, I'll turn your wife loose on you so she can keep an eye on what you are up to.' Seized with laughter, he fell back into his chair and said: 'I'm exhausted; I give in; business is killing me. Make out your note. . . .' "[21]

Finally, the musical soirées given by Betty helped launch the artists who performed there. Her support proved invaluable to Chopin. Since his arrival in Paris in 1832 the Polish pianist had failed to make a place for himself. Discouraged, in the aftermath of a disastrous evening at the Neys, he thought of leaving Europe for the United States, an idea he tried on Prince

Radziwill during a chance encounter along the boulevards. The Prince, who knew his *Tout-Paris*, took Chopin by the hand and led him straight to the Rue Laffitte. Several days later, Betty had him perform in her salon and extolled his talents so persuasively that next morning the great artist found himself the beneficiary of four influential protectors: Maréchale Lannes, Princesse de Vaudémont, Comtesse Apponyi, wife of the Austrian Ambassador, and a compatriot, Prince Czartoryski. Overnight mothers were clawing one another to have him for their daughters. Now he could be selective about his pupils, which prompted Betty to point out that it was absurd to charge only two francs per lesson. Soon delivered from his most pressing material worries, Chopin began composing again.

James' nephews admired that social aplomb mingled with indisputable authority. For them, James was *le patron*, and they called him simply "the Baron" or "the great Baron." Sometimes, carried away, they even referred to him as "the Great Mogul," always taking care, however, that Betty did not overhear them, since she disliked anyone making fun of Uncle-Husband! But when the Great Mogul was in a particularly good humor he did not take himself quite so seriously. On one occasion in Frankfurt, with the entire Rothschild clan gathered together, James appeared disguised as a Scotsman, complete "with tartan dress, the claymore in his hand, and exhibiting a flourishing view of stout legs and calfs."[22] Moreover, he did not reserve his pranks for the intimacy of his family. Once, while taking a cure in Germany, he became so gay and relaxed that the Elector congratulated himself "that the waters have produced such an effect upon Uncle James that he runs after all the girls. Perhaps we shall hear soon that Betty will have another little one."[23] But the true foundation of James' character remained his strength of will. He would tolerate no contradiction, and no one dared stand up to him. James de Rothschild had something of the tyrant about him.

The imperious side of James' character was much in evidence at the time of the drama caused by the marriage of Hannah, Nathan's daughter, to her handsome Englishman. The mother and brothers of the young woman, although disapproving, would not have gone so far as to disinherit her completely, but they allowed themselves to be intimidated by

James' rage. "This marriage makes me quite ill. . . . She has robbed our whole family of its pride. . . . We shall have to forget her and banish her from our memory."[24] When Nathaniel tried to intervene on behalf of his sister he succeeded only in having himself violently rebuffed. James explained why he considered it indispensable that the poor love-sick girl be disinherited: "We for our part, as well as our children, are determined not to come in contact with Hannah Mayer. . . . What sort of example for our children would a girl be who says: 'I marry against the wishes of my family'? . . . Why should my children or my children's children obey my wishes, if there is no punishment [for disobeying]? . . . Wouldn't my daughter one day, after she has married, say: 'I am unhappy be cause I did not marry a Duke, although my fortune was big enough?' "[25] His fury became so extreme that Anthony suggested to his brothers that they should not go against their uncle. "I would advise you," he wrote them, "for yourselves and also for the unity of the family not to receive Hannah for the moment."[26] Nathaniel, while admitting that his mother was free to follow her own inclinations, insisted that "it would be better if she did not invite Hannah for the present."[27] Fortunately, Betty understood how to calm the troubled waters. She affectionately congratulated her sister-in-law and in 1842, after their daughter's marriage to Nathaniel, even persuaded James to receive Hannah and her husband. But such crises could not be quickly forgotten, and it is hardly surprising to find one of James' English grandnieces remarking, in veiled terms, that the vast enlargement of Ferrières, made in order to shelter the entire family, struck her as a bit absurd.

James' relations were not the only ones to suffer from his irascibility. His employees paid dearly for the honor of serving him. Above all else, James insisted upon their total, unswerving loyalty. This was a matter less of principle than of elementary prudence. To work in a Rothschild bank was, inevitably, to acquire a valuable education. For anyone to leave and profit by that knowledge elsewhere amounted to stealing, in James' eyes. The tenacity of his rancor was enough to make any member of his staff hesitate about leaving. One of James' confidential agents, a certain Erlanger, resigned to set up his own banking house, only to have James pursue him with implacable hatred.

The Baron carried his resentment to the extent of asking Bleich-röder to have a malicious article on Erlanger published in the Prussian press. The banker sent his regrets that this was not within his power, assuring James, however, that Bismarck had been warned about the culprit.

To enjoy the advantages of representing James, his correspondents had to make enormous efforts. The Rothschilds, in keeping with a policy observed throughout their branches, retained the whole of the profits generated by the association. And the terms of association were such that the foreign representatives were often obliged to personally reimburse losses caused by unskilled trading. In the event of a crisis, they must volunteer to contribute a fraction of the commission if they wished to hold the Rothschilds' business. In addition, they had to endure the abusive tone of the brothers' letters of instruction. The Rothschilds did not seek relations of a professional nature but rather those of master and servant. Moreover, James employed a man as eminent as Bleichröder to take on tasks that had nothing to do with the bank. He was, for instance, asked to buy works of art whenever the market seemed propitious, and to make certain that journeys were well organized. He wrote letters whose form scarcely differed from the first missives sent by old Mayer to his powerful patrons at the court of Hesse-Kassel. "May I once and for all be permitted to lay before you my most profound, my most sincere thanks . . . it is you, Herr Baron, who picked me up from the dust. You are of a rare nobility, you who have made it possible for me to feed a large family. As long as I live, your image will flourish in my heart, and my last breath will be consecrated to you, oh my benefactor."[28]

In order to remain in the good graces of James, it was not enough merely to be accurate, scrupulous, and prompt in sending the most reliable information. Whoever served the Baron had to behave like a courtier. One of James' associates, Victor Bénary, who had developed a liking for Bleichröder, wrote to the latter urging him to come to Ostend, where James was having a few days' rest, and reminded his friend "how it was desirable and necessary to speak directly to Baron James from time to time. For business, that's worth more than twenty letters."[29] It was also advisable not to arrive empty-handed, for

James never declined propitiatory offerings. He particularly liked caviar, and to satisfy this taste Bleichröder even dispatched a special messenger to bear the exquisite food to Paris. Only a short time before, James and his brothers were begging Metternich to accept their gifts. Now it was they who were being offered precious baubles and bibelots "in frail witness to an immense gratitude."

With his inferiors James displayed a shocking boorishness. " 'Vat a pest you are! Vat do you know about dat? Get de defil out from here' were the civilities he addressed to me or to others," recalled Feydeau, "whenever we took it upon ourselves to make some observation concerning an order. I should point out that, given the dialect he spoke and his accent, it was not always easy to understand him. . . . And it would have been ungracious of me to resent his rudeness, since his behavior was even more uncouth towards others: 'Ah! Der you are, damned teefing Cherman Chew,' he said one day to a coreligionist, a bill broker who was entering his office. . . . The poor man stood there, crushed, without voice or expression. He may even have taken it as a compliment."[30]

Some years later an employee with keys to the safe avenged his fellow slaves when one evening he fled to America, never to be heard of again. He had embezzled the staggering sum of six million francs over a period of time by selling stolen shares and pocketing cash.

James, remarkably enough, had excellent rapport with his children, despite circumstances that might very well have placed the two generations at an all but unbridgeable distance from one another. It could not have been easy for a father with an overpowering genius, a rough and dominating personality, a man obsessed by his business, to establish easy and trusting relations with children who had grown up in a soft, luxurious atmosphere and whose task would be to follow in his footsteps, while also transforming themselves into elegant, distinguished, discreet men of the world. Yet, it seems that James did actually succeed in making his sons into men quite different from himself without their rebelling against his values, his style of life, and his authority.[31] The explanation lies in the fact that James was blessed with a warm nature. He did not allow a battalion of governesses, tutors, and servants to stand between him and his children. He carried paternal affection and pride to the point of preserving their first daubs and scrawls in his files. The slightest cold alarmed him and became an occasion for long letters of medical advice. James, the tireless toiler, always feared that Alphonse, once he had joined the business, would exhaust himself from overwork!

Born in 1845, James' last son, Edmond, grew up under a fond father who insisted that the noisy activities of his Benjamin be given free reign. Feydeau—who was forever horrified by the "remorseless and incessant parade of countless friends of three sexes, masculine, feminine, and beggar, all seeking news" that poured into James' office, and who always marveled that "the powerful banker's brain did not burst from the accumulation of figures and the battle of calculations"—recalled that "the youngest son, a big, chubby child . . . would come running in, riding his father's cane and blowing on a trumpet like the angel of Jehovah. And the poor Baron made no complaint; [he] didn't even frown."[32] Feydeau failed to take into account the excellent training James had undergone in his own childhood, in the pitiful, overpopulated house on Jew Street!

Early in their childhood James' boys began studying under a tutor, M. Thibaud, who remained with the family until the youngest, Edmond, had followed his elder brothers to the Collège Bourbon, the future Lycée Condorcet, the school that formed the sons of the *haute bourgeoisie*. The young Rothschilds knew English, German, and Hebrew, but French was their native tongue[33]— in fact, their maternal language since Betty spoke and wrote French quite spontaneously. James, on the other hand, continued to express himself in his Teutonic patois. He employed three secretaries to handle his correspondence in German, English, or French, but whenever he wrote by hand, in a script extremely difficult to decipher, he almost invariably slipped into Yiddish. Only rarely did he write in German, and still more seldom in French. French, however, was the language in which his sons replied, and thus the habit of corresponding in two languages took root in the family. Only the brothers communicated in the same language. Cousins preferred to remain in their own linguistic territories, with the result that the letters of Alphonse and Gustave to their English cousins are in French, while all the replies are in English.

Personal graces and refinements were also desirable in the elegant world that would be theirs. Thus the Rothschild boys, far from being prepared solely to read figures, took lessons in drawing, dancing, and gymnastics. By frequenting the fashionable stables in the Rue de la Chaussée-d'Antin, they became accomplished horsemen. Finally, James considered it important that his sons gain access to classical culture. The process got underway the year that Alphonse took his *baccalauréat*, when the young man found himself assigned to a celebrity, Désiré Nisard, who had begun his professional life as a republican journalist. After playing an active role in the July Revolution, Nisard turned his talents to letters. His accomplishments as a Latinist and his publication of a history of literature soon won him the post of director at the École Normale and eventually a chair at the Académie Française.[34] Some years before this election, however, James had engaged Nisard for his sons, offering him 1,000 francs a month, at a time when other teachers were earning no more than 100 or 150 francs and the salary of a professor at the Collège de France did not exceed 500 francs.[35] For James, apparently, there was no stinting when it came to *belles-lettres*. What a contrast to Salomon, who fifteen years before had halted his son's education as early as possible in order to make certain that the young man would follow in the same path as his father. James, however, realized that only the advantages of a traditional French education would enable his sons to become fully integrated. As far as he himself was concerned, it was too late, despite all the years spent in France, but this did not bother James, for his ambition lay elsewhere.

This imperious man, obsessed with a desire to excel, convinced of the universally corrupting power of gold, and determined to dominate a society that he heartily despised, felt secure enough to stand aloof from all factions. He gloried in being unclassifiable. He had no homeland and liked to believe that he belonged to no social category. This was the revenge of the Jew. But the children of James had never known humiliation, and it would have been absurd to perpetuate in them his own feelings of rage and retaliation.

Alphonse, therefore, made an untroubled transition into the world of adults. Following a brief period in law school, he joined his father in the large office, a long, low-ceilinged room, where he began learning his trade. At the same time, his father initiated him into his role as defender of Jewish liberty, taking the young man to the Ministry of Education "to inquire why no Jews had been appointed to the academic council of Bordeaux."[36] Finally, at the beginning of 1848, Alphonse became a naturalized Frenchman.

James' joy—and self-assurance—knew no bounds. So accustomed had the Baron become to seeing everyone bow before him that he even allowed himself to admonish Louis-Philippe on the occasion of a train journey he had organized for the royal family. Prince Philippe, one of the King's grandsons, recorded the incident in his diary: "I looked wide-eyed at the superb royal carriage. . . . *Bon Papa* lingered to speak with the Prefect and other notables, which considerably displeased M. de Rothschild, who announced that His Majesty was five minutes late. The King smiled. . . ."[37]

Louis-Philippe had been nicknamed "the Emperor of the five-percenters, the King of the three-percenters, the protector of bankers, the mediator of stockbrokers,"[38] and "the crowned calculator."[39] Consequently, there was nothing very surprising about his richest subject behaving more like a lord than a vassal. Since James believed his opulence granted him every right, it would be as well to examine at this stage just how much he spent on business and pleasure. The figures used here have been drawn from the firm's balance sheets, which, unfortunately, do not survive for every year of the period in question, and from the agreements made for the distribution of assets among the brothers.[40] The capital value of the Paris branch on its own cannot provide a basis on which to calculate James' income, since the firm's capital was distributed in two ways: among the brothers and among the several branches of the bank. Depending on the possibilities for investment, capital passed from one house to another, which in the meantime had no effect on the assets of the particular brother in charge. Thus in 1824, when negotiations got underway for the conversion of government bonds (from a higher to a lower rate), part of the capital in the London house was transferred to Paris, giving this branch a total credit of 37 million francs. But the transfer did not alter James' personal share, which remained at about 20 million francs. Actually, the proportional distribution of the Rothschilds' capital remained fixed. From 1818 until 1836, the year Nathan died, James' share, roughly the same as that of Amschel, Salomon, or Karl, represented a sixth of the whole. Nathan commanded a larger share.[41] Thereafter the archives disclose no further balance sheets until 1863, the year the Neapolitan branch was closed. The redistributions of capital that occurred at this time gave James a quarter, and a quarter to the heirs of each of his brothers who had produced children.[42]

The principle adopted by the brothers was that they would transfer all profits generated by their activity to the firm, except that every year they would each pay themselves an amount equal to four percent of their invested capital. This system lasted until 1842. Beginning in that year, the capital of the firm was allowed to increase by no more than a certain percentage, based on net profits. Thus in 1842 the capital was augmented by one and a half percent and in 1846 by two percent. But annually, before the capital could be increased, profits had to be distributed. This meant that from 1842 onward the brothers and nephews had at their disposal sums that were not only much larger but also much more difficult to calculate in the absence of yearly balance sheets.

As we have seen, the Rothschilds increased their capital at a dizzy rate between 1815 and 1828, but exactly how they accomplished this cannot be explained from the documentation now available. For the following period, we have even less data, but it is known that the family capital had passed 118 million francs by 1829 and 558 million by 1863. From the time of the Restoration (1814–30) until the fall of the July Monarchy (1848), we can be reasonably certain, without fear of inflating the figures, that the capitalization of the Rothschild firm doubled and that James, with a growth in personal capital from 20 to 40 million, enjoyed a proportional increase in revenues, from 800,000 to 1,600,000 francs a year. Even these figures fall short of reality, since they do not take into account such assets as the house on the Rue Laffitte, a mansion in the Rue Saint-Florentin, the first floor of which the Baron leased to Princesse Lièven, the Boulogne property, or the Ferrières estate, not to mention jewelry, objets d'art, and the proceeds from Betty's 1,500,000-franc dowry. But however incomplete the figure, it gives us a point of reference.

How does this fortune compare with those of James' contemporaries? In 1847 the nobility could still command immense capital, and some eighteen titled heads of family possessed assets of between one and ten million.[43] But capital in the form of land was proportionately much greater in the estates of the aristocracy than in those inherited by equally wealthy bourgeois, and during the Restoration and the July Monarchy, the nobility progressively enjoyed fewer of the truly great fortunes of France. This relative shrinkage of titled wealth between 1820 and 1847 can be explained by the reluctance of nobles to invest in industry and commerce and by their withdrawal from public life after 1830. Under Louis-Philippe, French aristocrats once again became idle. No longer did they assume the direction of ministries or take other top posts in the government and army. They denied themselves the extraordinary opportunities created by the century's economic development. Thus their fortunes were different, in size, structure, and evolution, from that of James.

In the absence of figures to show the massive wealth of Louis-Philippe, a fortune that was probably about the size of James',[44] we must turn for comparison to the great bourgeois bankers. Only one of these belonged in the same class with James, and that was Jacques Laffitte.

Laffitte, who without the Revolution would probably have remained a notary's clerk in Bayonne, estimated his fortune in 1820 at between 25 and 30 million.[45] If the capital of his bank, J. Laffitte et Cie, which amounted to 12 million in 1827, did not approach the overall size of the Rothschild firm, the style of life cultivated by Laffitte was certainly comparable to that of James, embracing as it did a mansion in the Rue d'Artois and a château at Maisons. But Laffitte also wanted a brilliant marriage for his daughter, matched by an illustrious title. The groom he chose was Joseph-Napoleon Ney, Prince de Moskowa, who was distinguished by being then in the service of the King of Sweden, and by having a father who had been one of Napoleon I's legendary Marshals. The marriage cost Laffitte dear, because the bride was not only of humble origins but slightly dim-witted as well. The settlement made by her father included a 50,000-franc trousseau and a dowry of 4 million, paid (circumspectly enough) as an annual income of 20,000 francs, this amount diminished by half as long as the couple resided in a family mansion. But Jacques Laffitte could not live long in the manner of the Rothschilds. Unable to survive the 1830 crisis, he had to liquidate his banking house and carve up his landed estate (which became Maisons-Laffitte). He only avoided going bankrupt through an advance from the Banque de France.

The other great bourgeois fortunes, while more stable (some indeed remain considerable even today), could not approach the figures built up by Laffitte. The bankers, who constituted the élite of the financial community at the time of James' arrival in Paris—the society that young Rothschild had courted so assiduously—could each claim capital assets varying from 5 to 10 million francs. The richest of them, Baron Seillière and Bernard Delessert, were worth 11 million in 1847. The charitable bequests made by Delessert in his will came to 451,000 francs, an amount then considered nothing less than fabulous. Jean-Charles Davillier, "venerable patriarch of commerce and industry," Baron of the Empire, left his heirs a little more than 6 million. Jean-Conrad Hottinguer had accumulated wealth equal to 4 million by the time he died in 1841, while Guillaume Mallet had less to leave, barely 2 million.[46]

These were the people who composed the professional milieu in which James operated, but it was not his social milieu, for several reasons. First of all, his fortune was so much more substantial than that of his competitors in banking. Among the bourgeois, gold constituted the only standard, unlike among the nobility, where the values that counted were the antiquity of the family and the origin of the title. For a true aristocrat, wealth was extremely convenient, well worth looking out for, but in a sense an accessory. A penniless Duke always remained a Duke, whereas a bourgeois who lost his money lost his social status as well. The rank of a bourgeois was the direct product of his income. Wealth alone distinguished the high bourgeoisie from the middle bourgeoisie and the middle from the lower. James, with his millions, his five-headed firm, his reserves that exceeded those of the Banque de France, his immense freedom in the movement of funds, shattered the moneyed middle-classes' own social scale. Yet his style of life did not approach that of the nobility, a fact that had nothing to do with wealth. Aristocrats had always known how to handle with ease and spend with flair the millions that came to them by way of dowry. But James had a penchant for work and for being engaged in activities of a particularly lucrative nature, both of which created a deep chasm between him and the landed aristocracy. A noble in the nineteenth century, especially under Louis-Philippe, did little more than oversee the collection of farm rents by his steward. A lordly landowner might well be a miser, but he would not want to give the impression of being overpreoccupied with financial matters.[47] Such scruples seemed absurd to James, whose proclaimed objective was to earn money and still more money. To attain such a goal, work was necessary, and James never regarded this as something to be regretted. In sum, it is impossible to fit him into any niche; he was a law unto himself.

Feeling in no way obliged, therefore, to adapt himself to any particular social etiquette, James continued to parade his luxurious scale of life with a lack of restraint that among the more sober bourgeois would have passed for bad taste. He went so far that he astonished even the young Orléans Princes. During the train journey organized by James, the King's grandsons took note of the lavish arrangements: "After the tunnel came the meal, and what a meal! Everything was on massive gold plates, of superb craftsmanship. Even the servants ate from gold plates and had as much champagne as they wanted!"[48] Then, there was the Baron's collection of paintings, which steadily grew by acquisitions from prestigious sources. From the collection of England's George IV he acquired *The Standard Bearer* by Rembrandt in 1840. The following year he bought the *Chartreux Madonna* by Jan van Eyck and Petrus Christus. In 1845 he sent agents to the sale of Cardinal Fesch's estate[49] in Rome and there picked up, among other pictures, a van Dyck, a Luini, a Rubens, a Murillo, and another Greuze, *La Petite Fille au bouquet*. Well-connected amateurs were allowed a tour of the apartments and salons of Rue Laffitte. A published guide to Paris, with a preface by Victor Hugo, provides considerable detail in its description of the décor. For her sitting room, Betty chose *A Young Man* by Rembrandt, a Ruisdael, a Teniers, a Wouverman, and a Hobbema. Dutch artists also predominated in James' rooms. For their bedchamber, however, the senior Rothschilds favored family portraits and a Moses in the Bullrushes by Paul Delaroche. In the grand salon, Jewish and family subjects gave way to a Virgin and Child by Luini, an exquisite Infanta by Velázquez, a portrait of a nobleman by Franz Hals, an ensemble of six Nattiers, the other Rembrandt, and the Greuze. The entire collection was insured for 10 million francs.[50] At one time or another James' walls displayed pictures from the collections of William III of Holland, Christian of Denmark, Prince Demidov, and the Duc de Berry. When the Versailles collections were put up for sale, he chose, among other things, two *secrétaires* that had once belonged to Marie-Antoinette. The poetry of provenance touched James and Betty so deeply that when their children wanted to give them a present for their silver wedding, they decided on a seventeenth-century crystal and ivory casket from Venice. This precious and extremely rare object (only fourteen of them were known to exist) had been made to contain baby linen. The Popes used once to have these made as presents for Kings at the birth of their eldest sons.

Showing no prejudice against contemporary masters, James had his only daughter painted by Ary Scheffer. In 1848, Ingres finally promised that Betty's portrait, on which he had been working since 1841, would be finished without further delay. Delighted, James asked the painter to make five copies, on a smaller scale, one for each of his children. But Ingres suddenly found himself interrupted. Once again, revolutionary France was reawakening.

9
A Republican
Veneer

The year 1848 found James, one of the best-informed men in Europe, calm and optimistic. Business was good: "Our weekly gains are a third greater than those of a year ago. We made 19 million in 1847; if things hold firm, we'll do 20 million this year," he predicted.[1] While he may have felt some anxiety about events in Italy or Germany, he never doubted the continuing stability of Louis-Philippe's regime. As if to prove his faith, he began the year by having the Rothschild bank underwrite a 250-million government bond issue paying three percent. The contract stipulated that James would transfer funds to the French Treasury in annual installments and that he would resell on his own account the bonds the government had issued to him. Then, given a steady rise in the bond market, he stood to reap a handsome profit.

Perhaps the prospect of this gain obscured his judgment. It seems surprising that a financier as sensitive to circumstances as James—always on the alert for the latest news, knowing so well the need for an exact assessment of the political situation— could have been so resoundingly wrong. Revolutions are, of course, never foreseen by anyone. It is impossible to anticipate the incident that triggers riot, or the accident that determines the victory or suppression of revolt. Consequently, there is no contradiction in perceiving the general malaise of a time yet simultaneously being surprised when it explodes. But James' correspondence shows no evidence that he was aware of popular discontent.

Social and political crisis had been discussed too much and too long for anyone to take it seriously. "Every day for several years," wrote Tocqueville, "the majority said that the opposition was placing society in peril, and the opposition kept repeating that ministers were losing the monarchy. Each side had reaffirmed its position so often, without really believing in it, that they ended up believing in it not at all, at the very moment when events would prove them both right."[2] This erosion of concern is revealed by the fact that the most pessimistic of observers were, paradoxically, those most taken by surprise when revolution erupted. Thus on March 10, 1848, after the insurgents had carried the day, young Count Apponyi, who as the Austrian Ambassador's nephew had close ties with James, wrote: "We must have been dreaming. It is impossible to believe that what we have just seen could be true. . . . A thunderbolt. A cyclone has destroyed and swept everything away. It's Providence, and God has willed it thus."[3] He forgot that three weeks earlier he had declared Europe to be "on the eve of a great explosion," and that he had predicted a "war by those who have nothing against those who have something." In 1830 the demands had been political; now, in 1848, they were social.

Chateaubriand, even in retirement, saw it coming and perceived "a vengeful world lurking behind society and making it tremble."[4] Balzac too had detected "a deadly terror . . . [welling up] from those people horrible to behold, haggard, sallow, leathery . . . [from those] men whom death cuts down more often than others and who are reborn just as hard-bitten as ever, whose misshapen, twisted faces exude through every pore the spirit, the desires, the poisons that bloat their brains, ineradicable signs of a panting greed."[5] It was a greed justified by misery and despair, the difficulty of finding work, and the blatant inadequacy of pay. It has been estimated that the average salary of the worst-off, for a thirteen-hour workday, came to 1.78 francs, the price of a Pont-l'Évêque cheese or two of those beautiful apples from Calville that the Baron loved so much. People were literally dying of hunger. Within two years the mortality rate went from 25.4 per 1,000 to 29.3,[6] a statistic that seems to have held little meaning for the nation's leaders. Again Tocqueville is worth quoting: "Don't you listen to what is said at the core [of the working classes]? . . . Don't you hear what is constantly repeated . . . that the division of assets which has always prevailed in the world is unjust; that property rests on foundations that are not equitable?"[7] Those in power neither listened nor heard. Reassured by the deceptive calm of the streets, they imagined that the absence of disorder guaranteed the permanence of the established order. Moreover, the certainty that authority would protect privilege helped suppress all fear of a red terror. The worker insurrections that occurred periodically throughout Louis-Philippe's reign, which was otherwise a time of peace, were put down, in Paris as well as in the provinces, by means cruel enough to keep them down. This too contributed to the blindness of the well-off. The split between real France and political France had deepened with every passing moment.

James derived most of his information from political circles and the King's entourage. These milieus—the product of that bourgeoisie which had taken such advantage of the new regime to grow quietly richer, steeped in self-satisfaction, isolated by power and egotism—thought less about social issues than about how to turn public affairs to their own profit. And the King had ceased to be the accommodating, clear-sighted person of 1830. Content to have acquired considerable power—which some called absolute—without imperiling parliamentary freedom, Louis-Philippe considered himself immune to all danger. Tocqueville thought he had succumbed to "senile imbecility." Mme de Boigne was more specific. "For some time," she wrote, "audiences were becoming pointless, because the King seized the floor, and it was often impossible to raise the subject for which one had asked [to be received]."[8] James, happy in his ready access to the sovereign, may have seen him too often to maintain a lucid, objective view, or to assess how much the regime suffered from its lack of moral and intellectual values.

A monarch ruling by Divine Right—who once inspired his followers to religious veneration—had been succeeded by a chief executive. Despite the exalted conception he entertained of his function and his person, Louis-Philippe had never managed to fill his supporters with absolute loyalty. The image he projected was so ordinary—so banal—that had he transferred the trappings of power to another person, performing the same functions as the King, the change would scarcely have been noticed. "By dint of his middleclass nature, one ceased to see the royalty. Why not, then, a President?"[9] asked Victor Hugo, sensibly enough. But James was too indifferent to doctrinal quarrels to recognize this disenchantment. Even if he had been less so, the thought of the difficulties of replacing the Orléans dynasty would have persuaded him of the desirability of the status quo. Reinstalling the Bourbons was unthinkable, except to a handful of Legitimists, and the two initiatives made by Louis-Napoleon, the Emperor's nephew, had failed lamentably. This left only the Republic.

Among conservatives the idea of a Republic automatically stirred up memories of the guillotine. The Republican legend, unlike the Napoleonic, had not enjoyed a good press among the bourgeois, high, middle, or low. No one in such circles would think of returning power to the heirs of Robespierre. In the salon of M. Dambreuse, Flaubert's financier in *L'Education sentimentale*, everyone made cruel fun "of men who longed for social upheaval . . . [who] demanded that work be organized. . . . The Republic is impossible in France."[10] One guest, however, shook the confidence of the property owners by declaring: "Watch out, people have Revolution too much on their minds. Too many books are published on the subject." He wasn't far wrong. Almost imperceptibly, the image of the Republic—that First Republic born in 1794, the short-lived, violent child of the Revolution—began to assume a different character, taking on the colors of courage, generosity, and justice.

Students, intellectuals, and artists accustomed themselves to the idea of the Republic much more than those in power imagined. A publication like the *Revue indépendante*, edited by George Sand and Pierre Leroux and dedicated to opposition, helped disseminate opinions ranging from sentimental liberalism to the most radical socialism. Finally, the working classes of Paris, unlike their counterparts in the provinces or the peasant masses, possessed true political consciousness. Not only in 1830, but again in 1832, 1834, and 1838, they had taken to the streets in bloody, short-lived riots. Completely detached from the monarchy, they supported the efforts of those who dreamed of a more just regime. Republican newspapers, socialist or communist sheets were all read and discussed by the workers of Paris.

These, however, were not sources from which diplomatic salons, financial bureaus, and official publications drew their information. Businessmen, insensitive, imperturbable, and indifferent, continued to live with their eyes fixed on the fluctuations of government bonds. They were as blind as the Princes who ruled them. "The government," wrote an astonished Tocqueville, "felt less anxiety than the leaders of the opposition. . . . There were no truly concerned people at this moment in Paris, other than the chief radicals or the men relatively close to the people and the revolutionary party, who could have known what was happening on that side. . . . It was not, certainly, the least bizarre element of this curious revolution that the incident which produced it . . . had not been foreseen or feared by any but the men who would come out on top."[11] Thus if James staked everything on the monarchy in January 1848, he was not alone in this. As so often before, he took aggressive financial positions and went further out on a limb than his competitors, because it was contrary to his temperament to manage his wealth cautiously and thereby allow it to be rounded off, like a pebble, by slow natural motion. He wanted to make money, and a lot of it, and this necessitated risk. The policy of daring had always succeeded with him, and he was not going to abandon it just because he had become enormously rich. Hence, it was as a great banker loaded with business deals that James de Rothschild would approach his third change of regime.

Before placing James in the context of the Second Republic, it is worth briefly recalling the days and events whose unfolding would bring down the House of Orléans.

The revolution of 1848 was precipitated by supporters of electoral and parliamentary reform—the advanced, liberal bourgeois opposition—who had learned to join forces, in the classic manner of political expediency, with the republicans. In this instance, they were brought together by the feeling that political reforms—principally those designed to extent the right to vote—would never be passed by Parliament. The opposition therefore decided to carry the campaign to the people. It avoided organizing meetings that would have easily been banned by the government. Instead, it launched a series of political banquets at which orators hotly denounced the corruption of the regime. Meanwhile Thiers conducted a violent campaign of speeches in the Chamber of Deputies against Guizot's foreign policy, and two leading liberal newspapers called on the people of Paris to take up the struggle. But faced with the success of the reform campaign, the government took fright, reacted defensively, and refused to make even the slightest concession. Still worse, it prohibited the banquet that was to close the campaign in Paris on February 22. The organizers would have complied, but already overwhelmed by the movement's more energetic elements, they could not prevent students and workers from assembling to proclaim their views. A formidable column of people began moving from the poorer districts and the Latin Quarter towards the Place de la Concorde, since the banquet was to have been held in a hall on the Champs-Élysées.

The first day, although filled with confusion, seemed on the whole to pose little threat to anyone. As the onlookers and the demonstrators jostled together, "soldier and bourgeois met and joked with one another."[12] Nevertheless, emotions ran high enough in establishment Paris to cause the Bourse to stop trading—in the reign of Louis-Philippe a sure sign of disquiet. Now James reacted. All the disturbance drove him "mad," but left him with enough presence of mind that he quickly tried to reorganize things so as to protect his assets. "I think," he advised his nephews, "we should purchase some American Treasury bonds, because America is still the most secure country for the investment of capital."[13] His awakening came late, and events would rapidly overtake him.

On February 23 the National Guard, the quintessential bourgeois force, refused to disperse the crowd still thronging the streets. With this simple gesture—or nongesture—the middle-class, that spoiled darling of the regime, did not so much overturn the government as let it fall. The situation had become critical. The King, finally recognizing the gravity of the moment, discharged Guizot, his Premier, and appointed Comte Molé,[14] who had the reputation of being slightly more liberal. This concession, although "one week too late or one week too soon,"[15] inspired a tremendous burst of joy. The question was whether it would appease the rebels. James thought not, since "it was a dangerous precedent for a King to give way to a factious minority and to an unruly band of national guardsmen."[16] Louis-Philippe's hopes for a quick solution were not to be realized. The mob—clamorous and disorderly—now turned hostile. A police station on the Boulevard des Capucines thought it was under attack, and what had been a scuffle turned into a gun battle. With this, a public demonstration became a revolution. The bodies of the dead were thrown on to carts and paraded through the capital. The so-called *Promenade des Cadavres* kindled the rage of an indignant population. As night fell barricades were beginning to block the streets.

Now fighting broke out in the streets. When the shouting rabble encircled the Tuileries Palace, the King abdicated with shocking and inexplicable rapidity. "He left like a bankrupt merchant fleeing his creditors," observed Prosper Mérimée with contempt.[17] This made a regency impossible, despite the dignity and courage of the Duchesse d'Orléans, who went with her young sons to the Deputies and suggested it. The Orléans dynasty, having fallen "more from booing than from bullets,"[18] could no longer command the least respect. Insurgents poured into the Chamber of Deputies, and the Republic was proclaimed. The conquerors, "as astonished by their victory as the vanquished were by their defeat,"[19] patched together a provisional government of twelve members, among whom moderates—Lamartine being the most famous—outnumbered socialists.

The surprise felt by the losers was matched only by their fear, a fear, however, that is understandable given the suddenness of what proved to be outright revolution. In 1830, the crisis had been resolved in a few days and had not led to real disturbance. "Politics remained the privilege of a narrow élite, and the power of the notables was intact."[20] On February 24, 1848, the Charter, the constitution, and parliamentary power no longer existed. There was only *tabula rasa*—and the unknown. The forces responsible for maintaining order had disappeared from the capital, a fact that shook even the calmest bourgeois. "In all Paris," wrote Tocqueville, "I did not see one member of the militia, one soldier, one gendarme, or one member of the police. The National Guard itself had vanished. Only the people carried arms, guarded public places, stood watch, issued orders, punished offenders, and it was both extraordinary and terrible to see the whole of an immense city, filled with so much wealth, under the sole protection of those who possessed nothing. . . . Meanwhile, sheer terror gripped all other classes. I don't believe that at any time during the Revolution [of 1789–94] it was quite so great."[21] Obviously, memories of that Great Revolution had been revived. The deepest fear was for property. Nathaniel expressed the anxiety of "good folks" when he wrote to his brothers in England: "Everybody is afraid of course. . . . Here matters are not very comfortable, the town is greatly agitated. . . . The weather is most beautiful so that all Paris will be in the streets and what with planting *les arbres de la liberté* and the diverse *marches en plein air*, God knows what will happen. . . . Our worthy uncle and his lady left just now for Ferriers [*sic*] where it was quite necessary for them to go. It is almost heartbreaking to think of a place where one has so much enjoyment, being taken away from you, as will be the case some day or other."[22]

James, even more than others, felt threatened, and not without reason, for on February 23 rumors of the most ominous kind began circulating. Victor Hugo reported that a Deputy came to warn him: "The worst is that something dark seems to be brewing in the background. Last night, more than fifteen of Paris' finest mansions were marked, with a cross on the door, for pillaging, among them Princesse Lièven's in the Rue Saint-Florentin."[23] This town house belonged to James, of course, who merely rented a floor to the Princess. Even more alarming than these vague threats was the destruction of the Château de Suresnes, which Salomon owned. The Rothschilds shared with the royal family the dubious honor of being the sole victims of the people's wrath. The Tuileries had been stormed by an overexcited mob that sacked the private apartments, not so much to pillage (Prosper Mérimée, who as official inspector of historic monuments was careful to keep a record of the damage, noted that a good many objets d'art had been returned) as to insult the toppled Princes. "Since we have won, we might as well amuse ourselves!"[24] But the following day, when the crowd undertook to assault those symbols of power and opulence—the Château de Neuilly, Louis-Philippe's private property, and the Suresnes estate—the amusement turned ugly.

According to Garnier-Pagès,[25] future Finance Minister under the Second Republic, it was during a revolutionary assembly, held outdoors on the Place de Puteaux, that the march on the arsenal at Mont Valérien and then to the Rothschild château was decided upon, following a denunciation made by a Suresnes poultry merchant, Louis Frazier. The assailants broke the lock on the main gate and swarmed over the property. No one attempted to stop them. They pillaged the pheasant preserve and the stables, took over the horses, and then seized the works of art. With hatchets, iron bars, and clubs they laid waste furniture, mirrors, and pictures. The mob's fury could be measured by the obvious fact that they wanted not merely to loot but also to destroy. This was the most frightening thing of all. After several hours of mayhem, the aggressors set fire to the place and fled. Neighbors, horrified at such systematic destruction, ran to the scene but arrived too late to extinguish the blaze, which quickly reduced the château to a smoldering ruin. They then called the National Guard, which sent out patrols and succeeded in arresting the ring leaders. Frazier ended up with a sentence of twenty years at hard labor.

No wonder James hastened to send his wife and daughter to London, where they arrived in the middle of the night, trembling with fright and full of appalling stories. James' sons followed a few days later. After deliberating with Nathaniel, the Baron decided that the two of them would not leave unless their lives were threatened. It would have been irresponsible to give way to panic when the future of the bank could be saved. The possibility of financial ruin horrified James even more than revolution. He decided not only to stand his ground but even to have his nephew Lionel come over from London, on the 27th, to decide on a course of action. He was confident of his ability to adjust to new circumstances, disagreeable as these might be. Thus, while sharing profits with workers struck him as an abomination, he saw no reason to resist if such participation would prevent nationalization. The issue held special importance for the owners of railway companies, since these were threatened with outright confiscation. From the contemporary evidence now available, a James emerges in whom opportunism and dignity blend together in a curious mixture.

By the 25th, according to *Archives israélites*, James had already confirmed that he would not quit Paris and that he "would offer his cooperation to such a good and honest Revolution." The fire at Suresnes had no effect on his decision. The story goes on to say that, upon hearing of it, James assembled his household and told them: "My friends, if they come, open all the doors. Don't resist. I'll remain among you with my nephew, M. Nathaniel, and may God's will be done. I know that all your savings have been deposited with me. If you lose them, you will share my last bit of bread." As everyone dissolved in tears, James concluded: "I wouldn't miss my château, but I would miss Paris if I had to leave it." The scene is so touching that one is tempted to smile, but Feydeau, who could never be suspected of partiality towards the Baron, paints him in no less flattering colors during these revolutionary days: "On the 24th, after having spent two days fighting in the ranks of the National Guard, I found myself placed in command of the post . . . [at] the Place Vendôme. The *heroes* of the glorious revolution . . . having ransacked the private apartments in the Tuileries, were strutting about in the garden, grotesquely decked out in the shawls and cloaks of the Princesses . . . and amusing themselves by firing shots in all directions, except where the vulgar suppose that Heaven is to be found. Bullets whistled down the Rues de Rivoli and Castiglione and through the Place Vendôme. . . . Around noon . . . I saw two gentlemen, arm in arm, calmly appear out of the Rue de la Paix and move towards the Tuileries, and I recognized one of them as the Baron de Rothschild. I quickly went up to him.

" 'M. le Baron,' I said 'you would seem not to have chosen a very good day for taking a walk. I think it would be better if you returned home rather than expose yourself to bullets whizzing in every direction.'

" 'My younk frient,' he replied, 'I tank you for your hatfice. Put tell me, vy are you here? Isn't it your duty? Vell, I too, de Baron de Rothschild, haf gome for de zame reason. Your duty is to shtand harmt vatch und hassure de zafety of goot zitizens; mine is to go to de Ministry of Finance, to zee vedder dey may not neet my hexperience und my gounzel,' and with this he left."[26]

His presence at the Ministry of Finance, which seems to have been engaged in a dual negotiation, a process that ended with the appointment of Michel Goudchaux as Minister, was in fact noted by various newspapers. Socialists, moderates, and conservatives all agreed upon the urgent need to reorganize the nation's finances. Once the first shot had been fired, business everywhere came to a standstill, and everyone began smuggling gold out of the country. The same people tried to exchange their "paper"—bills and securities—for gold, while also, paradoxically, selling objects made of precious metal. A long queue formed at the Mint. In order to inspire confidence in the provisional government, Lamartine and Arago agreed that the man they needed was Michel Goudchaux, "florid, enormous, rotund, innocent-looking . . . with a modest expression,"[27] who happened to be both a radical and a banker, a rare and useful combination. The fact that Michel Goudchaux also happened to be Jewish seems not to have mattered one way or the other. The tendency of Jews in general was to adhere to the regime in power. In France, this meant accepting a revolution from time to time, which they did all the more readily in 1848 since two of their own, Crémieux and Goudchaux, became ministers. The Chief Rabbi of France walked in procession, during those dark days of February 1848, alongside members of the Catholic and Protestant clergy under a single banner, which read: "Religions United. Universal Brotherhood."

In the case of Goudchaux, however, a problem developed that had nothing to do with his origins. "By virtue of having been deeply involved in business," Tocqueville tells us, "he managed to acquire a few reasonable ideas that served to conceal a mind actually filled with rank nonsense."[28] But to be fair, Goudchaux himself did not feel he possessed the abilities necessary for this difficult job. Lamartine and Arago begged him to accept at least temporarily. They emphasized that "M. de Rothschild and the principal members of the banking community were preparing to leave Paris, and that, for the sake of the prompt reestablishment of commercial interests, it was vital that he accept the Ministry of Finance. . . . Upon his acceptance, M. de Rothschild called on him and declared that his presence reassured him and that he [Rothschild] would remain in Paris."[29] Another nomination guaranteed to reassure the Baron was that of Adolphe Crémieux to the Ministry of Justice, which would provide him with a source of reliable information.[30] Calmed by the appointment of his old friends to these posts, James decided to dramatize his approval of the new regime by making the most generous contribution of all to the fund opened on February 25 for the benefit of those wounded during the revolution. His subscription was fifty thousand francs, or almost a quarter of the total given by the banking community as a whole.[31] This gesture of goodwill was particularly appreciated by the government, which relied heavily on James' support, a support essential for winning the loyalty of others and for overcoming the economic crisis.

James could well have taken offense at the rumors that the House of Rothschild was under "strict surveillance," or have worried about the interest-free loan that he had supposedly been required to make in order to meet the people's most immediate needs. But Louis Blanc wasted no time in denying the allegations: "I hasten to assure you, Monsieur [de Rothschild], that my name has been brazenly used without my permission. The provisional government is ready to take any measures necessary to prevent the distribution of printed sheets that have not been officially authorized."[32] Still, Caussidière, the new Prefect of Police, remained skeptical about James' deeper intentions and decided to investigate the banker by getting closer to him. Thus on February 27, when James appeared at the Prefecture to see one of the divisional chiefs, Caussidière invited him into his own office and, straightaway, told him of his suspicions that James would leave France. According to the Prefect, the Baron replied that he had refused to accept the possibility of bankruptcy and regarded "flight as cowardice."[33] He insisted, quite correctly, that his family were preparing to send him the funds necessary to meet his obligations and offered to introduce him to his nephew, Lionel, who was expected to arrive from London at any moment.

Caussidière then declared himself ready to do all he could to calm the Rothschilds, guaranteeing that James had nothing to fear from the people of Paris. "Although poor, they are honest," he said.[34] If James quaked inwardly as he reflected on the fate of his brother's château, he betrayed no sign of it. While he refused to extend credit to a printing plant employing five hundred workers, a service requested by Caussidière "in passing," James did reappear next day with Lionel and gave the Prefect two thousand francs to be distributed as he saw fit. As in 1830, James chose his sides without undue agonizing and then stuck by his decision. Henceforth, he would behave like a "good republican."[35] Caussidière understood him immediately. "Messieurs de Rothschild left me," he concluded "with their minds more at rest. They were convinced that the republicans could not be so bad as their enemies have maintained."[36]

Indeed, the Republicans did not turn out to be the ogres that many had feared. On the contrary, they knew well that they would have died of starvation if the situation had not been quickly stabilized. Michel Goudchaux, after only six days, relinquished his ministry to Garnier-Pagès. It was a burdensome legacy: "Money poured out of the Treasury like water through open floodgates—minute by minute, visibly. . . ."[37] Inexperienced but energetic, Garnier-Pagès joined with Crémieux and Arago, the Naval Minister, to form the nucleus of a group of liberal republicans who would constitute what might be called the government's right wing. Lamartine, the Minister of Foreign Affairs, whose prestige was such that he became virtual Head of State, joined them in the formulation of a moderate policy. His peaceful declarations, his refusal to export the revolution or become involved in ideological quarrels, his opposition to the use of the red flag, that symbol of violence and blood, soothed the nervous conservatives like a balm. The new leaders of France quickly gave the impression that they were determined to sacrifice neither order nor property. James, who was "very unhappy at having to live in a republican country," claimed, but only to his nephews, that he would have preferred "to live with his family in Kamchatka rather than in Paris."[38] But he plucked up his courage—and he was to need plenty of it.

Betty, her first fears now assuaged, began to fidget in London and desperately wanted to return home. She hated leaving James alone at so trying a time. She knew that underneath his efficient and resolute exterior lay easily aroused anxiety. The state of Uncle James' nerves had always been a source of concern in the family, which dreaded his attacks of melancholy. For all his self-assurance in business, the Baron knew stress only too well and needed the presence and affection of his wife. His authorization for her to rejoin him came in a somewhat awkward letter, which illustrated both his tenderness and his unease:

"My beloved angel,

"I received a letter, my dear angel, that is very dear to me, dated the 2nd, in which you insist upon coming here for a few days. I admit that my heart beats faster, and I'm happy to consent to your promise. I repeat 'your promise.' We must remain quiet. . . . One never knows what to expect with a republican government. I feel much calmer now. I view the situation as still dangerous. All that we can do here is meet our obligations. I'm taking on new business. . . . All that I ask of you is that you obtain a passport under a different name for a round trip. If you bring Alphonse, he too should have a supplementary passport with another name, because I don't want the newspapers to print a headline saying 'Madame de Rothschild has returned to London,' if you decide to go back there. That would give rise to idle gossip. . . . My good Betty, I think we should rent a small house and live in peace. . . . Do as your heart dictates. Come, and bring Alphonse, although I wonder whether we shouldn't keep him out of politics. If they see him, he'll be required to enlist in the National Guard. He may come if he lies low. . . ."[39]

Betty crossed over to France with Alphonse. A few days later they were joined by Gustave—in a Paris that had lost its gaiety. "The workers are our masters; we might as well get used to it," deplored Alphonse.[40] The Bourse managed to reopen on March 7, but quotations fell so low that it would have been catastrophic to try selling shares. Even more disturbing were the acts of sabotage, directed particularly at railways, stations, and bridges, which were perpetrated all round Paris. The vandals probably came either from the ranks of those who had been ruined by the advent of train travel, such as coachmen and all those who lived by the old systems of transport, or were anarchists angered over the profits realized by successful entrepreneurs. The shares of the Nord fell dramatically. Balzac had dreamed of disposing of his holdings at 900 francs a share; now they were worth no more than 212. James, in order to meet his commitments, found himself forced to sell at 33 government bonds he had bought at 77.

James began suspending all credit, a drastic policy that caused panic, recriminations, and often bankruptcy among his clients. Apponyi could hardly believe it when the Baron refused money to the English Ambassadress, though he admitted that the banker hung "by a thread."[41] James de Rothschild was in fact fighting for his life. Just as in his early career, he feared for his reputation: "As long as I pay what I owe, no one will be able to find fault. . . . Let us be courageous, let us show our greatness. We can stand by ourselves. . . ."[42] Miraculously, he prevailed. Léon Faucher, a respected journalist and economist, wrote to Henry Reeves, an English financier, on March 30: "In Paris everyone is ruined. The bankers are tumbling one after the other. Rothschild alone stands erect, albeit bled white."[43] James still inspired confidence, despite the hard times. In March, the House of Cruse, one of the great wine dealers of Bordeaux, confessed: "Our problems are enormous. Only the House of Rothschild rises above the mess and moves through the crisis in a manner to amaze the world."[44]

If James bore up, it was thanks to what Amschel called "the magic of the brothers," the steadfast and effective support given by the other branches of the family firm. This "magic," of course, often had to be stimulated. "Are we strangers? Should the Paris and Frankfurt houses be allowed to go under?" cried James, when he sensed that the zeal of the "English" was cooling.[45] The crisis caused the quarreling over accounts to flare up again, but transcending the pettiness was the feeling that a threat to one of the banks must involve all the others. Amschel rose in indignation when it seemed that London might not come to the rescue. "London, which is rich, should send six million francs to Frankfurt." The eldest Rothschild also struggled to restore James' morale. "If you reassemble all the bits and pieces of your fortune," he wrote, "you'll still be richer than all the others combined." Then, once again expressing his old distrust of Parisian life, Amschel concluded by advising James to give up the French capital and "buy the most beautiful house in Frankfurt, where one can live on a hundred thousand francs a year."[46]

But despite his lassitude ("here each day seems a year long"[47]), James had no intention of retiring from business. Lionel sent the subsidies that would permit his uncle to raise his head again. Soon the "great Baron" would even regret his initial wariness: "If only we had not allowed ourselves to be intimidated. Even now money can be made. We are going to have riots, things will become cheaper; a few days later matters will get better and so will the prices. It will never become completely calm again. . . . We must just work on that basis."[48] Such an appetite for business appeared absurd to Nathaniel, whose attitude reflected the sentiments of the less dynamic and less ambitious second generation. The cousins lacked the touch of folly so typical of those great entrepreneurs, the five ghetto-born sons of Mayer Amschel Rothschild: "I think it downright madness to plunge oneself up to one's neck in hot water on the chance of making a little money," wrote Nathaniel. "Our good uncles are so ridiculously fond of business for business sake, and because they cannot bear the idea of anybody else doing anything, that they can't let anything go if they fancy another person wishes for it. . . ."[49] "Our good uncle is as active as ever and seems determined to lose no opportunity of regaining what he has lately lost."[50]

The most pressing problem for James was the government loan that he had recently underwritten. The abrupt collapse of the financial markets made it impossible for him to go on placing the bonds with the public or, consequently, continue making the payments owed to the state. Of course, the French Treasury might have seized the twenty-five million guarantee, put up by the House of Rothschild in the event that it could not, under normal circumstances, meet its obligations, but such a solution, while catastrophic for James, would have been equally unattractive to the Finance Minister. Once the first subscribers failed to receive the payments they expected, public credit in France would suffer a terrible blow. And with its desperate need of money, the government could not afford to compromise what little confidence it still enjoyed. So the two parties reached an agreement. The old contract was canceled and the loan refloated at five percent payable on the same par value as the three percent rate of the preceding year. The bond-holders, far from being put at a disadvantage, found themselves with a profitable investment. James saved his stake. New money came in, and the bank began doing business again.

All these negotiations unfolded against a background of political unrest and social violence. Revolution, "this political cholera that has infested the world," as Nathaniel put it,[51] spread throughout Europe. On March 14, Metternich had to take flight, delaying only long enough to borrow a thousand ducats[52] from his dear friend Salomon—who a few days later made his own hasty exit. This development took the banker's grandchildren by surprise, for in their naïveté the younger Rothschilds imagined that their "dear grandpapa was so be-loved in Vienna that no one felt any cause to be concerned about his welfare."[53] On March 20 demonstrators also appeared outside Amschel's house in Frankfurt. Fortunately, the occu-pants suffered nothing more than a good fright. Finally, the situation in Naples began to deteriorate.

James, determined as he may have been to struggle for the survival of his firm, had two great fears: war between France and Austria, and the outbreak of civil war. In the first even-tuality, he would be forced to leave Paris, where he ran too great a risk of being taken for a spy.[54] In the second—the more likely of the dangers—he would fear for his children. Alphonse had already been drafted into the National Guard, and his brother Gustave was to be called up immediately. Racked by anxiety, James could not sleep at night: "Every time I hear the drums beating, I tremble for the lives of Alphonse and Gus-tave.[55] . . . . My Alphonse, a gun over his shoulder, fighting for the Republic."[56] To fight in defense of his fortune might, if worse came to worst, be acceptable, but when James consid-ered how vulnerable his sons were, young Jews, only recently naturalized, millionaires several times over, forced to fire on other Frenchmen, only to die for the Republic, it all seemed too stupid. He decided to act, explaining to his nephews: "I don't want to wait until the National Guard may be obliged to go into action, with Alphonse having to fight other young men. As a father, I want to avoid all these uproars. What's more, I'm not all that much of a republican. This is why I've decided to send him to America; all the more willingly since Nathaniel thinks it could be useful for our business. The only problem is that he's still a bit young, and I think someone as resolute and efficient as Mayer ought to accompany him. . . . I want Alphonse to leave Paris quickly, and I also want him to begin working seriously and to become a man."[57]

Mayer refused to give up the good life of London, much to James' disappointment, and Alphonse embarked alone, while Gustave was dispatched to Frankfurt. Asking Betty to return to London, yet keeping the younger boys at Ferrières, James himself stayed put, with the faithful Nathaniel at his side. This time, James had been clear-sighted. The infamous *journées* of June, the cruelest and most violent "days" of the 1848 revolution, would soon explode.

The April elections, which had marked the defeat of the extremists, of the right as well as the left, and the installation of a legal regime, still failed to solve the most urgent problems of the Parisian population. Unemployment had attained such frightful proportions that the creation of national workshops—resembling charitable enterprises where idle workers were paid for performing tasks of relatively minor importance, such as road repair and the gardening of vacant lots—did little to alleviate the general distress. Yet there were those who thought the time had come to close the workshops, on the grounds that it was ridiculous to continue paying for labor of little immediate value. But their closure would have thrown unemployed people on to the streets and was certain to provoke a violent crisis. Lamartine's supporters believed it possible to resolve the problem by tying it to the nationalization of the railways, an event that would justify large-scale recruitment for the purpose of completing construction and undertaking repairs. However, in that political climate, the idea came too late. Parliamentary opinion was divided. The revolutionary socialists did not have a majority, and other Deputies wanted to slow down social reforms, rather than take them further. Thus when the Minister of Finance submitted the nationalization project, he found himself facing a hostile Assembly. Montalembert[58] denounced "this first breach in the impregnable wall that until now protected family and property."[59] The shareholders of the Compagnie du

Nord met in special session, presided over by James, and opposed the measure with all the energy of property owners sure of their legitimate rights.

Meanwhile, the Assembly grew increasingly alarmed over the continuing restlessness in streets thronged with jobless workers and layabouts. To ward off still more serious problems, the legislators decided to dissolve the national workshops. The decree, voted on June 22, ordered all men under twenty-five without a permanent job to join the army, and the oldest of these were to prepare for posting to the provinces.

The response was an immediate and massive protest. A huge crowd gathered in the Place de la Bastille—that shrine sacred to the memory of 1789—where, to cries of "liberty or death," the enraged populace began throwing up barricades. The politics of reform and civil rights no longer mattered; now the demand was for the right to eat. When Arago attempted to address the protestors, one worker lashed out with: "Ah! Monsieur Arago, you've never been hungry." Prosper Mérimée, a professed liberal, found himself retreating towards the right wing. To him, the June riot became an expression of rage, fury, and despair: "One fought only to take or to preserve. For the insurgents, the objective was to pillage Paris and set up a regime based on the guillotine; for us, it was a matter of saving our hides."[60]

Street fighting continued for three consecutive days, from the 23rd to the 25th of June. But the workers could not hold out long against the army and the National Guard, which waged a systematic and crushing campaign under General Cavaignac, whose swift and terrible expertise earned him the popular nickname of "the Prince of Blood." The brutality of the repression had become possible once the workers lost the support of the democrats, who could not allow a riot to compromise a decision taken by an Assembly elected through a process of universal suffrage. Notions of order and legality prevailed over compassion and generosity.

James, in his daily reports to his nephews, admitted that the gunfire was so terrifying that he had at one point considered leaving Paris. He was all the more relieved when it ended. "Things are better," he wrote on the 25th, "I hope that by evening the bandits will have been put down. If order can be restored permanently, confidence will revive. The Chamber of Deputies and the government will at last understand that power can be exercized only with force. I think that will do a lot of good for all governments. . . . It will no longer be possible to seize the railways.[61]. . . I think the whole world will benefit from what has happened here. Everything, everywhere, will change for the better. . . ."[62] In these lines James reflected the happiness experienced by all those who had feared the worst. The wealthy at once breathed more easily. As Victor Hugo remarked: "Bit by bit noses began to poke out of windows. It was as if everyone were saying: 'Well now, a republic, that's all it is? . . .' February has given France a republican veneer, under which the old society is still visible."[63]

Given these conditions, James saw no risk in playing the complete republican. The ease and rapidity with which the Baron resigned himself to the new government, and the astuteness with which he took advantage of it, won him not only the respect of Kings (Leopold I, King of the Belgians, expressed his appreciation by entrusting him with five million francs), but also the supreme tribute of an ironic attack from the extreme left, as for instance that published in *Tocsin des travailleurs:*

"You are a marvel, Monsieur. Despite his legal majority, Louis-Philippe falls, Guizot disappears, and the constitutional monarchy, as well as parliamentary eloquence, are obliged to give way, but you—you don't budge. . . . What's become of Arago and Lamartine? They've collapsed, but you remain standing. The monarchs of the banking world are in liquidation; their offices are closed. The great captains of industry and the railway companies totter. Millions of shareholders, stockbrokers, industrialists, and bankers are ruined. Only you remain unassailable in the midst of so many disasters. Even though your house sustained the first shock in Paris, and even though a rolling wave of revolution threatens it in Naples, Vienna, and Berlin, you hold firm. Fortunes drain away, glory withers, powers sink, but the Jew, the King of our time, retains his throne. And that's not all. You could have fled this country where, in the words of your Bible, mountains skip like rams. You remain, assuming your power to be independent of the old dynasties, bold in the face of young republics. And you cling intrepidly to France. . . . You are more than a statesman, you are the symbol of credit. Isn't it time that the bank, that potent instrument of the middleclasses, contributed to the realization of the people's destiny? If you don't become a minister, you remain simply the great businessman of our era. Your achievement would be greater, and your reputation even more prestigious than the one you already have. After the royal scepter of money, an apotheosis—doesn't that tempt you? You must admit that it would be marvelous if one day the French Republic should offer you a place in the Pantheon."[64]

One wonders whether James may not actually have relished such socialist sarcasm. He was not, of course, the only person who adjusted promptly to the Republic. All round him, in fact, people were making the same about-face. What else—other than the republican plank—was there to grasp in that stormy sea? The cowardice of Louis-Philippe's departure constituted sufficient excuse for any reversal of loyalty. Only the fear of reprisals could have encouraged emigration. After the June uprising had been crushed, even the most fearful of the bourgeois began sleeping more soundly. But where the journalist made no mistake was in pointing out the facility with which James stepped over the wreckage of each fallen regime. His relationship with the various administrations was always characterized by a transparent simplicity: the give-and-take of mutual accommodation and advantage. Those currently in power protected him and allowed his business affairs to proceed. In return, he offered the benefits of his advice and support. And James placed such importance on the fulfillment of his part of the bargain that it freed him in advance from all debts of gratitude. He felt bound by no traditional commitments to party or person, thereby evincing an absence of political principle that was inevitable, given the total, unquestioned primacy he accorded his fortune and the glory of his family. Disraeli saw in "that absolute freedom from prejudice . . . the compensatory possession of a man without a country."[65] James, of course, had deliberately kept his distance from the country where he had lived for almost forty years. But this intensely personal attitude was not shared either by his wife or, with still more reason, by his sons.

Betty—less obsessed than her husband with the bank's affairs, closer in age and outlook to her children, certainly more

French—felt a deeper identification with national causes. A Legitimist under Louis-Philippe, Orleanist under the Republic and Second Empire—therefore always one regime behind—the Baroness did not give the impression of being without political allegiances. For instance, she always showed great concern for Marie-Amélie during her exile, regularly sending the former Queen fruit and never forgetting her birthday. Such small kindnesses must have touched the Queen since she bequeathed to Betty her most sentimental mementoes of France: the mittens and little black silk coif that she had worn during her flight to Great Britain in 1848.

James, on the other hand, severed all relations with the Orléans family, and fumed that he had had the bad luck to pay the King four million francs against a mortgage on his forests. In 1848, moreover, he found himself required to disburse another five hundred thousand francs claimed by the trustee charged with liquidating the departed sovereign's private estate. "It's anything but agreeable, but I very much fear I shall be obliged to do what is asked of me," he moaned.[66] After that, James resisted all temptation to shed tears over the fate of Louis-Philippe.

The process of reconstituting his network of well-placed friends was made easier by the discreet return of the former political leaders, quiet conservatives, "tomorrow's republicans," who were ever ready to reweave the broken strands of old times. "We were yesterday at Cavaignac's [the home of the new Premier]. Same people as usual," Nathaniel wrote to his brothers in London.[67] How could it have been otherwise? France, great nation that she was, had always, until then, had an electorate and a secondary education too narrow to produce three teams of leaders capable of relieving one another in such close succession, in 1815, in 1830, and again in 1848. Naturally, therefore, James maintained good relations with what was called the "party of order," brought to power by the conservative elections of April 1848, and by the brutal conclusion to the June insurrection. "There is no hope for reasonable Frenchmen," he said, "if they don't range themselves frankly and unequivocally behind the present government."[68] The recall of General Changarnier,[69] who had assumed the functions of Governor of Algeria, struck James as a good omen. Changarnier, a moderate with Orleanist leanings who was made responsible for security in the capital, happened also to be an admirer of Betty de Rothschild. Indeed, he confided more to the beautiful Baroness than was politically prudent, reported Mme Dosne, Thiers' ascerbic mother-in-law.

But James did not restrict his offers of service to those moderates most congenial to himself. Louis-Napoleon, that troublesome adventurer, with his entourage of new men, exasperated and even frightened the Baron, but to play against or ignore him would have been absurd. Thus, on December 10, 1848, the election of Louis-Napoleon to the presidency of the Republic did not catch James unawares.

10
The Parvenu Is Always Someone Else

Louis-Napoleon, the son of Louis Bonaparte, former King of Holland, and Hortense de Beauharnais, daughter of the Empress Josephine, was an old acquaintance. In 1840, while confined to Ham Fortess, after an unsuccessful attempt to seize power, the nephew of Napoleon I dreamed up a scheme for building a canal across Central America and wrote to James, hoping to interest him in the project. Nothing came of it, but in 1846, after he had escaped and settled in London, the younger Bonaparte had further financial dealings with the Rothschilds. Entertaining little respect for him and disturbed by his activities, the Baron warned his nephews during the troubled days of June 1848 that "this man [will cause us] great sorrow"[1] Clearly, James did not expect wonderful things from this somewhat "pale" shadow of the great Napoleon,[2] but neither he nor Nathaniel had any illusions about the imminence of his accession to power: "The French are such fools as regards politics and always act against their own interests. . . . It is a serious thing that Louis Napoleon should have so many adherents. . . . If the President of the Republic is to be named by the people there seems to be no doubt that Louis Napoleon will be their choice."[3] James therefore resigned himself to the inevitable and, according to a Parisian informant of Metternich, lent money to Louis-Napoleon at the time of the electoral campaign, which pitted Bonaparte against Cavaignac, the official candidate of the right; Ledru-Rollin, the official leftist candidate; Lamartine, who now represented no one but himself; and Changarnier, backed by a handful of Legitimists.

The campaign unfolded without incident—and ended with the election of a man offering no definite program or noteworthy political experience but who symbolized a legend, a fact that gave Louis-Napoleon an infinite advantage on this, the first, occasion on which the French could exercise the right of universal suffrage. When James advanced him money, it was for reasons of elementary political prudence. He did not want to be caught short and even managed to place one of his men in the new President's entourage. "Persigny alone is listened to," Metternich heard. " He has replaced M. Ferdinand Barrot with one of his own men and one also to some extent favored by M. de Rothschild, a M. Auguste Chevalier, formerly traffic manager for the Chemin de Fer du Nord."[4] In this period James continued to wield such influence that the mere mention of his name sufficed for the Prefect of Police to grant a delay of several months in an expulsion order threatened against Herzen, a Russian philosopher and revolutionist who had been deported by the tsarist government.[5]

But instead of becoming too involved with the internal affairs of France (which did not strike James as being fraught with danger, if one can believe Betty in a letter she wrote to Metternich, encouraging the Chancellor to come to Paris, since "we grow stronger day by day; security returns, and our domestic politics move forward along the path of progress and order"),[6] James concentrated on rebuilding his business and on reestablishing his position in Europe. He resumed construction work on the railway system, mainly for the Nord, and also set about developing international loans. Work was picking up satisfactorily. "Business has never been so good," exclaimed Alphonse. "We have just finished handling a loan for Austria. Propositions come in from all sides. . . . Belmont[7] has a host of projects in America. . . ."[8] But the Rothschilds did not belong to the Prince-President's inner circle, and there is no reason to think that James regretted the distance placed between this government and his house, especially since it in no way impeded the expansion of his business.

James, like his Orleanist friends, felt no sympathetic rapport with the President. They had nothing in common. The half-socialist, half-authoritarian vision espoused by Louis-Napoleon seemed absurd to James, whose attitudes had been shaped by thirty years of parliamentary royalism. "His hobby-horse is the people"[9] was the unflattering phrase often repeated round Paris. James found himself put off by the opportunistic character of an individual who had always lived on the fringes of society, a man whose education left much to be desired and who, by design or by default, expressed himself in a confused manner and appeared to move along no perceptible course. "He is consistent only in his hesitation," remarked Zola. Deep down, James despised him and subscribed to Thiers' view: "He's a cretin who will be led round by the nose." Consequently, James made no great effort to gain the good opinion of the President.

Political events moved quickly, for Louis-Napoleon would not satisfy himself with the limited powers granted by the constitution. Having failed to obtain a revision enabling him to seek reelection, he disbanded the National Assembly and proclaimed himself Prince-President. The rapid organization of a plebiscite, where the vote was not anonymous, gave him a majority of 7,500,000 votes against 1,500,000. The coup d'état of December 2, 1851,[10] and the transformation of an imperial republic into an official Empire hardly troubled the pragmatic James, who could only applaud the famous declaration of Napoleon III: "It's time the bad trembled and that the good put their minds at rest." The Baron had no doubt that the "good" would benefit from the guarantee of order and stability. The morning of the coup a number of leading bankers gathered for a meeting in the Rue Laffitte. One of them reported that "no one exactly blamed Louis-Napoleon for abolishing the constitution of 1851; it was felt to be more or less inevitable; the only worry was that it might prove a dangerous adventure. There was talk of several Generals who had been arrested; there was fear lest there might be disputes in the army, which, it was said, would be the end of France, whoever came out on top. M. Péreire was bombarded with questions. He told of what he had seen: the good humor of the officers, the high spirits of the soldiers, the great development of the military forces, the indifference of those who read posters, and the tranquility in Paris, despite the surprise everyone had had on waking that morning. The great financiers took pleasure in listening to this reassuring news."[11]

In this the financiers did not depart from the commonly held view. The provinces produced somewhat more vigorous resistance than did Paris, but each effort disintegrated in the face of harsh repression. The preceding years' rebellion had left the reformers drained of energy. In *La Curée*, Zola wrote: "Saved once again, bourgeois society congratulated itself, lay back, and slept late, now that a strong government would protect it and even relieve it of the need to think and manage its affairs. . . . Politics seemed as terrifying as a dangerous drug. The weary in spirit turned to business and to pleasure. The haves dug up their money, and the have-nots poked about in corners hoping to discover forgotten treasures. In the great silence of order, in the peaceful vacuum of the new reign, all sorts of pleasant rumors, of golden and voluptuous promises arose. . . . That handful of adventurers who had just stolen a throne would of necessity bring a reign of adventures, shady deals, and bartered consciences. . . . "[12]

Indeed, it seemed that the obsession with money knew no bounds. Whereas the recent regime had been largely self-serving, the Second Empire would offer new possibilities of financial gain to a much larger section of society. Paris became a fully fledged financial center, and within thirty years the number of securities traded on the Bourse was to increase threefold. Speculators had their appetite whetted by the upsurge in the Bourse that followed the coup d'état. All sorts of small investors—employees with modest salaries—succumbed to the speculation fever. No newspaper could be without its financial column, and no novel, it was said, ever had so many readers as the daily exchange quotations. According to the younger Dumas, "the Bourse became for that generation what the cathedral had been in the Middle Ages."[13]

"Bathed by that rising tide of speculation, whose spume would spread all over Paris,"[13a] James had a renewed sense of his own superiority. More solidly grounded than all the new arrivals, he no longer needed to dirty his hands, nor plunge up to his elbows in other people's money. In contrast to the flashy, neophyte, and often questionable entourage of the new sovereign, the Baron, after forty years of managing his millions and playing the elegant, looked like old money. "He took business seriously, distrusted vain theories, and did not like adventures. This too separated him from the present, and endowed him with an air of antiquity in the midst of a generation more prone to take risks in business as well as in politics."[14] James himself now found it amusing to pose as a decent, modest type and to savor the comic effect this had. One evening at Count Walewski's, he was asked why stock prices had declined the day before. "Do I know," he replied, "why the market rises and falls? If I knew that, I would have made my fortune."[15] Stock market or economic crises left him undaunted, at least outwardly, and his house became the very model of good form. "It had to be seen to be believed how, in that enormous banking house, he ruled with a rod of iron!" wrote Feydeau. "What marvelous order everywhere! How docile the employees were! And how intelligent! What submissive sons! What a sense of hierarchy! What respect. . . . I can't imagine it would be possible to find another banking house where everything would bear the stamp of such regularity, order, fitness, or respectability. Everything there smelled of great affairs, of a hard-won fortune acquired and well secured. Every head of department was *comme il faut*. The offices had an immaculate air that was a joy to behold. Finally, with the exception of a few slightly eccentric outbursts on the part of the boss, I never, in the fifteen years that I frequented the house, saw anything that was not altogether honorable, correct, and suitable."[16]

James had at last earned his gold braid of dignity. A Morny[17]—the true representative of the regime, tainted by a double bastardy, reveling in a fortune extorted from an old mistress—was not likely to impress "this all-powerful King," as Zola called him, "feared and obeyed in Paris and everywhere else . . . seated upon a throne more solid and more respected than that of the Emperor."[18] The Baron had served as banker, and therefore to some extent as confessor, to the Countess de Montijo, the mother of the future Empress Eugénie, who asked him to escort her daughter on the occasion of the young woman's presentation at court. With some affectation, James maintained that such tributes bored him. Invited to hunt at Compiègne, he liked to pretend that the whole affair was an agony to him: "I was dragged, against my will, in a carriage to follow the mounted hunt and watch that poor stag seeking a watery refuge from his enemies. . . . I swear in all candor that I'm too old to be amused by these frivolous diversions, and I shall end up by renouncing everything that vanity can offer. . . . Tomorrow and Wednesday there is a shoot, when everyone will pay more attention to my presence. If possible, I will leave on Wednesday and return to Paris. To be so near and yet not see those one loves is intolerable."[19]

James profited from this ordeal to speak privately with the Emperor for more than two hours on the subject of his railway interests. Still, he maintained a condescending attitude. The House of Rothschild refused, for instance, automatically to underwrite all government loans. Once, he was congratulated on remaining aloof from an operation that failed to yield the expected results. "He said quite modestly," wrote Prosper Mérimée, " 'I have noticed that on these occasions the Good Lord always takes great care of me.' "[20] When the Baron participated in a bond issue, it was primarily, he insisted, to show that "we do not scorn the government and that we don't want to stand in its way."[21]

With this conceit, James masked the genuine repugnance he felt for the manner in which Napoleon III and the more serious members of his inner circle, notably the Péreires, envisioned the future. For their part, the Emperor's entourage would have been happy to push the old banker to one side. "It is imperative that you free yourself from the tutelage of the Rothschilds, who reign in spite of you," Achille Fould advised the monarch.[22] Easier said than done!

By reinforcing the international character of the Rothschild firm, instead of allowing each branch to blend into its adopted country, James had succeeded in creating a supranational role for himself. Most of his contemporaries, in that century of nascent nationalism, would have been too fearful of the consequences to maintain such detachment from their own countries—and even James, as we have seen, acknowledged the risk since he took care that his children did not run it—but he himself felt secure enough to derive a formidable advantage from his independence. During the Second Empire, this aloofness earned him, if not the stature of a statesman, then at least that of a special Ambassador whose credentials were not limited to a single nation. Thus he served as unofficial link—and for the most important business—between the Emperor and the governments of the various countries where his financial operations had given him special influence.

In 1852, while on a visit to Vienna, James was received by the Emperor Franz Joseph, who entrusted the banker with a friendly message for Louis-Napoleon, a message that the French Emperor found all the more agreeable in that it was the first gesture of recognition made by a legitimate sovereign. In Prussia as well, James functioned as an intermediary until the end of his life. Bismarck always used the Bleichröder-Rothschild line of communication, rather than normal diplomatic channels, whenever he wanted to stress an important point. This was because the Chancellor's advisors understood that James "always had free access to the Emperor, who allowed [Rothschild] to speak with him openly, not only on financial matters but also about politics."[23] Such freedom in dealing with Louis-Napoleon was possible because James had access to enough capital to carry out his operations alone—a rare phenomenon at this time. Paradoxically, the years in which he was not intimately involved with the French government—when his pacifist views could do nothing to prevent the Italian war of 1859 or the expedition to Mexico in 1861, or again the war between Austria and Prussia in 1866—happened to be the very period when he appeared most powerful, having achieved a kind of social freedom, symbolized by Betty's refusal to appear at court. The first time she saw the Emperor was in her own home, at the famous Ferrières reception in 1862. This independence of James and, above all, the arrogance with which he exercized it could be explained, as we have seen, by his financial means, but also by the strength that continued to hold the Rothschild family together. In that second half of the nineteenth century the great-grandchildren of Mayer Amschel reached adulthood. Did the ties that bound them remain as taut as ever?

Frankfurt had ceased to have the sentimental value of a home port after the death of *Grossmutter* in 1849. Losing old Gudule put James in mind of that rare species—the poor Rothschilds—and he suggested to his brothers that they divide their mother's money and jewelry "among the members of the family who have known adversity and, unfortunately, are not completely comfortable, whether this be our sister Worms and her three daughters[24] or our sister Beyfus and her four children. . . ."[25] He then went further, displaying commendable generosity: "I also note with regret that our late mother's personal maid has, after so many years of faithful service, been left an inadequate annuity. For my part, therefore, I want to settle upon her a sum of 500 florins.[26] . . . I hope, my dear brother, that you will not reproach me and that perhaps you will do the same. The Almighty has blessed us with an abundance of riches and helped us through the difficult times we have just experienced, and it seems only fair that in settling this estate we think of those of our relatives who might need our help."

Amschel, to whom this was addressed, did not reply. Other problems were troubling him. The wife he never loved, and who moreover gave him no children, had died the year before. As soon as his mother was buried, Amschel took it into his head to remarry and began casting lustful eyes upon his grandniece, Julie, the daughter of Anselm and thus the granddaughter of Salomon. When the young woman energetically repulsed his advances, Amschel threatened to marry a certain Fräulein Ratisbon. By now the whole family was upset. When James and Salomon saw their eldest brother tampering with his will, they became truly alarmed. Illness, however, soon put an end to this whim, and poor Amschel lingered on, solitary and sour, until 1855. Salomon and Karl died the same year, leaving James the sole survivor of his generation, a pillar of authority within the Rothschild clan. One of Karl's sons assumed direction of the Frankfurt house, while the others remained in Naples until 1863, the year that branch closed, after the political reshuffle had rendered it useless. Anselm stayed on in Vienna, where he had been in charge since his father's departure in 1848.

By this time all the cousins, with the exception of the disobedient Hannah, Nathan's daughter, had intermarried, thereby cementing the joint ownership of the family enterprise. James had had no difficulty establishing his children according to his wishes. Alphonse married his fashionable second cousin, the beautiful Leonora, eldest daughter of Lionel and the future ornament of elegant soirées at Compiègne. While the young couple moved into a sumptuous establishment on the Rue Saint-Florentin, James and Betty continued to hold court in the Rue Laffitte. Gustave, made miserable by the unfamiliar solitude into which his elder brother's marriage had cast him, did not want to wait until a cousin of marriageable age appeared. He therefore took as his wife Cécile Anspach, whose father, one of the most prominent intellectuals within Paris' Jewish community, sat on the Supreme Court of Appeals. Quick and self-confident, more intelligent than pretty, Cécile won the heart of her father-in-law by "her even temper and kindliness, her eagerness to please without any loss of dignity,"[27] and by the art with which she could transport her husband *aux anges*. She was also clever enough to allow herself to be guided by her sister-in-law through the intricacies of her new family. Cécile thus rapidly became "rothschildized." James even trusted her to sign official papers for him and his sons when they were all away at the same time.[28]

This union offers a certain sociological interest, suggesting as it does that James preferred an alliance with a family whose Judaism was authentic and Orthodox to one with the Jewish financial aristocracy. Only in the next generation would the Rothschilds have sons-in-law named Ephrussi, Lambert, Leonino, or Sassoon.[29] Cécile and Gustave too established a separate household, before settling in the Avenue de Marigny. Finally, Salomon married his cousin Karl's daughter in 1862. James, however, kept a tight rein on his sons. "This Titan, forever overburdened, would never shift to [his sons] the least part of his colossal labor and . . . they would never permit themselves, however minor the occasion, to give a signature, that cabalistic signature which committed the house, without first consulting their father. 'Ask Papa,' answered these forty-year-old men, almost as experienced as their father, to the smallest request."[30]

James hovered over his sons and left them so little freedom that he managed to stifle their spirit of enterprise, the very quality that he admired above all others. Had his children displayed more energy and their father been more inclined to urge them on towards new frontiers, the Rothschilds would certainly have opened a branch in New York. Belmont met with such success there that he considered himself more the family correspondent than an agent. Alphonse realized this at the time of his visit in 1848: "Belmont is a real *grand seigneur*, with a sumptuous house, carriages, and footmen, and I counted myself lucky that he was willing to allow me inside his office. . . . This gentleman is consumed by conceit and vanity. . . . He has cultivated an independent air, more particularly a style and a manner that are the result of his escape from all active control. . . . The problem with Belmont is that he has spent twelve years as absolute master of 12,000 miles [*sic*] away from his employer."[31]

The twenty-year-old Alphonse, fired by youthful enthusiasm and alerted by the 1848 revolution to the instability of Europe, desperately wanted to open a banking house in New York: ". . . the country has all the elements of prosperity in such abundance that one would have to be blind not to recognize them, and one cannot but admire the intelligence and the energy with which the people know how to exploit them. In Europe there are many antiquated ideas about America, but [they] must vanish when one is confronted by the facts. . . . I have no hesitation in saying that a Rothschild house and not a mere agency should be established in America."[32] What could be clearer, more obvious, or more sensible? In 1857 a London banker sent his son Pierpont Morgan to New York, where he would become one of the most powerful financiers in the United States. James, however, was not one of those men who fling their sons out of the nest, thereby forcing them to make good on their own, and Alphonse, for his part, never renewed his campaign. He, his brothers, and all his cousins allowed themselves to be seduced by the sweetness of a good—but obedient—life. Nonchalance is the price one may pay for gentlemanly refinement.

Authoritarian and possessive, James remained the traditional Jewish patriarch. Every evening he brought his brood together round the dinner table in the Rue Laffitte. Reading Leonora's letters, one gets the impression that despite their splendid houses spread throughout Paris' smartest areas, the young couples enjoyed scarcely any autonomy. James was enchanted by the growing number of his grandchildren, and when it came to naming them, he made the final decision. He always arranged to have some of them with him whenever he left for a cure, finding their game of charades one of his favorite distractions. The death of Charlotte and Nathaniel's son in 1850 plunged the Baron into such depression that he canceled important meetings because of it. During Leonora's visits to her parents in England, James wrote her many sweet and endearing letters: "I should like to tell you about us all, and keep you up to date on all the little events of our family circle, from which you are never absent, for one instant, my adored child . . . my ever charming Laurie, do kiss our adorable baby, whose absence pains me. . . ."[33] Obviously it was James' mood that set the atmosphere in which the entire family lived.

The young generation could only admire the incredible energy and drive of that little old man. "Wherever he may be, [our good Uncle] puts life into everything and makes his party lively; we have been taking long walks and playing whist, but as the baths tire him, we go to bed rather early," wrote Lionel from Wildbad, where he had joined James.[34] Leonora added to the picture: "The great Baron keeps up wonderfully. He is in fine form. He does not complain about his bad eyes or gout now that he is here *en garçon*. He goes to the play every night with some lovely woman and he is *désolé* when between three and four in the day time he does not find Mme Walewska or some other flame of his at home."[35]

James did not pursue women, and none of the famous cocottes could boast of having caught him in her net. But Alphonse, a true fashionable Parisian, was known to sup with La Païva, while Gustave indulged in a flirtation with the beautiful Castiglione, the Emperor's mistress, who rather liked prowling the corridors of the Rue Laffitte—whenever Cécile was away. James was content merely to idolize Mme Walewska, innocently and above board, and to tease the pretty salesgirls, while munching his pralines, at Bonnet's sweetshop in the Place de la Bourse.

This reservoir of good nature, this gaiety, this capacity to enjoy and to make the most of all the marvels offered him by a smiling fate, this determination to lead a full and rich life—

all these contributed towards preserving the happy intimacy that James had always had with his children. Thus he succeeded, despite their overflowing coffers, in convincing his sons of the need to continue his work, a rare accomplishment in banking families.

Once grown-up, James' sons also followed their father's example in assuming leadership roles within the Jewish community. Alphonse took his place in the Central Consistory in 1850, when he was twenty-three, and became president of that body in 1869. Elected to the Paris Consistory in 1852, Gustave was chosen president only six years later, at the age of twenty-eight.

As the dominant figure of French Jewry, James was not an ardent partisan of the total assimilation of his coreligionists. In the debate that arose between the champions of Orthodoxy, eager to maintain all their distinctiveness, and the liberal elements, who favored the progressive elimination of the most conspicuous differences, James ranged himself on the side of the conservatives.

Herein lay a paradox, for James himself had adopted a completely occidental style of life, and had encouraged his sons to become French gentlemen. The Rothschilds, in Paris as well as in London, became so casual in their everyday attitude towards religion that the appearance of their stricter cousins from Frankfurt always created a commotion. "Willy and Natty arrived yesterday. . . . The special kitchen, for the preparation of kosher meals, has never been put to work. However, the cook having got the strictest orders, bought a whole new set of utensils, and, that not being all, she had to take the lot, glass and china as well, to a washing place on the Seine or to some big cleansing place and there dip every single piece thrice in the river. It seems that a sizable crowd gathered to observe the propitiatory ceremonies of these Egyptians, Nepalese, or God knows what kind of prehistoric people."[36] But when it came to founding a shelter or a hospital for the Jews of the capital, James would not only finance the whole institution, but he even saw to it that all the rules of religion were observed there.

The inauguration of the Rothschild Hospital caused quite a stir in Paris. *L'Illustration*, the bimonthly publication that anticipated the big present-day magazines, devoted two full pages to the event, there extolling the generosity of the donor, while also pointing out the danger of such segregation: "We understand . . . that Salomon Heine in Hamburg and the Rothschild brothers in Frankfurt have had the charitable idea of sheltering all sick Jews in special establishments. In those two cities the government is driven by caste consciousness. In the midst of such competition between the various groups of society, it is natural that well-intentioned men should concern themselves with the lot of their unfortunate coreligionists. Nor are we surprised that the city council of Berlin has, as a consequence, decided to build a special hospital for poor Jews. Wherever civil liberty is denied the Jews, the latter must of necessity form a people apart.

"Thank Heaven, in France the Jews do not have the same reasons for perpetuating their isolation among us. . . . We join those who applaud the civil and religious emancipation of the Jews in France. We join those who cry out wholeheartedly for the complete liberation and rehabilitation of that unfortunate and submissive race, oppressed as it is by barbaric prejudice. . . . We believe that if anything can be efficacious in helping to destroy this monstrous prejudice, it is a complete and sincere fusion of the Jewish race with the great French family. . . . To try to maintain a line of demarcation between the Jewish community and Christian society is to justify the very bias that we deplore—it is to perpetuate the ancient condition of the Jews."[37]

These sentiments followed a liberal, modern, intellectual line of reasoning, which advocated the abandonment of all practices that tended to separate Jews too manifestly from their neighbors. Terquem, for example, wanted to abolish circumcision—a "questionable operation, bloodthirsty, cruel, dangerous, bearing the stamp of African savagery and contrasting violently with the customs of Western peoples"[38]—or even to shift the Sabbath to Sunday. James would have nothing to do with such innovations, relishing his pleasant role as unofficial chief and official benefactor of the community. That role helped to endow him with a rank unlike that open to anyone else.

One can imagine the euphoria that possessed James throughout the pomp and circumstance that accompanied the inauguration of the hospital. "The ceremony," reported *Univers*

israélite, "was one of the grandest that Judaism has ever celebrated within its midst. . . . The Minister of Public Works, the
Director of the Department of Religion, the Prefect of the Seine,
the Mayor of the eighth *arrondissement*, persons of all ages and
social conditions, wanted to attend the magnificent spectacle
and to offer sincere homage to the sponsor of this beautiful
and forever memorable day. . . . M. de Rothschild and his family . . . were saluted in the garden with brilliant
symphonies. . . . Everyone had taken his place, and a religious
silence reigned over the assembly as in the temple of the Lord
on the highest holidays. Then several little girls . . . presented
Mme la Baronne with a bouquet and compliments, which the
noble lady received with the greatest kindness." Next came
grandiloquent orations expounding on "everything the Jews
owe to this great house that, by its integrity and eminent vir-
tues, has contributed so much to our moral emancipation."[39]
We may assume that, by the end of this three-hour ritual, James
considered himself a Prince and, like a Prince, translated his
goodwill into immense largesse, all the while remaining completely aloof from the crowd.

By the end of the Second Empire the Rothschilds were dis-
tributing more than eighty thousand francs in official donations
to the Jewish community,[40] a sum equal to half the total subsidy
made by the government, to cover its administrative costs: rabbinical salaries, seminary expenses, and the upkeep of synagogues.

But the community found itself confronted with financial
obligations of an entirely different sort, created by the growing
number of needy Jews arriving from Central Europe. In 1842
the Relief Committee, which distributed aid, came under the
direction of Albert Cohen, who had long been in charge of the
Rothschilds' charitable works. Right away the Committee's
budget began to swell, from 51,000 francs to 133,000 in ten
years, thanks mainly to James.[41] When it came to exceptional
expenditure, like that for the construction of the hospital,
amounting to 400,000 francs, the Baron assumed the full bur-
den. Not content merely to pay the bills, he developed a certain
panache and learned the art of flamboyant publicity. Thus,
while he had little contact with Jews on a social level, James

made certain that everyone knew of his concern for all Jews, whatever their origins. On Yom Kippur he would attend services and then invite to "a grand dinner"[42] every Jewish officer in the French army who had appeared at the temple in uniform. Even after fifty years in France, James de Rothschild still identified himself with the Jewish community, which for him remained a vital and compelling entity. How different this was from the psychological evolution of the Jewish bourgeoisie, enlightened, wealthy, and truly assimilated. Ludovic Halévy spoke for this class when, in response to anyone citing the difficulties still endured by Jews in the world, he would reply that he was happy "to have left that hell and to have escaped Judaism."[43]

James, by contrast, liked to believe himself at the apex of the pyramid formed by that part of Jewish society which was forced to live in isolation, subject as always to the agonies of poverty and prejudice. He willingly assumed the responsibilities of such a position, but, once again, in the manner of a Prince secure in his own freedom from servitude. And James could play such a role all the more readily since not only did he do much to support the oppressed Jews, but he also represented a dream come true, the spectacular and unique success that every unfortunate Jew visualized as the ultimate vendication of his own degraded position. Too remote from James to be jealous of him, the Jew saw "in [the Rothschild] name . . . for all of dispersed Israel, a steadfast protector, an unbreakable shield, a column of iron, and a wall of bronze. The long reach of James de Rothschild's arm across seas and deserts often aids our brothers in danger and distress and makes our enemies tremble and recoil. Like Jacob in the Bible, he has struggled against superior beings who wished ill to Israel and has prevailed over them."[44]

Such hyperbole, excessive as it may seem even in the light of James' generosity, did not displease the Baron. It simply matched his style of living, made possible by a fortune that, in terms of the total capitalization of the Rothschild bank, had reached 560 million francs by 1863.

James' wealth had always been perceived by the public as a prodigious phenomenon. It now became the foundation of the modern myth of the financier. "In less than a century," wrote Zola of Gundermann, his imaginary banker who among all such contemporary creations most resembles James, "the monstrous fortune . . . had been born, had welled up and overflowed in that family, from thrift but also from a lucky combination of circumstances. It seemed like the product of predestination, aided by lively intelligence, desperately hard work, as well as by prudent and invincible effort, all continually directed towards the same end. Now whole millions poured into the bottomless depths of one man's ever-increasing wealth. And Gundermann was the true master, the omnipotent king, feared and obeyed in Paris and all over the world."[45]

Throughout his career, James had used his fortune to impress the great of the society in which he moved. At the end of his life, he limited his competitiveness to the members of his family, a rivalry made all the more keen by the similarity of their tastes.

Beginning in the 1850s the Rothschilds conceived a passion for building, whether in London, in Vienna, in town, or in the country. Curiously, they were all infatuated with the same architect, and the great Victorian piles he erected for them seem, in their disproportionate scale, perfectly suited to a family determined, it was said, to astonish one another. The author of these ambitious structures was Joseph Paxton, the gifted gardener turned architect who had become famous as the builder of the Crystal Palace, the gigantic iron-and-glass greenhouse-like pavilion put up for London's Great Exhibition of 1851. The first Rothschild to engage Paxton was Mayer, Nathan's youngest son, who wanted to build a new house and transform the gardens on his estate at Mentmore. So grandiose was this undertaking that it required more than ten years to complete. The entire park—all 865 acres of it—was drained by hand and then worked over with the most modern machinery. Finally, after miles of hedgerows had been uprooted, the terrain was replanted according to a design prepared with extreme care.[46] Meanwhile, Anthony, Mayer's elder brother, asked Paxton to enlarge Aston Clinton House, which he had purchased in 1851, and Adolph, Karl's son, entrusted the English master with the work on his Château de Prégny, near Geneva. James, on seeing the Mentmore plans while on a visit to England, became so enthusiastic that he decided to commission Paxton again, this time for the reconstruction of Ferrières.

Actually, James had been constantly rebuilding Ferrières since 1829, the year he acquired the property from the Fouché heirs. The estate extended over 9,880 acres, all drained by a network of pipes embedded in the earth, a scheme then hardly known in France, but familiar in England, and one that had had the happy result of doubling the revenues produced by Ferrières.[47] New farm buildings, stables, etc., had contributed toward making the place "a model property."[48] Now, however, James wanted more. "Make me a Mentmore, only grander," he instructed Paxton. This "genius," as the family called him, complied, even though complaining of "the Baron's irresolution" and insisting "that the palace—it really will be a palace— will not be finished for seven years."[49] Paxton underestimated himself and succeeded in completing the château in 1859. The plan recalled that of Mentmore, with its square shape defined by four corner towers, its crowning pinnacles (later replaced at Ferrières by cupolas), and its monumental central hall surrounded by a gallery, which served to diminish the sense of height in a disproportionately vast ensemble.

At Ferrières James and Betty affirmed their sense of family in a set of five private apartments and their sense of hospitality in eighteen suites reserved for guests. The château could house a hundred servants, while the stables were large enough to accommodate eighty horses. Betty assumed responsibility for the interior and entrusted its decoration to the fashionable artist Eugène Lami.[50] Eager to get it right, the Baroness and her advisor prepared themselves with a trip to Venice "to visit the sublime patrician houses."[51] There the painter-decorator found inspiration for several projects, most notably the grand staircase, whose ceiling, with its coffering and its central medallion painted in shades of blue, evokes that of the Doge's Palace. Ferrières presented a challenge, since problems would inevitably arise in the attempt to impose a Second Empire style on a Victorian country house derived from an Elizabethan plan. But Lami overcame the problems and succeeded in making Ferrières a triumphant expression of Second Empire taste. Philippe Jullian described it as "the magnificence of a Veronese adapted to a grand hotel."[52] Actually, Lami's achievement lay in combining English comfort with decorative motifs from the Italian sixteenth century or the French seventeenth.

Of course, James could not let the occasion go by without using it to enhance his own glory, as in the obsessive repetition of his initials integrated with the image of Atlas supporting a globe over which hangs the Rothschild coronet. The solemnity of certain rooms—especially the state dining room which, according to Leonora, evoked "the great chapel of the Knights of the Garter at Windsor"—was sometimes to seem overwhelming. Still, a festive spirit—a sense of ease, something almost intimate—reigned at the château. The watercolors that Lami painted at Ferrières show an imposing Louis XIII salon brought to life by an umbrella and a bouquet of flowers left on a small chair. In another corner we see a rocking chair, a thoroughly bourgeois touch, alien and reassuring. Ferrières was no museum, despite its glut of masterpieces.

One thing could not be doubted: James' satisfaction. Visitors, however, expressed a variety of opinions which reflected their attitude towards the master of the house as much as their aesthetic judgment. The Goncourts didn't like it at all. "We're just back from Ferrières. Trees and waterworks created by the squandering of millions, round a château costing eighteen million, an idiotic and ridiculous extravagance, a pudding of every style, the fruit of a stupid ambition to have all monuments in one! Nothing superlative, nothing outstanding on this land where one man's fantasy has sown banknotes . . . ."[53]

Apponyi and his smart titled friends proved more indulgent, appreciating as they did the English comfort and the technical innovations. An entry in his journal notes: "There was dinner and then a carriage ride with M. and Mme de Rothschild. The banker showed off the model wash-house, a masterpiece of elegance, picturesque and convenient. Eighty thousand pieces are laundered there every year, a normal amount for this house. . . . The interior arrangements leave nothing to be desired. Everything is in good taste and quite magnificent. There are fine pictures and an infinity of beautiful things of all sorts—armor, statuettes, goblets in vermeil, ivory, or gold, embellished with pearls and semiprecious stones; chests in bronze, in iron, in silver, in old lacquer; every kind of vase, ornamented with precious stones; old armoires, inlaid with ivory and silver, and mosaic from Florence. The rooms for friends are comfortably furnished, without too much luxury, but with beautiful rugs, large sofas, easy chairs, mirrors, excellent beds, wash stands, and an abundance of towels. . . ."[54]

The whole world wanted to have a look, and Prince Napoleon himself requested, through Prime Minister Nigra of Italy, "the honor of visiting" Ferrières. Tours were organized, one of which prompted a grandniece, Evelina, the sister of Leonora, to make this enthusiastic, if somewhat tongue-in-cheek, report: "I own I was quite astonished and *éblouie*. I had never seen Ferrières in foliage and besides the great Baron is always buying new treasures. We found Aunt Betty in better spirits, the contrary is so distressing that one often dreads paying a visit. . . . We, which means Julia and Natty and I were shown all over the place, estate and gardens and when we came back I pleased Uncle James by telling him that I could find only *one* fault—the place was too royal to be without sentinels. . . ."[55] Clearly, this child had mastered the art of winning the old man's heart. Criticism, however, was not likely to trouble James, since he found Ferrières the perfect instrument of power. Never did it work to greater effect than when Napoleon III came for a visit in December 1862.

The event was generally seen as evidence of a desire for reconciliation on the part of an Emperor anxious over the growing financial difficulties that were clouding his reign. James staged the reception with such pomp and solemnity that he obviously viewed the occasion as a meeting between two great powers. Napoleon III responded by making every effort—of courtesy, tact, and savoir-faire—to eliminate all trace of condescension. He greeted Betty, superb and triumphant in violet velvet, with a *"Je vous remercie de votre bon accueil"* so sincere that the Baroness declared, with satisfaction, that he could not have spoken better had he been addressing the Empress of Austria.[56]

Following a luncheon served in the record time of one hour and twelve minutes, Napoleon planted the traditional cedar and then took part in a great shoot. He and the other gentlemen proceeded to kill more than nine hundred pheasants. "The poor birds," wrote Leonora, "are so tame that they come and meet the cartridges. The prefect of police declared: '*Ce sont les gladiateurs qui viennent saluer César.' "*[57] On their return the guns were saluted by the chorus of the Paris Opéra performing under the direction of Rossini. Finally, the Emperor said goodbye to the entire family. A comment by Prosper Mérimée perfectly summarizes the entire affair: "As the Emperor left for Paris, Rothschild said to him in the accent and the Germanic French that you are familiar with: 'Sire, my chiltren and I vill nefer forget dis day; de memory of it vill remain tear to us,' " characteristically misusing the masculine article with *mémoire*—or perhaps using it deliberately as a joke since *un mémoire* means "bill" or "dun."[58]

Inasmuch as Napoleon III was not Louis XIV, Ferrières did not suffer the fate of Vaux—confiscated by a jealous monarch— and continued to delight James. If Betty, as her daughter-in-law implied, had her head somewhat turned by all the compliments, the Baron kept his composure. He was now sixty-six, and often immobilized by severe rheumatism. "We did not see much of Uncle James. He was suffering from great pain, so one hour he walked in the gardens and the next he went to bed. He was wheeled about in a little chair, ditto Aunt Betty, and they each had three attendants, a pair to carry the bread and chestnuts for their deer, fish and birds."[59] James had to spare his eyes and could read newspapers only with difficulty. Moreover, he suffered from the most frightful *crises de foie*. Still, the great reception at Ferrières, instead of being an apotheosis signaling the host's retirement, gave the Baron a new lease of life. He had had the satisfaction of making the sovereign call on him, as well as the joy of seeing his predictions come true, including the ruin of Péreire. Calmly he returned to his business, to "his dear, pretty little money."

Despite fatigue that obliged him to take cures ever more frequently, James never gave up the direction of his banking house. In a letter typical of this period of his life, he began by complaining of his health: "I'm back from Wildbad, and I leave for Dieppe tomorrow. I don't feel at all well, my dear nephews. . . . I'm going to have to resign myself to old age."[60] Having given vent to his regrets, however, he went on to more serious matters. Once again, he wanted to take a bold step forward and chafed at his nephews' prudence: "I thoroughly disapprove of timidity in business matters and greatly regret that we did not negotiate the Swedish loan. I would have liked to conclude it."[61] It astonished everyone that the old man had not begun to flag. Feydeau wondered what drove him on: tyrannical force of habit or laudable professional ambition? Whatever the cause, James continued to receive all and sundry, to dictate, to work out deals, to figure and calculate forever and ever. The true explanation is probably a simple one, that nothing amused James so much as making money.

Money had, from his childhood, been the obsession of James de Rothschild. Money alone had made it possible for him to find fulfillment and taste the heady fruits of power. Of course, he was not so single-minded that he could not enjoy his splendid residences, pictures, and objects. Several months before his death, the Baron undertook the redecoration of his salons in the Rue Laffitte so as to install the great Gobelins tapestries that until then had ornamented the walls of Ferrières. Such work interested and distracted him, but it could never replace his principal activity, which was banking. To ask James de Rothschild to give up making money would have been as absurd as suggesting to a painter that he throw away his brushes, to an author that he give up writing, to a mathematician that he stop thinking about equations. James was fully conscious of the fact that he could produce profits better than anyone alive, and nothing gave him greater pleasure than proving this to himself and to others, day after day. His attitude is beautifully illustrated in his short management of Château Lafite.

The reader may remember that thirty-eight years earlier James had dreamed of acquiring the estate of Lafite. At that time, however, the proprietors had been unwilling to sell. Finally, in 1868, they decided to divest themselves of the château and its vineyards. Thus James succeeded, at last, in procuring his beloved Premier des Premiers Grands Crus, for the very considerable sum of 4,140,000 francs.[62] He then began immediately to speculate in his wine! Nathaniel wrote to his brothers in London: "I sold my wine the other day at Mouton at a famous high price of 5,000 the tonneau. The quality must be extraordinarily good this year as the merchants are buying it all up. Our worthy Uncle has not yet disposed of his Laffitte [*sic*]. He expects a further rise."[63]

James died twenty-seven days later, succumbing to an attack of jaundice. "With my father in his present state, it is not possible to talk business with him, and we avoid anything that might upset him,"[64] wrote Alphonse to his cousins by way of explaining the paralysis that settled over the Rue Laffitte during the Baron's short illness. A worn-out body could not long support James, and the old fighter breathed his last in the early hours of Sunday, November 15, 1868.

Epilogue

The doors had to be opened at ten in the morning, since the crowd pressing into the Rue Laffitte could not be held back. In the salons Alphonse, his brothers, and the cousins received condolences from four thousand people, arriving in a steady stream. Another two thousand mourners, less energetic, could not gain entry to the Rothschild mansion and jammed the street. "I never saw such an assembly of people," declared a great-nephew.[1] Within this multitude, however, he could distinguish the Duc de Cambacérès, the Emperor's representative, seen in a brief exchange with Prince Metternich, accompanied by all the secretaries and attachés of the Austrian Embassy. Also caught in the crush were ministers, ambassadors, and generals. Meanwhile, official delegations came from the Banque de France, the Chamber of Commerce, the Bourse, and, most of all, the Jewish corporations of France. Even the Chief Rabbi of Belgium, M. Astruc, made an appearance.

Finally at noon the hearse, simple and totally unadorned, as Jewish tradition would have it, began moving forward, pulled by a pair of horses. The family had declined military honors, to which James, as a recipient of the Great Cross of the Legion of Honor, would have been entitled. The corre-

213

spondent for *The Times* of London reported that he could not remember having ever seen so many people crowding the pavements and spilling on to the street, all the way from the Rue Laffitte to the Porte Saint-Denis. The police had to draw on every ounce of their energy to clear a path for the convoy. Parisians loved funeral processions, and James' aroused more than the usual curiosity.

The crowd was calm, almost respectful. That morning the newspapers had filled their front pages with long articles on James, recalling the circumstances of his rise in the world and noting his integrity, his importance in the political life of his time, and, most of all, his inexhaustible and intelligent generosity. The tone throughout was laudatory, whatever the paper's political orientation, showing that the animosity of the 1840s had disappeared. James had ceased to be contested; he had been accepted. Even more, he was missed. Fully conscious of the astonishing adventure that had taken James de Rothschild from the anonymity of Frankfurt's Jew Street to the pinnacle of fame, Parisians jostled one another to witness the long cortège composed, first, of the Baron's three personal valets, then the men of the family, employees of the bank and the Compagnie du Nord, and finally the representatives of the two Consistories, central and local, the Jewish seminary and schools, the temple, and the Jewish hospital, old-age home, and orphanage. On its arrival at Père-Lachaise Cemetery, the procession turned towards the Jewish section. At the graveside, Albert Cohen, President of the Benevolent Society, the three Chief Rabbis, and M. Delebecque, vice-president of the Compagnie du Nord, delivered eulogies. But there was no "official" address, and no government representative attended. James was buried, as his father had been, in the bosom of his synagogue, his firm, and his family. He had traveled a long way, but always under the banner of fidelity to his forebears.

I am the great-great-granddaughter of James de Rothschild. My mother is the eldest daughter of Gustave's only son. We find her in the old family photograph reproduced on pages 140–141, the tiny baby perched on the back of the couch where Gustave and Cécile sit enthroned, surrounded by all their progeny: the slightly tense young couples, mischievous granddaughters dressed in organdy, and clean-shaven youths, elegant and rakish. Cécile, the reigning Baroness, stout, severe, swathed in heavy velvet, seems the very incarnation of those sated dowagers of the Belle Époque. Gustave, still handsome with his regular features and short, well-groomed beard, sits erect, his clenched hands resting on his knees, avoiding any show of affection for the pretty little girls seated at his feet. He is posing. The scene is Paris, some years before the Great War. No caption is needed. The picture alone suffices.

My father was born in the Warsaw ghetto, the child of a pious rabbinical family. "Every moment that I do not spend studying the Torah is a moment stolen from God," was a phrase my grandfather often repeated to his son. With his long beard, his black caftan, and his faraway look, he is, in the only photograph I have seen of him, impossible to place in time or space. Doubtless he existed at the antipodes of the Rue Laffitte. My father crossed that distance with rapidity and ease. At the time of his marriage to my mother, he had become something unique for a Jew of his country, an Ambassador representing the young Polish republic.

We never ask our parents enough questions while they are alive. My father died some twenty-five years ago, and I never cease to wonder at the extraordinary nature of his life, the contradiction between the world of his childhood and that of his adult career, and the metamorphosis that he chose to undergo and that ended with his happy adaptation to a new existence. It is even more difficult to grasp the much greater anomalies presented by my maternal ancestor, James de Rothschild. Coming from equally obscure origins, the Baron not only found his place in French society but also left his mark on it, actively participating in its economic and political life, all the while refusing, unlike my father, to become assimilated. The conditions that he found and created in Paris had nothing in common with those of the Frankfurt in which he grew up; yet his values could hardly have remained more constant: the abiding obsession with his work, his proud love of family, and the commitment to his religious community.

The Baron's priorities have withstood the erosion of time. When I wrote these words the bank in the Rue Laffitte was still absorbing the sons of the fifth generation. Ironically, nationalization has since made the Banque Rothschild a true state bank. Other traditions have fared better. Such is the present size of the family that a number is assigned to each member, signifying his generation and his place within the generation, as well as the number of his father's generation, in order to locate that particular Rothschild on the comprehensive family tree. Even so, a vigorous *esprit de corps* unites the entire clan. The current head of the French branch has married twice, each time to a second cousin, thereby honoring the tradition of intrafamily alliances that began when James married his niece Betty in 1824. If the vast and anachronistic residences have had to be abandoned, the collections remain intact. Naturally, one keeps one's Rembrandts and Fragonards, if at all possible, but I confess to being touched even more by certain personal and intimate memorabilia: a set of curtains from the Rue Laffitte now hanging at the windows of a great-grandson; a tooth glass and a shaving bowl, decorated with the interlaced initials "JR" and still in use; and the bed in which James died, preserved in a small room at Château Lafite.

Finally, the Rothschilds have never ceased to accept responsibility for leadership within the Jewish community. Despite the changes that have occurred in this society, James' descendants have continued to serve in the presidency of the Consistory and on the committees that direct its activities. When Alain de Rothschild, who had been particularly devoted to the organization of the rapidly growing world of French Judaism, died in 1982, the shopkeepers of the poorest Jewish district in Paris closed for an hour in a sign of mourning. But the contemporary Rothschilds make no attempt to emulate their ancestor's astonishing concentration on business. The Rothschild personality has burst those bonds. Intellectuals or dilettantes, writers or sportsmen, Zionists or atheists, they all relish the pleasures of relaxation, a word that the Great Baron did not even know.

The archives of the Continental branches of the House of Rothschild have suffered considerable abuse over the years. Those in Vienna and Frankfurt were all but totally destroyed during the Second World War. In France, they could be recovered only in part, and, unfortunately for my purposes, that part excluded most of the personal letters. The banking papers, meanwhile, went to the Archives Nationales, and I cite them as RAP (Rothschild Archives Paris). London, by contrast, has preserved its correspondence intact, which makes the English archives a rich and varied source, mixing commercial papers with the most intimate letters. I have cited them as RAL (Rothschild Archives London). At present, however, that resource cannot be fully exploited until the letters of the five original brothers have been translated from Yiddish (or even decoded), a task that has been accomplished only for a fraction of the available material. The material is there, however—great piles of letters awaiting the interest of future linguists and historians.

Among the twenty published works devoted to the Rothschilds, I must single out that of Egon Corti (*The Rise and Reign of the House of Rothschild*), which appeared in 1929–30 and constitutes the sole access that we have to documents now destroyed. Scarcely less valuable is the book by Bertrand Gille (*Histoire de la maison Rothschild*, 1965), whose search of the archives in Paris was exhaustive.

Rich as a Rothschild? An Introduction

1. The rate adopted by the INSEE (Institut National de Statistiques et d'Études Économiques) and published in the *Annuaire statistique de la France* for 1979. 2. Jean Fourastié has estimated that in the course of the nineteenth century the French national per capita income rose from 290 francs to 1,530. See *Machinisme et bien-être*

(Paris, 1962). 3. The "real" price for any one year is the current price divided by the lowest hourly wage paid for manual labor in that year. The formula makes it possible to calculate all prices for a given year in relation to the same base. It also provides a constant basis on which to consider the evolution of prices from year to year. For example, if we can assume that a train ticket cost $10 in 1970 and the lowest hourly wage for that year was $5, then the real price becomes 2, or 10 divided by 5. If in 1980 the same train ticket cost $15, while the hourly wage remained $5, the real price can be seen to have gone up, since 15/5 = 3. 4. Victor Hugo, *Choses vues* (Paris, 1972), Vol. II, 254. 5. *Annuaire statistique de la France*, 1979. The reader should not confuse the current price used for this calculation with the real price cited above. The first is an actual amount, while the second is derived from the price-wage equation. 6. These figures, rounded off for the sake of clarity, have been drawn from Adeline Daumard, *La Bourgeoisie parisienne de 1815 à 1848* (Paris, 1963). 7. During the period in question, the dollar was worth around 5 francs. 8. Moses Yale Beach, *The Wealth and Biography of the Wealthy of the City of New York* (New York, 1855). 9. Gustavus Myers, *History of the Great American Fortunes* (New York, 1939), Vol. I, 194.

1 Jew Street

1. The title borne by the son of Napoleon I and Empress Marie-Louise from 1811 until 1814, after which he was styled the Prince of Parma (1814–18) and finally the Duke of Reichstadt (1818–32). 2. François-Nicholas, Comte Mollien (1758–1850), was one of Napoleon's key advisors, serving as Finance Minister from 1806 until 1814 and during the Hundred Days. Thereafter he declined all invitations to reenter public life. 3. Mollien

to Napoleon, March 26, 1811. Archives Nationales, Paris, AF IV 1089a. **4.** In a genealogical tree reconstructed by Lord Rothschild. **5.** B. R. Mitchell, *European Historical Statistics: 1750–1970* (New York, 1975). **6.** Wilhelm IX of Hesse (1743–1821), who succeeded his father in 1785, was elevated to the rank of Elector in 1803. **7.** To avoid confusion among all the Mayers, Kalmanns, Gutles, Gutelches, Jentles, and Jitles, the Europeanized variants of the original Jewish names have been used throughout this study. Thus Gutle Schnapper becomes Gudule, just as Schönche, Belche, Salman, Breinliche, Kalmann, and Jacob appear as Jeannette, Isabella, Salomon, Babette, Karl, and James, reflecting the changes that occurred gradually with the passage of time and the growth of the Rothschild millions. **8.** Many of these Hessians fought for the British in the American Revolution and then settled in the United States after the war. **9.** Egon Corti, *The Rise and Reign of the House of Rothschild* (New York, 1928–30), Vol. I, 22–23. **10.** The Schiff family, who shared the house with the Rothschilds, would also achieve fame, after a son, Jacob, emigrated to the United States in 1865 and became a railway tycoon. **11.** Cited by Isaiah Berlin, *Personal Impressions* (New York, 1981), 147. **12.** Henriette, as a consequence of several infatuations with men her brothers called "crooks," was packed off to England and there married to Abraham Montefiore, Nathan's brother-in-law. This alliance, which placed Henriette at the center of London's most distinguished Jewish families, so went to the young woman's head that by sheer insolence she became a trial to her brothers and sisters. Of all Mayer Amschel's daughters, however, she alone reattached herself to the family by marrying her daughter to a Rothschild nephew. **13.** Gudule to Karl, July 29, 1804. RAL T 27. **14.** Gudule to her sons, *passim.* RAL T 27. **15.** Mayer Amschel to Nathan, undated except by reference to Jacob's bar mitzvah. RAL T 27. **16.** Cecil Roth, *Histoire du peuple juif* (Paris, 1980), *passim.* **17.** Cited by Fernand Braudel, *Civilisation matérielle, économie et capitalisme: XVe-XVIIIe siècle* (Paris, 1980), Vol. II, 336. **18.** Mayer Amschel to Nathan, 1805. RAL T 27. **19.** Mayer Amschel to James, 1808. RAL T 27. **20.** Charles-Theodore, Baron von Dalberg (1744–1817), was the last Elector of Mainz. A firm advocate of the unification of Germany, Dalberg placed himself at the disposal of Napoleon I, for which the Congress of Vienna stripped him of all official power. **21.** Heinrich Graetz, *History of the Jews* (Philadelphia, 1941), Vol. V, 504. **22.** Karl to James, June 18, 1814. RAL T 29(1)a. **23.** The Jewish religion imposes very strict dietary laws, which require that the faithful abstain from eating pork and from meat and dairy products mixed at the same meal. Moreover, animals must be slaughtered in accordance with a specific rite. **24.** James to Salomon, Nov. 3, 1814. RAL T 29(2). **25.** Mayer Amschel to James, Dec. 13, 1808. RAL T 27. **26.** *The Foundation of the English Rothschilds: N. M. Rothschild as a Textile Merchant* (London, n.d.), 15, 17–18. **27.** Police report made on March 3, 1812, and cited by Jean Bouvier, *Les Rothschild* (Paris, 1967), 43.

2 A New World

1. Salomon to his brothers, July 14, 1814. RAL T 29(1)a. **2.** Béatrice Philippe, *Être Juif dans la société française* (Paris, 1979), 15. **3.** *Ibid.*, 112–118. **4.** *Ibid.* **5.** RAP: personal account books. **6.** Salomon to Nathan, Feb. 28, 1815. RAL T 30. **7.** Salomon to Nathan, n.d. RAL 109/10. **8.** Salomon to Nathan, Aug. 1814. RAL T 29(1)b. **9.** In the period 1815–18 the total capital of the firm increased from 3,332,000 to 42,528,000 francs. Bertrand Gille, *Histoire de la maison Rothschild* (Geneva, 1965), Vol. I, 458. **10.** Davidson to Nathan, June 24, 1814. Cited in Lord Rothschild, *The Shadow of a Great Man* (London, 1982), 6. **11.** Salomon to Nathan, June 24, 1814. RAL T 29(1)a. **12.** James to Nathan, May 19, 1817. RAL T 27. **13.** James to Nathan, March 25, 1813. RAL T 29(2). **14.** James to Nathan, Jan. 24, 1817. RAL T 27. **15.** James to Salomon, March 1, 1817. RAL T 27. **16.** James to Nathan, March 3, 1817. RAL T 27. **17.** For the whole of this development I am indebted to Romuald Szramkiewicz, *Les Régents et censeurs de la Banque de France nommés sous le Consulat et l'Empire* (Geneva, 1974).

3 Old France and Young Barons

1. Honoré de Balzac, *Le Cabinet aux antiques* (Paris, 1972), 460. **2.** Hugo, cited by Jean-Louis Bory, *La Monarchie de Juillet* (Paris, 1972), 74. **3.** Richelieu to Osmond, July 13, 1818. Cited by Gille, *op cit.*, 71. **4.** James to Hannah, his sister-in-law in London, Oct. 2, 1815. In a touch of cosmopolitan gallantry, James opened his letter in English: "My dear and good sister." He then went on in Yiddish. RAL 109/2/3. **5.** Robert, Earl of Liverpool (1770–1828), served as Prime Minister of England from 1812 to 1827. **6.** James to Nathan, March 11, 1818. RAL 109/8. **7.** Arthur Wellesley, first Duke of Wellington (1769–1852)—Governor of Mysore. Member of Parliament and Irish Secretary, author and commander of the British expedition against the French on the Iberian Peninsula (1808–13), Ambassador to France during the First Restoration, British delegate to the Congress of Vienna, commander of the allied forces against Napoleon at Waterloo, and commander of the occupation army in France—opposed the dismemberment of the French nation. **8.** James to Nathan, March 8, 1818. RAL 109/8. **9.** James to Nathan, March 11, 1817. RAL 109/6. **10.** Amschel to James, Jan. 16, 1816. RAL T 34. **10a.** *Ibid.* **11.** James to Nathan, Oct. 6, 1817. RAL 133/2. Leopold of Saxe-Coburg-Saalfeld (1790–1865), the future King Leopold I of the Belgians, was at the time of James' letter married to Princess Charlotte, the daughter of George IV and heiress presumptive to the throne of England. Leopold had long been a client of the Rothschilds. **12.** Élie, Duc Decazes (1780–1860), lawyer and advisor to Louis Bonaparte, rallied to the Bourbon cause in 1814. Made Prefect, he replaced Fouché as head of the French state police. From 1818 to 1820. Decazes served as Premier of France. **13.** Metternich, *Mémoires* (Paris, 1880–84), Vol. IV, 15. **14.** It should be remembered that the net worth of the House of Rothschild grew from 3,332,000 francs in 1815 to 42,528,000 francs in 1818. Such an increase cannot be explained from the available documentation, according to Bertrand Gille, the firm's financial historian. *Op. cit.*, 449. **15.** Cited by Corti, *op. cit.*, 205. **16.** *Ibid.*, 183. **17.** Amschel to Salomon, June 23, 1817. RAL 109/8. **17a.** *Ibid.* **18.** James to Nathan, March 1, 1817. RAL 109/6. **19.** Gille, *op. cit.*, 61. **20.** Cited by Bouvier, *op. cit.*, 70. **21.** Comte de Castellane, *Journal* (Paris, 1896), Vol. II, 200. **22.** Victor Boniface, Comte de Castellane (1788–1862), fought in the Napoleonic wars, rallied behind the Bourbons, and ultimately became a supporter of Napoleon III, who made him a Senator and a Marshal of France. **23.** Castellane, *op. cit.*, 201. **24.** Goncourts, *Journal* (Paris, 1887), Jan. 17, 1863. **25.** George Sand, *Mémoires de ma vie* (Paris, 1854–55), Vol. III, 7. **26.** Metternich, *op. cit.*, Vol. III, 6. **27.** *Ibid.*, Vol. VI, 94. **28.** Corti, *op. cit.*, Vol. II, 56. **29.** James to David Parish, Aug. 18, 1819. State Archives, Vienna. *Ibid.*, I, 212. **30.** Amschel to James, Jan. 30, 1817. RAL 109/6. **31.** Corti, *op. cit.*, Vol. II, 292. **32.** Salomon to Nathan, c. 1818. RAL 109/10. **32a.** *Ibid.* **33.** Auguste de Frenilly, *Souvenirs* (Paris, 1908), 232. **34.** Charles Bocher, *Mémoires: 1760–1848* (Paris, n.d.), Vol. I, 134. **35.** Corti, *op. cit.*, Vol. I, 280. **36.** *Ibid.*, 361. **36a.** *Ibid.* **37.** Fritz Stern, *Gold and Iron* (New York, 1977), 115. **38.** Alphonse to his cousins, June 1867. RAL T 10. **39.** Corti, *op. cit.*, Vol. I, 360. **40.** This legend was inculcated in the children and grandchildren. As an illustration for her memoirs, entitled *Reminiscences*, Constance Battersea, Nathan's granddaughter, chose an engraving that showed Mayer Amschel solemnly returning to Wilhelm of Hesse all the assets the Prince had left in Rothschild's safekeeping.

4 A Wife, a Chef, and Millions

1. Jules Michelet, *Journal* (Paris, 1959), Vol. I, 458. **2.** Castellane, *op. cit.*, 200. **3.** Heinrich Heine (1797–1856) was born into a Jewish Family of Dusseldorf, but converted to Christianity "in order to gain an admission ticket to European civilization." In 1831 he moved to Paris. Superb poet and mordant, witty observor, Heine left an indelible portrait of Parisian mores in *Französische Zustände* and *Lutezia* (*Lutèce* in French), the first a collection of newspaper articles written in Paris for publication in Germany and the second a volume of political essays. **4.** Heinrich Heine, *Religion et philosophie* (Paris, 1837), 2. **5.** Amschel to Nathan, Jan. 15, 1816. RAL T 34. **6.** Salomon to Nathan, Oct. 23, 1817. RAL 109/8. **7.** Amschel to Nathan and Salomon, April 20, 1818. RAL 109/9. **8.** Bocher, *op. cit.*, 34. **9.** Amschel to James, June 17, 1814. RAL T 29(1)a. **10.** Karl to Amschel and James, Nov. 9, 1816. RAL 109/53. **11.** Karl to Salomon, April 20, 1818. RAL 109/9. **12.** Amschel to Salomon and Nathan, April 20, 1818. RAL 109/9. **13.** Karl to Salomon, April 20, 1818. RAL T 17. **14.** A prolific mother, Adelaide Herz made a good wife and an elegant hostess. However, she became a bit of a problem towards the end of her life when, somewhat dotty, she thought herself a teapot, and "Teapot" is the name by which she continues to be known in the oral history of the Rothschild family. **15.** Contract dated July 10, 1824. RAP. **16.** Here one is reminded of a witticism made, at a much later date, by Boni de Castellane when, upon entering the home of Maurice de Rothschild, one of James' grandsons, he exclaimed: "*Cher Baron! Vous! Chez vous!*" **17.** Betty to Charlotte, Sept. 26, 1821 RAL 109/10. **18.** Charles-François, Comte de Rémusat (1797–1875), was a French philosopher and liberal politician who served as Interior Minister in 1840, supported the Republic, went into exile after Louis-Napoleon's coup d'état in 1851, but obtained amnesty in 1859. Later in life he devoted himself to literature and published his memoirs. **19.** Delphine de Girardin, *Lettres parisiennes* (Paris, 1861), 283. **20.** Stendhal, *Lucien Leuwen* (Paris, 1901), 46. **21.** *Ibid.*, 58. **22.** Mme de Beauséant, one of Balzac's unforget-

table creations, was an elegant lady of nineteenth-century Paris whose role in *La Comédie humaine* was to guide her country cousin, Eugène de Rastignac, through the intricacies of society and thus speed him on his way to a successful career. **23.** Lady Morgan, *La France en 1829 et 1830* (Paris, 1830), Vol. II, 20. **24.** Jean-François Revel, *Un Festin en paroles* (Paris, 1979), 229. **25.** *Ibid.*, 284. **26.** Morgan, *op. cit.*, 20. **27.** Goncourts, *op. cit.*, July 1858. **28.** Vicomte de Launay, cited by Louis Coperchot, "La Société sous Louis-Philippe," *Revue de Paris*, July 1927. **29.** Castellane, *op. cit.*, 320. **29a.** *Ibid.* **30.** Daumard, *op. cit.*, 391. **31.** Nathan to his brothers, Jan. 2, 1816. RAL 109/4. **32.** Heine, *Lutèce* (Paris, 1855), 33. **33.** Corti, *op. cit.*, Vol. II, 39. **34.** *Ibid.*, 152. The donation was around 2,500 francs. **35.** Jean-Baptiste, Comte de Villèle (1773–1854), was a naval officer who spent the Revolution on the islands of Maurice and Réunion. Upon his return to France he became a powerful advocate of the Bourbon restoration, a position that induced him to retire from political life in 1830. **36.** Bouvier, *op. cit.*, 86. **37.** *Ibid.*, 87. **38.** Balzac, *La Maison Nucingen* (Paris, 1838), 15. **39.** John Reeves, *The Rothschilds: The Financial Rulers of Nations* (New York, 1975), 192. **40.** Gille, *op. cit.*, 186. **41.** *Ibid.* **42.** Heine, *Lutèce, op. cit.*, 22. **43.** Comtesse de Boigne, *Mémoires* (Paris, 1907), Vol. III, 312.

5 The Revolution of 1830

1. Karl to Salomon, May 20, 1817. RAL 109/8. **2.** Karl to Salomon, Nov. 11, 1817. RAL 109/8. **3.** Constance Battersea, *Reminiscences* (London, 1923), 9. **4.** Salomon to Metternich, June 19, 1830. Austrian State Archives, Vienna. Cited by Corti, *op. cit.*, Vol. I, 387. **5.** See Louis Bergeron, *Les Capitalistes en France* (Paris, 1978), 166–167. **6.** Hugo, *Les Misérables* (Paris, 1862), Vol. IV, 1, 5. **7.** Louis-Philippe, *Mémoires* (Paris, 1973). **8.** René de Chateaubriand, *Mélanges historiques* (Paris, 183), Vol. II, 10. **9.** Eugène-François d'Arnauld, Baron de Vitrolles (1774–1854), emigrated during the Revolution, returned to France under the Consulate, and thereafter served as a chief spokesman for the ultra-rightists. **10.** Salomon to his bank manager, Wertheimstein, in Vienna, July 31, 1831. Cited by Gille, *op. cit.*, 204. **11.** *Moniteur universel*, Aug. 3, 1830. **12.** Charlotte, Nathan's daughter and the wife of Anselm, Salomon's son, to her mother Hannah, Sept. 24, 1830. RAL, 109/15. **13.** James to Salomon, Nov. 29, 1830. Cited by Gille, *op. cit.*, 208. **14.** James to Salomon, Nov. 27, 1830. *Ibid.* **15.** Corti, *op. cit.*, Vol. I, 396. **16.** Alexis de Tocqueville, *Souvenirs* (Paris, 1964), 32. **17.** Boigne, *op. cit.*, 211. **18.** Tocqueville, *op. cit.*, 31. **19.** Louis-Philippe claimed to have more of Louis XIV's blood in his veins than Louis XVIII and Charles X. In this he was not wrong, but the blood happened to be somewhat tainted by bastardy. Although legitimately descended from Louis XIII, Louis-Philippe was related to Louis XIV only through the Sun King's illegitimate children. And this was true twice over, since the new monarch's father, Philippe Égalité, had been the grandson of Anselm, iselle de Blois, a daughter of Louis XIV and La Vallière, and his mother a great granddaughter of the Comte de Toulouse, one of the sons born of the long liaison with La Montespan. **20.** Tocqueville, *op. cit.*, 32. **21.** *Ibid.* **22.** Corti, *op. cit.*, Vol. I, 396. **23.** Salomon to Gentz, Sept. 9, 1830. Cited by Corti, *op. cit.*, Vol. I, 398.

24. Memorandum circulated by James to his brothers, March 9, 1831. Cited by Gille, *op. cit.*, 211. **25.** Rudolph Apponyi, *Vingt-cinq ans à Paris* (Paris, 1913). **26.** Heine, *De la France*, Dec. 1831. **27.** Speech made by Casimir Périer before the Chamber of Deputies. **28.** Sand, *op. cit.*, Vol. IV, 14. **29.** *Ibid.* **30.** *Ibid.*, Vol. V, 2. **31.** *Archives israélites*, 1842.

6 A Public Figure

1. Charles-Robert Vasilievitch, Count Nesselrode, *Papiers*, Dec. 1840. **2.** Michelet, *op. cit.*, 458. **3.** Nesselrode, *op. cit.* **4.** James to Richtenberger, Feb. 2, 1839. **5.** James to Amschel and Salomon, Dec. 21, 1839. RAL T 27. **6.** Cited by Gille, *op. cit.*, 214. **7.** Salomon to Richtenberger, Feb. 2, 1839. **8.** Gille, *op. cit.*, 222. **9.** *Ibid.*, 234. **10.** *Ibid.*, 246. **11.** *Ibid.*, 491. **12.** Alfred de Vigny, *Daphné*, July 20, 1837. Cited by Léon Poliakov, *Histoire de l'antisémitisme* (Paris, 1968), Vol. III, 374. **13.** Alexandre Weil, "De l'état des Juifs en Europe," *La Revue indépendante*, 1844. **14.** Heine, *Lutèce*, *op. cit.*, 8. **15.** Corti, *op. cit.*, Vol. II, 164. **16.** *Niles Weekly Register, 1835-36.* Cited by R. Glanz, "The Rothschild Legend in America," *Jewish Social Studies*, XIX (1957), 20. **17.** *Ibid.*, 1829-30. **18.** *Archives israélites*, March 1844. **19.** Ernest Feydeau, *Mémoires d'un coulissier* (Paris, 1873), 217. **20.** Heine, *Lutèce*, *op. cit.*, 22. **21.** Mayer to his brothers, June 17, 1839. RAL T 7. **22.** Albeit an English Rothschild, Nathaniel, Nathan's third son, spent more time in Paris than in London after 1830. Very close to his uncle, whom he loved and admired, and whose only daughter, Charlotte, he married in 1842, Nathaniel drew a vivid and affectionate portrait of James in the course of a long correspondence with his brothers on the other side of the Channel. **23.** Nathaniel to his mother and brothers, 1846. RAL T 7. **24.** F. A. Seillière to his father. Cited by Gille, *op. cit.*, 394. **25.** James to his nephews, June 17, 1839. RAL 101/2. **26.** Bouvier, *op. cit.*, 135. **27.** *Ibid.*, 137. **28.** Tocqueville, *op. cit.*, 44. **29.** James to his brothers and nephews, Feb. 2, 1839. RAL T 35. **30.** Prince de Joinville, *Vieux souvenirs* (Paris, 1894), 87. **31.** Heine, *Lutèce*, *op. cit.*, 56. **32.** Balzac, *Lettres à l'etrangère*, Oct. 2 and 5, 1846. **33.** Letter dated May 28, 1845. Cited by Bouvier, *op. cit.*, 126. **34.** James to Apponyi. Cited by Corti, *op. cit.*, Vol. II, 227. **35.** Alphonse to his cousins, 1846. RAL T 7.

7 Pariah King

1. Cited by Gille, *op. cit.*, 303. **1a.** *Ibid.* **2.** *Ibid.*, 304. **3.** Nathaniel to Anthony, June 4 and 12, 1840. RAL 109/40. **4.** *Le Constitutionnel*, Oct. 12, 1840. **5.** *Ibid.*, Oct. 13, 1840. **6.** S. Posener, *Adolphe Crémieux* (Paris, 1934), 217. **7.** *Ibid.*, 212. **8.** Heine, *Lutèce*, *op. cit.*, 8. **9.** Cambridge required that the oath be taken, but only at the time of final exams rather than at registration. The system permitted young Jews to attend lectures and thus improve their minds, albeit without the hope of receiving a degree. Not until 1871 would the exclusionary rule be suppressed. **10.** Conversion always provoked the severest criticism within Jewish circles,

which considered the act an expression of rank cowardice. Around 1860 it was estimated that the number of converts did not exceed five hundred. See Patrick Girard, *Les Juifs en France de 1789 à 1860* (Paris, 1976), 159. **11.** P. Lévy, *Les Noms des israélites en France* (Paris, 1960). **12.** Girard, *op. cit.*, 89. **13.** Bernard Lazare, cited by Michael R. Marrus, *Les Juifs de France à l'époque de l'affaire Dreyfus* (Paris, 1972), 199. **14.** Salomon Reinach, *L'Émancipation intérieure du judaïsme français*. Cited by Marrus, *ibid.*, 33. **15.** Girard, *op. cit.*, 92. **16.** Samuel, the great prophet and judge of ancient Israel, gave the Jewish nation its monarchy and placed Saul on the throne. **17.** Response made by Thiers to Fould, June 2, 1840. **18.** Heine, *Lutèce*, *op. cit.*, 8. **18a.** *Ibid.* **19.** James to Nathaniel, July 16, 1839. RAL T 35. **20.** Isaac Goldsmid competed with the Rothschilds both professionally and socially. When granted the title of baronet in 1841, he was the first English Jew to be ennobled. Lionel, annoyed that he had not been the first Jew to enter the English peerage, refused a baronetcy when it was offered in 1846. See Lord Rothschild, *You Have It, Madam* (London, 1980), 4-5. **21.** A legendary figure in English Judaism, Sir Moses Montefiore (1784-1885) was born in Italy but made his fortune in Great Britain trading on the London Stock Exchange. In 1824 he retired to devote the rest of his life to philanthropy and to the defense of Jews everywhere in the world. Sir Moses lived to the noble age of 101. **22.** Salomon Munk (1803-67) was a brilliant philologist who left Berlin when it appeared that he could never hope to receive an appointment there. Helped by James, he moved to Paris, where he became librarian at the Bibliothèque Nationale. Eventually Munk succeeded Renan as Professor of Hebrew at the Collège de France. **23.** *Le Figaro*, Dec. 6, 1857. **24.** Chateaubriand, *Mémoires d'outre-tombe* (Paris, 1849), Sept. 17, 1833. **25.** Olry Terquem, *Huitième lettre d'un Israélite français à ses coreligionnaires sur la religion des riches au XIXe siècle, sous la forme d'un dialogue entre un riche et un pauvre* (Paris, 1836). **26.** *Univers israélite*, April 1845. **27.** By, respectively, Heinrich Heine and Ludwig Börne. **28.** Ludwig Börne, *Lettres de Paris*, (1832). Born in the Frankfurt ghetto, Börne converted to Christianity for the sake of his career in journalism. By 1830 his socialist ideas made it expedient for him to seek refuge in France. **29.** *Ibid.* **30.** Heine, *Pensées et souvenirs.* Cited by Corti, *op. cit.*, Vol. II, 201. **31.** Eugène de Mirecourt, *Rothschild* (Paris, 1855). **32.** Börne, *op. cit.* **33.** Étienne Cabet, *Le Populaire de 1841* (Paris, 1846). **34.** Obituary notice, *Archives israélites*, Nov. 1868. **35.** *Le National*, Aug. 1846. **36.** It is of course difficult to generalize about the reactions of a community as diverse as that formed by the Jews of France. I have decided to base my view of the situation upon the *Archives israélites*, since that review represented the opinion of pious Jews, devoted to their religion, secure in their identity, but reformist and convinced of the need for political and social assimilation, thus eager to participate in French political life. In brief, *Archives israélites* stood for those Jews most sensitive to the consequences of an anti-Semitic movement. *Univers israélite*, the other, relatively conservative review, was more concerned with problems of religious reform and ventured less into the thicket of contemporary politics. **37.** *Archives israélites*, 1868. **38.** Alphonse Toussenel, *Les Juifs, rois de l'époque: histoire de la féodalité financière* (Paris, 1845). See introduction. **39.** *Ibid.* **40.** Pierre Leroux, *Revue sociale* (1846). Cited by Poliakov, *op. cit.*, 385. **41.** Georges-Marie Mathieu-

Dairnvaell, *Histoire édifiante et curieuse de Rotschild Ier, roi des juifs* (Paris, 1846). **42.** *Archives israélites*, 1840. **43.** The creation of the dramatist Caron de Beaumarchais (*Le Barbier de Séville*, 1775; *Le Mariage de Figaro*, 1784), Figaro represents a type well known under the *ancien régime*—a scheming, high-spirited underling whose cleverness and enterprise enable him to prevail over the aristocracy that would deprive him of the love and life to which his superior qualities entitle him. Many have regarded the character as a true harbinger of the French Revolution. **44.** *Le Globe*, 1846. **45.** *Réponse de Rotschild Ier, à Satan, roi des imposteurs* (Paris, 1846); *Nouvelle réponse du prince des Israélites, Rothschild Ier, à un pamphlétaire* (Paris, 1846); *Première réponse officielle de M. le Baron James de Rothschild* (Brussels, 1846); *Que nous veut-on avec ce Rothschild Ier? par un banquier* (Paris, 1846). **46.** Heine, *Lutèce, op. cit.* 33. **47.** *Ibid.* **48.** *Ibid.*, 31.

8 The Great Mogul

1. Lionel to Anthony and Nathaniel, June 15, 1836. RAL F FAM C/4/114. Cited by Lord Rothschild, *The Shadow of a Great Man* (London, 1982), 49. **1a.** *Ibid.* **1b.** *The Times* of London, Aug. 4, 1836. **2.** Corti, *op. cit.*, Vol. II, 292, Shrewder than he appeared to be, Amschel distrusted his elegant nephews and stipulated in his will that the bequests he made to them must be canceled in the event the young men should forsake Judaism. See *Archives israélites*, 1855. **3.** Anselm to Anthony, May 13, 1840. RAL T 24. **4.** James to his English nephews, June 15, 1839. RAL 101/2. **5.** James to Nathaniel, Nov. 6, 1839. RAL T 7. **6.** James to his nephews, Nov. 6, 1839. RAL T 7. **7.** James to Anselm, Jan. 10, 1839. RAL T 35. **8.** Nathaniel to his brothers, June 23, 1842. RAL 109/50. **9.** James to Nathaniel, March 13, 1840. RAL 109/38. **10.** James to Nathaniel, Oct. 29, 1839. RAL 109/37. **11.** Amschel to Anthony, March 22, 1830. RAL 109/14. The "official" owner at the time, Sir Samuel Scott, was merely a "straw man" for a Hollander named Vanderberghe, who had bought the château after its seizure as national property in 1794. James, being determined to own nothing less than the *premiers des premiers grands crus*, had to wait until 1868, the year he died, to acquire Laffitte. Nathaniel had purchased Mouton, the adjacent château, in 1855. **12.** James to Mayer, April 30, 1847. RAL T 7. **13.** Mayer to Hannah, July 21, 1839. RAL T 25. **14.** James to Anthony, May 12, 1840. RAL T 24. The Rembrandt in question may have been the self-portrait bought at Christie's on May 8, 1840. **15.** Balzac to his mother, Sept. 27, 1832. **16.** James to Balzac, Jan. 21, 1833. **17.** Balzac to Werdet, May 18, 1835. **18.** Cited by André Maurois, *Prométhée ou la vie de Balzac* (Paris, 1965), 291. Edmond Werdet must have had ample occasion to reflect on James' advice. He had left the bookstore where he worked in order to become Balzac's exclusive publisher. Incapable of resisting the incessant demands for money made by his author, Werdet had to file for bankruptcy and finally left the publishing profession altogether. **19.** James to Balzac, March 17, 1842. **20.** Balzac never learned to spell James' name correctly, and left a long series of variants running from 'de Rostchil' to 'Rotchild.' It should be noted however that Nucingen, the banker in *La Comédie humaine*, was not, despite the Germanic accent, inspired by James. The son of converted Jews and unsupported by a large family like the Rothschilds,

he engaged in the kind of questionable operation that seems more characteristic of Ouvrard than of James. **21.** Balzac, *Lettres à l'étrangère* (Paris, 1899), Vol. III, 218. **22.** Anselm to his cousins, Sept. 11, 1843. RAL 109/55. The claymore is a large "dress" sword. **23.** Anthony to his brothers, Aug 27, 1841. RAL 104/1. **24.** James to Nathaniel, June 29, 1839. RAL T 35. **25.** James to Nathaniel, July 16, 1839. RAL T 35. **26.** Anthony to his brothers, July 17, 1839. RAL T 7. **27.** Nathaniel to his brothers, n.d. RAL T 7. **28.** Cited by Stern, *op. cit.*, 9. **29.** *Ibid.*, 34. **30.** Feydeau, *op. cit.*, 138. **31.** Only Salomon, James' third son, tended to kick over the traces. Gambling debts and troubles with women resulted in his confinement to Ferrières for several months, after which he was dispatched to the United States and ultimately married to a cousin. Salomon died at age twenty-nine, his demise attributed by Paris gossips to a heart attack brought on by stock market speculation. **32.** Feydeau, *op. cit.*, 134. **33.** Some years later Bismarck, intent upon insulting Alphonse in the course of negotiations related to the indemnity imposed by Germany after the Franco-Prussian War (1870), rudely refused to reply to Alphonse in French and even assaulted him in German. For Bismarck, Alphonse—Rothschild though he was—could never be anything but a Frankfurt Jew, therefore impossible to deal with in French. **34.** Comparable to an American liberal arts college, the École Normale is the most exclusive such institution in France, its students selected by means of stiff competitive examination. **35.** Founded by François I (r. 1515–47), the Collège de France is the most prestigious institution of the entire French educational system, and a chair at the Collège represents the crowning glory of a brilliant academic career. **36.** *Archives israélites*, 1847. **37.** Journal kept by Prince Philippe of Württemberg, an unpublished document transmitted by the Duke of Württenberg to Baroness Élie de Rothschild. **38.** Letter written by Ludwig Börne while in Paris in 1832. **39.** Stendhal, *Lucien Leuwen*, Chap. LX. **40.** The figures cited here have all been taken from Gille, *op. cit.*, the amounts rounded off for the sake of clarity in establishing their relative sizes, from brother to brother and from period to period. **41.** The distribution (in francs) of the Rothschilds' capital in the period 1815–28, as reported by Gille, *op. cit.*, 458:

	1815	1818	1825	1828
Amschel	441,000	7,776,000	18,943,750	19,693,750
Salomon	441,000	7,776,000	18,943,750	19,693,750
Nathan	2,205,000	12,000,000	26,875,000	28,200,000
Karl	122,500	7,488,000	18,643,750	19,393,750
James	122,500	7,488,000	18,643,750	19,393,750
Anselm				2,083,332.5
	3,332,000	42,528,000	102,050,000	118,458,332.5

42. Amschel died without issue in 1855, the same year that claimed the lives of both Salomon and Karl. **43.** For the whole of this development, see Daumard, *op. cit.* **44.** According to the correspondence of James and Nathaniel (RAL 109/67), the forests owned by Louis-Philippe were themselves worth 24 million francs in 1848. **45.** Szrankiewicz, *op. cit.* **46.** All figures have been drawn from Szrankiewicz, *ibid.* **47.** On this subject see Jean Lhomme, *La Grande Bourgeoisie au pouvoir: 1830–1880* (Paris, 1960). **48.** Prince of Württemberg, *op. cit.* **49.** Joseph Fesch (1763–1863), the maternal uncle of Napoleon I. **50.** *Paris-Guide* (Paris, 1867).

9 A Republican Veneer

1. James to his nephews in London, Feb. 9, 1848. RAL 109/65. 2. Tocqueville, *op. cit.*, 40. 3. Apponyi, *op. cit.*, Vol. IV, 171. 4. Chateaubriand, cited by Adrien Dansette, *Deuxième République et Second Empire* (Paris, 1943), 17. 5. Balzac, *La Fille aux yeux d'or* (Paris, 1913), 1. 6. Roger Price, *The French Republic: A Social History* (Ithaca, 1972), 1. 7. Tocqueville, *op. cit.*, 38. 8. Boigne, *op. cit.*, Vol. IV, 396. 9. Hugo, *Choses vues, op. cit.*, 268. 10. Gustave Flaubert, *L'Éducation sentimentale* (Paris, 1870), 2. 11. Tocqueville, *op. cit.*, 46–48. 12. *Ibid.*, 51. 13. James to his nephews, Feb. 22, 1848. RAL 109/65. 14. Louis Mathieu, Comte Molé (1781–1885), served, in succession, Napoleon I, the Bourbons, and Louis-Philippe. Hostile to Napoleon III, he retired from public life after 1851. 15. James to his nephews, Feb. 23, 1848. RAL 109/65. 16. Nathaniel to his brothers, Feb. 23, 1848. RAL 109/65. 17. Mérimée to Countess de Montijo, April 12, 1848. 18. Mérimée to Countess de Montijo, March 3, 1848. 19. Tocqueville, *op. cit.*, 83. 20. René Rémond, *La Droite en France* (Paris, 1954), 88. 21. Tocqueville, *op. cit.*, 93. 22. Nathaniel to his brothers, Feb. 23, 1848. RAL 109/65. 23. Hugo, *Choses vues, op. cit.*, 272. 24. Flaubert, *op. cit.*, Vol. III, 1. 25. L. Garnier-Pagès, *Histoire de la Révolution de 1848* (Paris, 1861–72). 26. Feydeau, *op. cit.*, 159–161. 27. Hugo, *Choses vues, op. cit.*, 447. 28. Tocqueville, *op. cit.*, 163. 29. *Archives israélites*, April 1848. 30. James to his nephews, June 5, 1848. RAL 109/66. 31. Fould, Mallet, Périer, Gouin, Delessert, and Hottinguer made up most of the rest of the contribution. See Garnier-Pagès, *op. cit.* 32. *The Times* of London, March 3, 1848. 33. Marc Caussidière (1808–61), who had participated in various worker insurrections, mounted the barricades in 1848, when he also took possession of the Préfecture de Police and held it against the wishes of the provisional government. *Mémoires* (Paris, n.d.), 210–212. 34. *Ibid.* 35. Report made by the Austrian Ambassador to Brussels, March 1848. 36. James retained a sense of gratitude towards Caussidière and expressed it several years later when the latter had to seek exile in Great Britain after the coup d'état of 1851. The Baron sent Caussidière 30,000 francs along with a gracious note: "Pay me back in the next ten or twenty years, or whenever you can." Thus provisioned, Caussidière left for the United States and settled in New York, where he became a wine and cognac merchant. Salomon, James' third son, visited him in 1860 and was happy to report that the former rebel had captured the city's "most aristocratic clientele." Sigmund Diamond, *A Casual View of America* (Stanford, 1961), 23. 37. Garnier-Pagès, *op. cit.* 38. James to his nephews, March 10, 1848. RAL 109/65. 39. James to Betty, March 4, 1848. RAL 109/65. 40. Alphonse to his cousins, March 29, 1848. RAL 109/65. 41. Apponyi, *op. cit.*, Vol. IV, 376. 42. James to his nephews, March 17, 1848. RAL 109/65. 43. Léon Faucher, *Correspondance* (Paris, 1867), Vol. I, 234. 44. Cited by Gille, *op. cit.*, Vol. II, 35. 45. James to his nephews, April 1848. RAL 109/66. 46. Amschel to James, May 3, 1848. RAL 109/66. 47. James to his nephews, March 29, 1848. RAL 109/65. 48. James to his nephews, May 1, 1848. RAL 109/65. 49. Nathaniel to his brothers, June 27, 1848. RAL 109/66. 50. Nathaniel to his brothers, June 9, 1848. RAL 109/66. 51. Nathaniel to his brothers, June 4, 1848. RAL 109/66. 52. Around 4,250 francs. 53. Alphonse to his cousins, March 19, 1848. RAL 109/65. 54. James to his nephews, May 4, 1848. RAL 109/66. 55. James to his nephews, May 17, 1848. RAL 109/65. 56. James to his nephews, June 4, 1848. RAL 109/65. 57. James to his nephews, May 5, 1848. RAL 109/65. 58. Charles Forbes, Comte de Montalembert (1810–70), was a Catholic liberal who supported the cause of religious and educational freedom. He rallied behind Napoleon III. 59. Cited by Bouvier, *op. cit.*, 144. 60. Mérimée to Countess de Montijo, June 28, 1848. 61. James to his nephews, June 25, 1848. RAL 109/67. 62. James to his nephews, June 27, 1848. RAL 109/67. 63. Hugo, *Choses vues, op. cit.*, 325, 355. 64. Corti, *op. cit.*, Vol. II, 250. 65. Benjamin Disraeli, *Sidonia*. Cited by Lord Rothschild, *op. cit.*, 3. 66. James to his nephews, n.d. RAL 109/65. 67. Nathaniel to his brothers, July 7, 1848. RAL 109/67. 68. Cited by Gille, *op. cit.*, Vol. II, 52–53. 69. Nicolas Changarnier (1793–1877) was a career officer in the French army who entered the Chamber of Deputies in 1848, only to be stripped of his posts and banished by Louis-Napoleon. But Changarnier made a return in 1850, and after 1871 he headed a parliamentary group loyal to the royalist cause.

10 The Parvenu Is Always Someone Else

1. James to his nephews, June 16, 1848. RAL 109/66. 2. An unsigned report from the Paris branch of the Rothschild firm to the branch in London, Dec. 10, 1848. RAL 109/69. 3. Nathaniel to his brothers, Sept. 1848. RAL 109/68. 4. Metternich papers, cited by Gille, *op. cit.*, Vol. II, 53. 5. Alexander Herzen, *My Past and Thoughts* (New York, 1974), 409. 6. Metternich papers, cited by Gille, *op. cit.*, Vol. II, 52. 7. August Belmont (1816–70), when only fourteen, took an unsalaried job at the Rothschild bank in the hope of learning the business. When he was seventeen his employers sent him to Naples. Then, in 1837, he went on assignment to Havana, after which, instead of returning to Europe, he settled in New York. There, while continuing to represent the Rothschilds, he met with immediate success in his own right. He even became an influential member of the Democratic Party. In 1849 Belmont married Caroline Perry, the daughter of Commodore Perry, who in 1854 would open Japan to the West. From 1853 to 1857 Belmont served as American Ambassador to The Netherlands. 8. Alphonse to his cousins, June 10, 1851. RAL 109. 9. A *mot* attributed to Mme Dosne, Thiers' mother-in-law. 10. English-speaking readers may be familiar with the situation from *Ratapoil*, a character created in lithography and sculpture by the artist Daumier for the express purpose of satirizing the kind of unscrupulous *agent provocateur* that the Bonapartists sent about the country to play upon the fears of Frenchmen, and by this means to intimidate them into accepting the coup of December 2, 1851, as well as the restoration of the Empire that followed. 11. Cited by Bouvier, *op. cit.*, 168. 12. Émile Zola, *La Curée* (Paris, 1871). 13. Alexandre Dumas, cited by Alain Plessis, *De la Fête impériale au mur des fédérés* (Paris, 1973), 98. 13a. Zola, *La Curée, op. cit.* 14. *Journals des débats*, Nov. 1868. James' obituary was written by Prévost-Paradol. 15. Goncourts, *Journal*, March 29, 1863. 16. Feydeau, *op. cit.*, 149–150. 17. Charles-Joseph, Duc de Morny (1811–65), was the natural son of Hortense de Beauharnais (thus the half-brother of Napoleon III) and Comte Flahaut de la Billanderie. After an army career in North Africa, he entered politics and became the

leading organizer of the coup d' état that gave Louis-Napoleon dictatorial powers. As Minister of the Interior, Morny used intimidation to assure the outcome of the 1852 plebiscite, which transformed the Prince-President into Emperor Napoleon III.   **18.** Zola, *L'Argent* (Paris, 1891), Chap. III. In this novel Zola quite candidly modeled his banker, Gundermann, upon the character and personality of James, his Judaism and cult of the family, his physical traits and mentality. In certain passages the novelist drew on the eye-witness accounts of Feydeau.   **19.** Letter dictated in French, from James to his children, Dec. 21, 1852. RAL 109/83.   **20.** Mérimée to Countess de Montijo, Jan. 12, 1851.   **21.** James to his nephews, Dec. 16, 1852. RAL 109/83.   **22.** Cited by Gille, *op. cit.,* Vol. II, 98.   **23.** Cited by Stern, *op. cit.,* 37.   **24.** The children of James' sisters married into the same Frankfurt families as their parents and grandparents—the Schnappers (Gudule's family), the Beyfusses, the Sterns, etc.   **25.** James to Amschel, n.d. RAL T 8.   **26.** About 1,000 francs.   **27.** James to Leonora, April 22, 1859. RAL 109/84.   **28.** *London Illustrated News,* Jan. 1863.   **29.** The Sassoons originated in the Jewish community of Baghdad but made their fortune in Bombay. Like the Rothschilds, the four sons of the Sassoon who founded the family fortune dispersed to seek careers in different cities: Calcutta, Shanghai, Hong Kong, and Japan. Once established, they made themselves the protectors of the Jewish communities throughout the Near and Far East. In 1860 a Sassoon grandson settled in London, after which his son married Aline de Rothschild, one of Gustave's daughters.   **30.** Feydeau, *op. cit.,* 146–147.   **31.** Alphonse to his sister and parents, April 11 and 21, 1849. RAL, cited by Gille, *op. cit.,* Vol. II, 581.   **32.** Alphonse to his sister and parents. Cited by Gille, *op. cit.,* Vol. II, 582.   **33.** James to Leonora, April 22, 1859. RAL 109/84.   **34.** Lionel to Anthony, Aug. 15, 1849. RAL T 8.   **35.** Leonora to her parents, n.d. RAL, Fonds Baronne Alphonse de Rothschild.   **36.** Charlotte to Nathaniel, n.d. RAL T 8.   **37.** *L'Illustration,* May 15, 1852.   **38.** Olry Terquem, *Projet de règlement concernant la circoncision* (Paris, 1821).   **39.** *Univers israélite,* May 1852.   **40.** Figures cited by Marrus (*op. cit.,* 87) and drawn from the lists of donations published every week in *Univers israélite.*   **41.** Girard, *op. cit.,* 203.   **42.** *Archives israélites* and a letter from Leonora to her parents, n.d. RAL, Fonds Baronne Alphonse de Rothschild.   **43.** Ludovic Halévy, *Carnets* (Paris, 1898). Cited by Marrus, *op. cit.,* 56.   **44.** *Univers israélite,* Dec. 1868.   **45.** Zola, *L'Argent, op. cit.*   **46.** George F. Chadwick, *The Works of Sir Joseph Paxton* (London, 1861), 189.   **47.** *Archives israélites,* 1849.   **48.** *Illustrated London News,* Jan. 1863.   **49.** Leonora to her parents, n.d. RAL, Fonds Baronne Alphonse de Rothschild.   **50.** Eugène Lami (1800–90) studied under Baron Gros and then Horace Vernet before making a long stay in Great Britain. Later he became famous as the visual chronicler of contemporary Parisian life, a role that prompted Baudelaire to call him "the poet of official dandyism."   **51.** Leonora to her parents, n.d. RAL, Fonds Baronne Alphonse de Rothschild.   **52.** Philippe Jullian, cited by Mario Praz in *Psychologie de l'ameublement* (Paris, 1964), 362.   **53.** Goncourts, *Journal,* July 1858.   **54.** Apponyi, *op. cit.,* Vol. IV, 44.   **55.** Evelina to her father and brothers, n.d. RAL T 9.   **56.** Leonora to her parents, n.d. RAL.   **57.** Leonora to her parents, n.d. RAL.   **58.** Mérimée to Countess de Montijo, Jan. 15, 1863.   **59.** Evelina to her father and brothers, n.d. RAL T 9.   **60.** James to his nephews, July 18, 1868. RAL T 10.   **61.** *Ibid.*   **62.** For this price to be meaningful, it should be noted that in 1858 Nathaniel had purchased Mouton for 1,125,000 francs, while Margaux went to the Aguados, financiers with origins in Spain, for 1,300,000 francs. In 1853 the Péreires had paid 425,000 francs for Château Palmer.   **63.** Nathaniel to his brothers, Oct. 18, 1868. RAL 109/96.   **64.** Alphonse to his cousins, Nov. 3, 1868. RAL 109/96.

Epilogue

1. Nathaniel, Lionel's son, to his parents, Nov. 19, 1868. RAL T 10.

223